HILDEGARD
OF BINGEN,
1098–1179

1 Hildegard of Bingen, 1098–1179. Statue of the Saint, parish church, Eibingen.

HILDEGARD OF BINGEN, 1098–1179

A Visionary Life

Second Edition

SABINA FLANAGAN

 Routledge
Taylor & Francis Group

LONDON AND NEW YORK

First published 1989
by Routledge
11 New Fetter Lane, London EC4P 4EE

Simultaneously published in the USA and Canada
by Routledge
29 West 35th Street, New York, NY 10001

First published in paperback 1990

Second edition 1998

Reprinted in 1998, 1999, 2001, 2003

Routledge is an imprint of the Taylor & Francis Group

Typeset by Keystroke, Jacaranda Lodge, Wolverhampton
Printed and bound in Great Britain by
T. J. International Ltd, Padstow, Cornwall

British Library Cataloguing in Publication Data
A catalogue record for this book is available from the British Library

Library of Congress Cataloguing in Publication Data
A catalogue record for this book has been requested from the Library of
Congress

ISBN 0–415–18551–3

FOR MY MOTHER AND FATHER

CONTENTS

PLATES

PREFACE TO THE FIRST EDITION

The relics of one of the most remarkable women of the Middle Ages now lie in Rüdesheim, a town on the picturesque middle reaches of the River Rhine, well known for its proximity to the Rock of the Lorelei and its extensive vineyards. Yet pilgrims do not continually flock to the parish church in Eibingerstrasse where the heart and tongue of St Hildegard of Bingen († 1179) are preserved in a golden reliquary. Unlike the patient and self-effacing St Bernadette of Lourdes, or the surpassingly meek and ordinary St Theresa of Lisieux, Hildegard has not attracted a large popular following. Her virtues were indeed of a different order. There were limits to her patience, and her humility, though real enough, was of the paradoxical kind which gives authority and assurance. 'Meek' and 'ordinary' are the last words to describe her, as even slight acquaintance with her story will show.

Hildegard was born into a noble family in Germany in 1098. Although destined from an early age to live a life of total enclosure, literally walled up in her cell, she left its shelter to found her own convents at Rupertsberg, on the Rhine near Bingen, and later at Eibingen on the opposite side of the river. From Rupertsberg she corresponded with secular and ecclesiastical leaders, as well as a vast range of people of lesser rank and standing, and went forth as monastic troubleshooter, consultant exorcist, and visiting preacher. Had Hildegard confined herself to these activities she would have been unusual enough among the women of her day. But Hildegard was even more remarkable in producing an extensive body of writings. At a time when few women wrote as much as the occasional letter, Hildegard's written works not only surpassed those of most of her male contemporaries in the range of their subject matter (from natural history, medicine, and cosmology, to music, poetry, and theology), but also outshone them in visionary beauty and intellectual power.

Hildegard's achievements are thrown into prominence by the fact that, as an author, she stood virtually alone among the women of her time. Why do we have almost no other writings by women from this period? Even allowing for the ravages of time, deliberate suppression, or mere negligence, it seems that women were responsible for only a tiny proportion of the entire twelfth-century literary output. What were the factors, internal or external, overt or covert, which militated against women writers? How did Hildegard overcome them, and if she could, what prevented her female contemporaries from doing likewise? I hope some answers to these questions will emerge in the course of this book.

My own interest in Hildegard was first kindled over a decade ago by reading Peter Dronke's account of one of her poems. When I tried to find out more I discovered both that the field of her activities was much wider than I had imagined and that it had been only patchily cultivated. Although different aspects of her work had received varying amounts of attention there was nothing which gave a satisfactory overview of Hildegard's life and work. I decided then that some day I should make a study of Hildegard for myself. Several years later I wrote a PhD thesis about some aspects of Hildegard's prophetic persona. By the time this was complete, my own need for a general introduction to Hildegard had passed. Nevertheless there still seems to be some need for such a work, especially for those who are making their first acquaintance with Hildegard.

While microfilm and jet aircraft have facilitated antipodean study of medieval history, I have often felt disadvantaged by my geo-graphical remoteness, not only from the subject of my study, but from others engaged in the same field. If we add to this the chronological and cultural distances, not to mention the religious distance between Hildegard and myself, the whole undertaking seems somewhat presumptuous. Yet in seeking to describe and understand what Hildegard was doing, being so far removed from the scene may have had some benefits. At least it means that there are no easy expla-nations waiting to be assumed, such as came so readily to some of her nineteenth-century hagiographers. It may also make an overview easier to achieve, where those closer to the subject, in both senses of the word, may fail to see the wood for the trees.

A further objection to such an enterprise as mine might be raised – that Hildegard's writings have not yet been studied in sufficient depth to make a proper assessment of her place in medieval life and thought possible. Indeed, most of her writings still lack modern critical editions, the prerequisite for any such detailed study. Some of these are expected to appear in the next few years, but others are still so far from publication that they have not been assigned even a tentative date. Yet to put off writing about Hildegard for another decade at least would disappoint those who, having come in contact with this remarkable figure through her music, poetry, theology, writings on women or the natural world, now wish to find out something more. My intention, then, is to provide a comprehensive introduction to Hildegard, in the light of current scholarship, from which readers may be inspired to read, or even to produce, more specialized studies.

A NOTE ON READING THE BOOK

While Hildegard's writings are remarkable in themselves, the question of how she came to produce her works and have them accepted by her contemporaries is almost more intriguing. I have tried in this book to give an account of both what she wrote and how she did it. Since even Hildegard's major works are not well known or readily accessible, I have described them at some length. These descriptions form the central chapters of the book (chs 4–7). Here I have been more concerned to indicate the interrelations of her ideas and theories within the total body of her work, than to identify their possible sources or compare them with those of her contemporaries. To provide a general account of twelfth-century natural history, cosmology, or theology is beyond the scope of my book. The chapters on Hildegard's writings are contained within an argument about how Hildegard was able to enter domains generally seen as the preserve of men, such literary activity being the major one. Those readers wishing to follow the sociological argument may thus go from chapter 4 to chapter 8 and then turn back to complete the picture with the account of Hildegard's later writings. Those wanting to get an idea of the nature and range of Hildegard's work could start with the central chapters. On the other hand, since the descriptions and the argument proceed more or less chronologically, the book can be read with profit straight through.

Sabina Flanagan
Adelaide, 1988

PREFACE

Over the last nine years there has been an amazing outpouring of scholarly activity on the life and work of Hildegard of Bingen. Yet, despite this, or perhaps for this very reason, there is still clearly a place for an introductory book on Hildegard which presents her life and writings in the context of her times.

I have taken the opportunity offered by this second edition – published in the year of the 900th anniversary of Hildegard's birth – to correct some errors of fact or emphasis, detected partly by myself and partly by vigilant reviewers. I have also reconsidered some aspects of the story in the light of the discovery of new information, and the appearance of critical editions of Hildegard's works, though some of these are still wanting – notably the medico-scientific writings and the correspondence. I have also updated the citations of primary sources from the older, often inadequate, texts to the new critical editions where they exist, and have in addition, included references to important secondary studies on particular aspects of Hildegard's thought which have subsequently appeared. To this end I have replaced a section, 'The Works of Hildegard', which nine years ago had perforce to refer to a number of unpublished manuscripts, with a select bibliography of both primary and secondary sources. A discography, distinguishing the recordings which seek to reproduce the style of Hildegard's time from more modern departures using Hildegard as a starting point for what are essentially new compositions, is also provided. Such material may be consulted by those interested in further exploring this fascinating subject for themselves. Some may even be inspired to produce more specialized studies – a hope which I expressed in the Preface to the first edition of this book, and which has already been amply realized.

Proper acknowledgment of the intellectual and personal debts I have incurred over the last decade would require several pages.

Suffice it to say that these studies have brought me into contact with an international circle of students of Hildegard whose generosity, intellectual liveliness and mutual support have made my investigations not only a challenge but a delight.

Sabina Flanagan
Adelaide, 1997

ACKNOWLEDGEMENTS

Many people have helped me in the writing of this book. I owe special thanks to Peter Dronke, both for his work, which has been an inspiration to me for many years, and his hospitality and advice in Cambridge in 1985; to Henry Mayr-Harting, who encouraged me to write about Hildegard, although this might not be quite the book he expected; to Barbara Newman and Werner Lauter, who generously sent me their publications; to the family von Racknitz of Disibodenberg who helped me with an elusive photograph; to my colleagues at the University of Adelaide; to Greta Mary Hair, who shared her musicological expertise with me; and finally to Alison, Cassie, and Chris for their enthusiasm and to my husband, Wilf Prest, for his critical support and supportive criticism.

Author and publisher gratefully acknowledge permission given to reproduce illustrations by the Biblioteca Statale di Lucca (plates 7 and 8) and Brepols, Turnhout, Belgium (plates 5, 6, 9, and 10).

Map of Germany showing places mentioned in the text.

1

LIFE AND DEATH

When Henry, fourth of that name, ruled the Holy Roman
Empire, there lived in hither Gaul a virgin famed equally for the
nobility of her birth and her sanctity. Her name was Hildegard.
Her parents, Hildebert and Mechthilde, although wealthy and
engaged in worldly affairs, were not unmindful of the gifts of the
Creator and dedicated their daughter to the service of God. For
when she was yet a child she seemed far removed from worldly
concerns, distanced by a precocious purity. (*Vita*, Bk 1)

I

This is how Godfrey, a monk from Disibodenberg who acted as
Hildegard's secretary and provost to the nuns at Rupertsberg,
introduces his subject in the first book of his *Vita Sanctae Hildegardis*
(*Life of St Hildegard*). When he died in 1176 he left the work unfinished
and it was not until a decade later, when Hildegard herself had
been dead for some years, that Theodoric of Echternach, a famous
monastery in the diocese of Trier, wrote the second and third books
and added the prefaces.

Although one of her biographers had been in daily contact with
Hildegard and in a position to ask about her early life, much
information which might be considered important or even essential
by a modern reader is missing from the *Vita*. The date and place of
Hildegard's birth, for instance, are not given. Such omissions arose
because the authors were more interested in Hildegard's spiritual
credentials than her secular ones. Even here much of the description
is stereotyped. On the other hand, selections from Hildegard's
correspondence are included in the *Vita*. Even more valuable is
Theodoric's incorporation, in the second and third books, of lengthy

1

autobiographical passages from an otherwise unknown work by Hildegard. Other major sources of biographical information are Hildegard's letters, and the prefaces to her works which describe when and how they came to be written. Additional information of more questionable reliability is to be found in the *Acta Inquisitionis*, a document drawn up for submission to Rome in the early thirteenth century when the nuns at Rupertsberg were seeking Hildegard's canonization. The recently discovered *Vita* of Hildegard's mentor, the anchoress Jutta of Sponheim, while useful for suggesting the background to Hildegard's early life, further complicates the picture by providing a chronology which seems incompatible with most of the other sources.[1] There is also an incomplete *Vita* written by the Walloon monk, Guibert of Gembloux, Hildegard's last secretary. Various archival evidence, in the form of charters and records of gifts to her monasteries, provide further details. For reasons which will become obvious, there is more information about the second half of Hildegard's life than about her early years.

II

Hildegard began her earthly pilgrimage not far from where her mortal remains rest today. She was born in Bermersheim, near Alzey (about 20 km south-west of the important cathedral city of Mainz), in the summer of the year 1098. Nothing more is known of her parents than their names and that they belonged to the nobility.

The sources tell us little of Hildegard's childhood. Godfrey's assertion that she displayed a precocious spirituality sounds like a pious stereotype. Lives of the saints are full of impossibly well-behaved children who either never played at all, or if they did, built mud churches rather than castles. On the other hand, according to Hildegard's own account, included in the second book of the *Vita*, she had her first visionary experience before she was 5 years old. Indeed, it may well have been this unusual event, coupled with her apparently precarious health, which suggested to her parents that their daughter should be dedicated to the religious life. So, as Godfrey wrote:

> when she was about eight years old she was enclosed at Disibodenberg – buried with Christ that she might arise with him to immortal glory. Here Jutta, a pious woman dedicated to God, introduced her to the habit of humility and innocence. (*Vita*, Bk 1)

Rather than choosing to enter their daughter formally as a child in a convent where she would be brought up to become a nun, Hildegard's parents had taken the more radical step of enclosing their daughter, apparently for life, in the cell of an anchoress, attached to the Benedictine monastery at Disibodenberg. Jutta, it should be said, was not merely a pious woman, but the young and beautiful daughter of a local count. She undertook to instruct Hildegard in the recitation of the psalter, the major part of the anchoress's day, and no doubt in other womanly occupations in the time left over from their programme of prayer.

But as with other religious movements and institutions, such as the Egyptian hermits and the Cistercians, extraordinary spirituality soon attracted a large following of would-be disciples, with the result that the original institution was forced to diversify. So it was at Disibodenberg, where the daughters of the local nobility were sent by their parents, and the cell which had sufficed for Jutta, Hildegard, and one or two others now had to accommodate a much larger number of people than at first intended. Thus by the time Hildegard had reached the age of thirteen or fourteen (c. 1112), the recluse's cell had become, to all intents and purposes, a small Benedictine convent, attached to and dependent on the monastery at Disibodenberg.

Between that time and the death of Jutta in 1136, when Hildegard was about 38 years old, the sources provide no information about her life except for the blandest of platitudes. Thus, according to Godfrey, she 'went from virtue to virtue' and 'the tranquillity of her heart was demonstrated in modest silence and economical speech'. Hildegard, when recounting the history of her visionary experiences, says that during this time she ceased talking about what she saw by supernatural means, as such openness had only caused her embarrassment when younger. Now she confided only in Jutta, who in turn informed 'a certain monk', presumably Volmar of Disibodenberg, who was to become Hildegard's teacher, trusted assistant, and friend until his death some thirty years later. In view of Hildegard's later talent for organization, it would not be surprising if she had some part in the administration of the convent. At any rate, when Jutta died in 1136 Hildegard became head of the establishment, the unanimous choice of the sisters, according to Guibert.

Although the election of Hildegard to head the convent suggests some recognition of her gifts and abilities by her immediate circle, at this stage of her life they were apparently not such as to distinguish her from hundreds, perhaps thousands, of her worthy but now forgotten contemporaries. The real turning point in her career came a few years later, in 1141, as she recalled in the preface to her first major visionary work, which she was to call *Scivias*, apparently a contraction of *Sci vias Domini*, 'Know the Ways of the Lord':

> And it came to pass in the eleven hundred and forty-first year of the incarnation of Jesus Christ, Son of God, when I was forty-two years and seven months old, that the heavens were opened and a blinding light of exceptional brilliance flowed through my entire brain. And so it kindled my whole heart and breast like a flame, not burning but warming . . . and suddenly I understood the meaning of the expositions of the books, that is to say of the psalter, the evangelists, and other catholic books of the Old and New Testaments.

This is how Hildegard described the sudden access of understanding by which she felt able to penetrate to the inner meaning of the texts of her religion. Of even greater importance for her subsequent career was the command she received at the same time: 'O fragile one, ash of ash and corruption of corruption, say and write what you see and hear'. So there might be no mistaking the directive to write down and publicize what she understood from her visions, it was repeated three more times in similar terms.

Yet Hildegard hesitated to act, fearing she was unequal to the task. She described her predicament as follows:

> But although I heard and saw these things, because of doubt and a low opinion (of myself) and because of the diverse sayings of men, I refused for a long time the call to write, not out of stubbornness but out of humility, until weighed down by the scourge of God, I fell onto a bed of sickness. (*Scivias*, Preface)

Interpreting her illness as a sign of God's displeasure, Hildegard finally told Volmar about her difficulty. With his help, and the permission of Abbot Kuno of Disibodenberg, she was encouraged to begin writing down the visions which formed the basis of the *Scivias*. Immediately her illness lifted and as she subsequently wrote: 'rising from my sickness with renewed strength I was just able to bring the work [*Scivias*] to a conclusion in the space of ten years' (ibid.).

It may seem from the last quotation that Hildegard was able to devote herself to a career of writing as soon as she rose from her bed of pain. But both Godfrey and Hildegard in their respective portions of the *Vita*, indicate that her establishment as a writer was not quite so straightforward. At some stage Abbot Kuno informed Archbishop Henry of Mainz about Hildegard's work and it was through him that Pope Eugenius (1145–53), a Cistercian *protégé* of St Bernard, came to hear about it at the synod held in Trier between November 1147 and February 1148.

A commission was sent to Disibodenberg to find out more about Hildegard and her writings (Godfrey names Albero, Bishop of Verdun and his deputy Adalbert as members). Satisfied that the visions were authentic they returned to Trier with a completed portion of the *Scivias*. Here the pope, 'holding it in his own hands . . . read (it) aloud to the archbishop and cardinals'. It was subsequently resolved that Hildegard should be commanded to transcribe and make known whatever she received in this way from the Holy Spirit. A letter to this effect was sent to her and such papal approval no doubt served as a spur to her finishing the work, although it still took another three years.

We should not wonder at how long the *Scivias* took to write, since Hildegard, with her responsibilities as a nun and in the running of the convent could spend only a limited time on the task each day. Moreover, Hildegard's increasing fame did nothing to lessen the numbers of candidates attracted to the establishment at Disibodenberg and a severe shortage of accommodation developed. Rebuilding was not a novelty at Disibodenberg (the monastery had been in an almost continual state of alteration during Hildegard's time there), so plans for expanding and relocating the women's quarters were already in the air. Then Hildegard suddenly announced that she had received a command from God to move her nuns to Rupertsberg, a hill overlooking the junction of the River Nahe with the Rhine at Bingen, some 30 km from Disibodenberg.

That her proposal was strenuously resisted by the monks at Disibodenberg is hardly surprising. Quite apart from a natural disinclination to recognize the independence of one whom they had nurtured (more or less) from infancy, there were more pressing reasons for opposition. The property (usually in the form of land) which the nuns brought with them when they entered the convent contributed to the wealth of the monastery as a whole, not to mention the gifts of the faithful attracted by Hildegard's evident holiness. It must have seemed to the monks that they were about to lose their chief spiritual and material asset, for once the nuns were physically distant from Disibodenberg the exercise of spiritual and temporal authority over them would be difficult to maintain.

The proposal was also unwelcome to others besides the monks, most probably the parents of her nuns, as Hildegard's comment from the *Vita* indicates:

> But when my abbot and the brothers and people of the district understood what sort of change this was to be – that we wished to go from lush fields and vineyards and the comforts of home to a desert place, devoid of amenities – they were amazed and they conspired together to prevent and thwart us. They also said that I was deceived by some illusion. (*Vita*, Bk 2)

In the face of such opposition Hildegard took to her bed once more, withdrawing into utter immobility and silence. According to Godfrey, Hildegard finally prevailed when Abbot Kuno, entering her bedchamber in a sceptical frame of mind, found himself unable either 'to lift her head up, or to turn her from side to side'. This convinced him that Hildegard was suffering from no ordinary illness but a visitation of 'divine correction'. Nor was it only God who was at work behind the scenes for Hildegard. She had enlisted secular support in the person of the widowed marchioness Richardis of Stade (the mother of one of her nuns) who had intervened on her behalf with Archbishop Henry of Mainz. With his support Hildegard was able to purchase her chosen site at Rupertsberg from its owners, the canons of Mainz Cathedral and Count Bernard of Hildesheim and his brother.

When the arrangements had been completed (c. 1150), Hildegard, with some twenty of her nuns, made the day's journey from Disibodenberg to Rupertsberg. The contrast in physical environment between the well-established, stone-built complex they had left and the temporary dwellings to which they came must have been striking. In Hildegard's case this may have been offset by an improvement in the psychological environment which gave her increased control and autonomy. She had emerged from the shadow of the monastery of Disibodenberg into the sunlight of her own foundation. On the other hand there seems to have been some disaffection among the nuns and real financial hardship, which was made worse by the numbers of guests and pilgrims who became a charge on the convent. This is how Hildegard recalled the early days of Rupertsberg:

> so they said 'What is the point of this, that noble and wealthy nuns should move from a place where they wanted for nothing to such great poverty?' But we were awaiting the grace of God, who

showed us this place, to come to our aid. After the burden of these troubles God rained grace upon us. (*Vita*, Bk 2)

One such benefit, Hildegard went on to explain, was the granting of burial rights to laypeople in the convent cemetery. This was to prove something of a mixed blessing later on.

Apart from difficulties with her own flock, Hildegard had to reach an accommodation with the monks of Disibodenberg over their respective spheres of financial and spiritual influence. It appears from Hildegard's account that she did not finally confront Abbot Kuno over the matter of the nuns' dowries until shortly before his death in 1155. She pursued her case with his successor, Helenger, with results that were inscribed in a charter of 1158 issued by Archbishop Arnold of Mainz. Apart from regulating the distribution of assets between the two houses, Disibodenberg was given the task or privilege (depending on how you looked at it) of furnishing Rupertsberg with a provost of their choice to oversee the nuns' spiritual welfare.

Despite the claims of her administrative duties, Hildegard continued to write during the early years at Rupertsberg, though she concentrated on shorter works rather than a sustained piece of visionary writing like the *Scivias*. To this period can be attributed many of the hymns and sequences, for which she also wrote the music, and her medico-scientific works which survive in fragmentary and otherwise dubious forms as the *Physica* (*Natural History*) and *Causae et curae* (*Causes and Cures*).

While such works can readily be seen as arising from the needs and interests of the new foundation – music to give a sense of corporate identity, medical jottings reflecting her work among pilgrims and visitors – it is harder to place some of Hildegard's other compositions at this time. Her *lingua ignota* or unknown language, a series of invented words corresponding to an eclectic list of nouns, and her *litterae ignotae*, an alternative alphabet, may have found some place in the domestic economy as a secret code, if indeed they were anything more than an intellectual diversion on a level with crossword puzzles.[2]

In her autobiographical notes Hildegard was able to dismiss the initial dissatisfaction of some of her nuns following the move to Rupertsberg as a passing phase, by pointing to the support of her loyal followers. However, soon after she finished the *Scivias* in 1151, Hildegard experienced the defection of her most favoured assistant, Richardis of Stade. In the *Vita*, Hildegard gives the following laconic account of the affair:

While I was writing the book *Scivias* I held a certain noble girl . . . in great affection, just as Paul loved Timothy. She allied herself to me in diligent friendship in everything and consoled me in all my trials until I completed the book. But after this, because of her noble connections, she turned aside to the honour of a higher position and was elected head of an important foundation. . . . Soon afterwards she left me, and in another place far from me, she gave up the present life and the dignity of her appointment. (*Vita*, Bk 2)

Hildegard's letters, on the other hand, reveal a depth of feeling about the subject which might not be suspected from the passage just quoted from the *Vita*. The incident will be examined in more detail in a later chapter. I mention it here merely to complete the picture of the uneasy start to Rupertsberg, which Hildegard tended to attribute to human frailty, and, it must be remarked, that of others rather than of herself. Since this was the case, it does not seem fanciful to regard her next major work, the *Liber vitae meritorum* (*Book of Life's Merits*), written between the years 1158 and 1163, a book about the vices and their countervailing virtues, as reflecting her direct recent experience of human nature.

During the first decade at Rupertsberg Hildegard began to gain prominence in the world outside the convent. When Frederick Barbarossa was elected king of Germany in 1152 Hildegard wrote him a letter of congratulation and good advice. She seems to have maintained a close connection with him (in spite of the schism which began in 1159 with the disputed election of a successor to Pope Hadrian IV and continued for eighteen years) and accepted his charter of protection in 1163. It is true, however, that as the papal schism was prolonged, Hildegard's letters became less cordial. That she was in correspondence with others at this time is indicated by her claim in the preface to the *Liber vitae meritorum* that she had written many letters of advice and correction. Hildegard describes the years 1158–61 as being one long illness, but in spite of her poor health and while apparently engaged on her second major work, she embarked on a series of preaching tours.

Some of these would have entailed visiting different monasteries and addressing the assembled monks or nuns in the chapter house, as for example at Siegberg or Zwiefalten. Sometimes, however, she took a more unusual step, as on her second tour in 1160 where she preached in public in Trier, as well as visiting Metz and Krauftal. It need hardly be said that public preaching – indeed preaching at all – was a rare privilege to be accorded a woman. In 1163 the places she is said to have visited include Cologne, Boppard, Andernach, Siegburg, Werden, and Liège. Although river transport would have been available for parts of these journeys, some overland travel could not have been avoided, and such travel, whether by foot, horse, or litter, must have taxed the strength of the 65-year-old nun. This is especially true of her last great journey to Swabia in 1170, where she is said to have visited a series of monasteries including Maulbronn, Hirsau, Kirchheim, Zwiefalten, and Hördt – an overland circuit of at least 400 km.

In 1163 Hildegard began her third and most ambitious theological work, *Liber divinorum operum* (*Book of the Divine Works*). This came to her in a vision, as a commentary on the opening of St John's Gospel, taking up and refining several of the cosmological themes first explored in the *Scivias*. The writing of this work suffered frequent interruptions and it was not finally completed until about 1174, only five years before Hildegard's death. Not the least drain on her time and energy must have been the foundation in 1165 of a second convent, at Eibingen across the Rhine from Bingen, presumably to cater for nuns who could not be accommodated at Rupertsberg.[3] Hildegard apparently maintained close contact with the daughter house, visiting it twice a week. Indeed, several of the healing miracles attributed to her, involving her curing the blind by the application of Rhine water, were said to have taken place when she was travelling by boat across the river between the two houses.

Hildegard's health, although never robust, seems to have worsened at about this time. She refers to herself as 'lying for almost three years on a bed of illness' in her preface to the *Vita Sancti Disibodi* (*Life of St Disibod*), which she wrote in 1170 at the request of the abbot and monks of the parent house. Nevertheless, she also managed, during this period, to travel at least as far as Kirchheim and visited other places in Swabia where she dealt with monastic problems on the spot. The nature of Hildegard's illnesses, which could confine her to bed for weeks and yet allow her to undertake the most gruelling journeys, will be examined further below.

Hildegard is seen in another unusual role at this period, that of exorcist, although she may well have performed such services at other times in her life. A disproportionate amount of the third book of the *Vita* is given over to an account of the freeing of a woman from Cologne who had been harassed by an evil spirit for eight years. The account is especially interesting because it incorporates part of the correspondence between Hildegard and the monks of Brauweiler, to whom the woman had unsuccessfully applied for relief, as well as a description of what happened in Hildegard's own words. One of Hildegard's letters contains the text of a fascinating rite of exorcism which she composed for the occasion and sent to the monks. The incident, which was something of a *cause célèbre* at the time, is treated in more detail in chapter 8.

During this time Hildegard continued to work on the *Liber divinorum operum*, sometimes laying it aside in favour of shorter commissioned works, such as lives of St Rupert and St Disibod or her commentary on the Benedictine Rule. A much more severe interruption, both in practical and psychological terms, was caused by the death of the monk Volmar, Hildegard's original adviser, friend, and collaborator, who had been her secretary for over thirty years, as well as acting as provost for the nuns at Rupertsberg. From the time of his death until her own some five years later Hildegard expended much energy in finding a suitable replacement who might meet both her own needs for secretarial support, and those of the nuns for spiritual and material services. In the first instance she enlisted the help of Ludwig of St Eucharius at Trier, who was later to commission Theodoric to complete the *Vita*, and her own nephew Wezelin, at that time provost of St Andreas at Cologne.

According to the agreement concluded twenty years earlier, the abbot of Disibodenberg was bound to supply the nuns at Rupertsberg with the provost of their choice. Hildegard applied to Helenger, but a replacement was not forthcoming. Finally she took up the matter with Pope Alexander (1159–81), so that in the end, possibly after negotiations lasting as long as a year, the monk Godfrey was sent from Disibodenberg, late in 1174 or early 1175. While provost at Rupertsberg, Godfrey began to write the *Vita*, but died in 1176 before completing it.

It is at this point that we find Guibert, a monk from Gembloux, poised to make his brief but important appearance in Hildegard's life. From their correspondence, wordy and opinionated as it is on Guibert's side, much of the chronology of Hildegard's later life and the details of her visionary experiences and methods of writing are drawn. He first began writing to her in 1175, and, fired with enthusiasm, paid a short visit to Rupertsberg. When Godfrey died in 1176, Hildegard's brother Hugo was pressed into service as secretary, while a canon from St Stephen's at Mainz attended to the spiritual needs of the nuns. Hildegard invited Guibert to Rupertsberg in 1177. Shortly after his arrival both the Mainz clergy were carried off by a fever and Guibert assumed both vacancies, as secretary to Hildegard and spiritual father to the nuns. He remained at Rupertsberg, not without some misgivings, until recalled to Gembloux in 1180.

The last year of Hildegard's life was clouded by a dispute with the clergy of Mainz. It will be remembered that one of the benefits claimed by her monastery at Rupertsberg was that of the burial of the rich and noble inhabitants of the surrounding district.[4] The problem arose when the clergy of Mainz claimed that because a certain man buried at Rupertsberg had died excommunicate, his body should be disinterred and cast out of the sacred ground. Hildegard replied that the man had been reconciled to the church at the time of his death and that to do as she had been ordered would be a grievous sin. The response from Mainz was an interdict, forbidding the celebration of mass and permitting the divine office to be performed only in an undertone and behind closed doors. The course of the dispute can be followed in a series of letters, including one from Hildegard on the place of music in the divine economy, which is described in chapter 9.

Finally, in March 1179, the interdict was lifted and Hildegard spent her last six months free from major conflict. She died peacefully on 17 September 1179, having forecast her approaching end to the nuns. It is a pity that Guibert of Gembloux, although resident at Rupertsberg at the time, has left no account of her death – his *Vita*, for reasons that are not altogether clear, only takes the story as far as the proposed move to Rupertsberg. The account we have from Theodoric, who had to depend on what the nuns told him, unfortunately has nothing of the moving intimacy of some of the descriptions of the passing of other monastic saints.[5] He relies heavily on an account of the meteorological prodigies which accompanied her 'joyful transition to the heavenly Bridegroom'.

III

Clearly, the recipient of such charismatic gifts in life must have been considered a candidate for sainthood after death.[6] At the time of Hildegard's death the process of canonization was becoming more systematized and bureaucratic. Pope Alexander III's letter to King Canute (Knut) about the cult of his father, King Eric of Sweden (†1160), is generally held to be the first definitive statement of a policy which made all subsequent canonizations subject to the authority and approval of the Holy See. Henceforth canonical status was to be conferred by papal bull, rather than by popular veneration and diocesan approval. No such definitive statement of papal recognition exists for Hildegard. Instead we have, in the *Acta*, the documentation of some stages of the inquiry. Although this gives a fascinating insight into the process of inquisition, it proved ultimately inconclusive. The document we have arises from an approach made by the nuns of Rupertsberg to the pope in the first third of the thirteenth century. If earlier attempts were made there is no evidence of them.

In accordance with the new procedures a commission was appointed to take evidence from witnesses at Bingen about Hildegard's 'life, conversation, fame, merits and miracles, and in general about her circumstances'. The commissioners, all members of the Mainz clergy, reported back in a document dated 1233 (see P. Bruder, 'Acta Inquisitionis . . . ' *Analecta Bollandiana*. 2, 1883, 119). This is largely a compilation of miracles, some remembered by witnesses as having been performed while Hildegard was alive, and others effected by her relics or at her tomb. For some reason (probably a lack of sufficient detail), this submission was rejected and the document returned to the commissioners who then made extensive alterations. The additions detail further miracles and give (where possible) the names of those involved in the earlier ones. However, the amended version does not seem to have reached the Curia, since there is a later letter, from Innocent IV in 1243, asking for the claim to be resubmitted. There is no evidence of further progress towards Hildegard's canonization in the thirteenth century.

During the next century, however, Hildegard's name and feast day begin to appear in the martyrologies. Further evidence of her formal canonization, or at least express permission for her 'solemn and public cult' is found in an indulgence from John XXII dated from Avignon in 1324.[7] Here forty days' indulgence is granted to the faithful who observe certain feast days, including that of St Hildegard, at the church at Rupertsberg. Finally, her inclusion by Baronius in the sixteenth-century *Roman Martyrology* ensured her status as a saint. Her cult flourishes – particularly in monastic contexts, but also publicly – to this day, as can be seen from the glittering shrine in her church at Rüdesheim/Eibingen which rests on an altar inscribed: 'Heilige Hildegard Bitte für Uns' ('Saint Hildegard pray for us').

IV

Even from a brief survey of Hildegard's life, certain remarkable aspects emerge which stand in need of explanation. How are we to account for such prodigious activity in areas where women, if not actually forbidden to participate, were at least not actively encouraged? How many other women of the time do we find preaching with official approval, exorcizing, founding their own convents, and above all composing works which have given them a place among the 'fathers, doctors and writers of the Church'?[8] The answer is, very few indeed. Two other German nuns were among the few women of the twelfth century whose writings have survived, but their works are hardly comparable with Hildegard's. Herrade of Landsberg compiled an illustrated encyclopedia, the *Hortus deliciarum* (*Garden of Delights*), for the edification of her nuns, while Elisabeth of Schönau, inspired by Hildegard's example, related her visionary experiences to her brother, who set them down in Latin. How, then, was Hildegard able to overcome the obstacles which her female contemporaries seem to have found insurmountable? The answer to this question is complex since it involves, among other things, the effects of cultural conditioning on human behaviour. However, Hildegard possessed one overriding advantage which set her apart from other aspiring writers.

Ever since her experience of 1141, when she felt herself compelled by God to write down her visions, she believed that her life was set in a prophetic mould. Accordingly, she saw herself as the mouthpiece of the Lord, merely conveying his messages to her hearers and readers. Such messages were not concerned exclusively with the future, as the modern meaning of the word 'prophecy' might suggest. The medieval understanding of the term was much wider. To the people of the Middle Ages, as to the ancients, prophecy implied the revelation of divine secrets concerning the past, the present, and the future. Hildegard's belief that she possessed such privileged knowledge would not have been enough to ensure her success if her superiors had not seen it the same way. As Hildegard wrote in the first autobiographical passage in the *Vita*:

> When these things were brought to the attention of the church of Mainz and discussed, all agreed that they came from God and from the gift of prophecy which the prophets spoke forth in former times. (*Vita*, Bk 2)

2 Hildegard reliquary. Parish church, Eibingen.

There were both biblical and early Christian precedents for the role of female prophet. Moreover, a woman could be a prophet without upsetting the perceived natural order, since no particular attributes of her own were required, except, possibly, humility. Indeed, there was some suggestion that God might specifically choose the weak and despised to confound the strong. Thus, to be a female prophet was to confirm women's inferiority, rather than to deny it.

In this way Hildegard was able to participate in the field of theological writing by disclaiming any intention of operating on the same terms as those (men) who had appropriated it. But soon after this ground was conceded Hildegard began to adopt other apostolic prerogatives, usually, it should be noted, at the request of others. Thus we find her writing letters of advice, preaching, visiting monasteries, exorcizing, and healing. All these activities were justified on the same grounds: her privileged access to the *'secreta Dei'* – 'the secrets of God'. These secrets were both general, in that they covered the whole field of theology, and particular, when they had to do with courses of action to be taken in specific circumstances. Since ignorance and uncertainty about what to expect both of the natural and supernatural world were widespread, anyone who had a plausible claim to such privileged knowledge would be much in demand. What we must now consider is why Hildegard did not discover such a role for herself until relatively late in life, and to do so we need to re-examine the circumstances of her early years.

2

WORLD AND CLOISTER

For in the eleven-hundredth year after the Incarnation of Christ, the teachings of the apostles and the burning righteousness which He had placed in Christians and the religious began to grow sluggish and turn to vacillation. In such times was I born and my parents pledged me to God with sighs . . . . In my eighth year I was offered to God for the spiritual life. (*Vita*, Bk 2)

I

In these words Hildegard, in her old age, described the circumstances of her birth and entry into religion. What the description lacks in circumstantial detail is made up for by her evocation of the mood of the times, which she portrays as one of decline and decay. This characterization of the turn of the twelfth century may, however, strike the modern reader as being at odds with our view of the period as one of 'renaissance' or 'renewal' in secular as well as spiritual terms.[1]

We know, for example, that in the course of the eleventh century western Europe began to recover from a period of stagnation and contraction which had followed on the dissolution of the Carolingian Empire. Internal instability was exacerbated by a series of external attacks – from Saracens in the south, Magyars in the east and especially from Vikings in the north and west. The gradual cessation of such external threats brought a measure of security and the population then began to increase. Agricultural productivity grew at an even greater rate. Thus people were in a position to look beyond their narrowed horizons, both metaphorically and physically. This sense of renewed vigour and of increasing possibilities for action found expression in various ways: in the First Crusade, which triumphantly reached Jerusalem in 1099, in an increase of land under cultivation, in the growth of urban centres, the expansion of cathedral schools, and the founding of new religious orders, such as the Cistercians, Carthusians, and Premonstratensians.

The kingdom of Germany was comprised of five great duchies: Franconia, Swabia, Saxony (incorporating Thuringia), Bavaria, and Lotharingia. Probably because it suffered less disruption from the barbarian invasions than other parts of Europe, Germany was one of the first areas to recover from the resultant political chaos. Yet the apparent stability which allowed a series of Saxon and Salian kings to dominate the scene for over a century was built upon very infirm and shifting foundations.

Part of the problem lay in the composition of the kingdom itself. Because of the lack of centralized government, over the years a great deal of power had devolved upon the men on the spot and the authority of these dukes, margraves, and counts was usually in inverse proportion to the frequency of the king's visits to their territory. The position of the bishops, invested with temporal rights by the king from Carolingian times, had become more important with increased urban development and led to a greater potential for a conflict of interests with the nobility (not to mention the rising townsmen). A succession of eleventh-century kings allied themselves now with one faction and now with the other. The situation was further complicated by the lack of any clear-cut social boundary between the two conflicting groups, as the bishops were themselves generally drawn from the ranks of the nobility.

A new development which seems to have arisen because of the relative weakness of feudal ties (compared, for instance, with England or France), was the use of the so-called 'ministeriales' for the performance of royal business. This unique and anomalous class of servile or unfree nobility became increasingly influential and powerful in the course of the eleventh century, yet they were barred from marriage into the free nobility and excluded from positions reserved for this class, for instance, membership of certain cathedral chapters. Ministeriales were used increasingly during this period for garrisoning royal castles, and this was a particular source of resentment to the free nobility.

The rule of the Saxon and Salian kings, like that of the Carolingians, who saw themselves as representatives of God on earth and protectors of the church, was essentially theocratic. However, their reform of the papacy, by freeing it, at least temporarily, from the secular influence of warring Roman families, had the unintended consequence of putting in place a series of popes whose ideas on the reform of the church and its relation to the secular ruler inevitably brought the two spheres of influence into collision, culminating in the excommunication and deposition of Henry IV by Pope Gregory VII in 1075. During the reign of Henry IV (1056–1106) this contest combined with the social tensions sketched above to produce decades of civil war in Germany.

By 1090 the opposition to Henry at home, at first led ineptly by Herman of Salm and then with more effect by Eckbert of Meissen, showed signs of weakening. However, the successors of Pope Gregory had on the whole continued his reforming work and Urban (elected in 1088) renewed Henry's excommunication and the ban on lay investiture together with other planks of Gregorian reform.[2] It was he who proclaimed the First Crusade in Clermont which mobilized the forces of western Europe, with the exception of those of Germany, which was otherwise occupied, to undertake the defence of the Holy Places.

Such was the uneasy state of affairs in the kingdom of Germany when Hildegard was born. The closing stages of the drama, in which Henry IV's son, Henry V, finally revolted and after imprisoning his father in the castle of Bockelheim, began to rule in his stead, had yet to be played out. After his father's death in 1106 there was to be a lull in the civil strife as the younger Henry rallied the nobles to his cause and tried, in 1111, to settle the matter of investitures by marching to Rome with a large army. However, the pope later revoked the right of investiture granted to Henry under duress, and once more Germany experienced a period of civil war, a compromise solution only being reached with the Concordat of Worms in 1122.

The effect of such prolonged military and political disturbances on those not directly involved in the fighting is hard to assess. It should be remembered, however, that medieval warfare was usually quite localized. Much of the fighting during the civil war took place in Saxony, well away from the Rhineland, although some important towns, such as Cologne, were besieged on occasion. Away from such centres, the periodic rhythms of rural life doubtless continued largely undisturbed, together with the recurrent cycles of prayer offered up in the monasteries which dotted the landscape. Indeed, it is during these troubled years that monastic life in Germany underwent something of a renewal. This was largely due to the efforts of William of Hirsau († 1091) who introduced the observances of the French

Benedictine monastery of Cluny to Germany. A contemporary wrote of his work:

By the effort of this holy man, the monastic religion, which among those who had assumed the religious habit had almost grown cold in the Teutonic regions, began to grow warm again and to recover.[3]

How are we to reconcile this decidedly optimistic view of the spiritual climate of the times with that expressed by Hildegard in the auto-biographical excerpt quoted at the head of the chapter? Perhaps she was thinking of the large-scale politico-religious troubles, the conflict between the pope and emperor which caused such grave and widespread disturbances. There is, however, another possible expla-nation. In the passage quoted, Hildegard was considering history and her place in it from a different vantage point from either that of the biographer of William of Hirsau or even a modern historian. She was, in fact, locating the time of her birth in the broad sweep of salvation history, stretching from the creation of the world to its eventual consummation. Seen in the light of Christian historiography, the present, indeed all the time that had elapsed since the Incarnation, was being lived in the shadow of the world's approaching end. It was not so much that the end of the world was felt to be particularly imminent – there were different views on this difficult question and Hildegard was careful in her writings never to commit herself to a date. Nevertheless the world and all that pertained to it was thought to be in decline, having reached its last age. In this period of the world's senescence Hildegard saw a special role allotted to herself.

Since her interests were eschatological rather than historical, we should not expect to find Hildegard writing about particular contemporary events. There is, however, a convenient source of local information which can help us set the scene for the time of Hildegard's birth. Disibodenberg, the monastery to which Hildegard went as an anchoress, produced a chronicle, written some time in the 1140s, which covers these years.[4] What then, does the Disibodenberg monk record from this period?

The entries for the last decades of the eleventh century are much concerned with the conflict between Henry IV and his opponents. Rather than follow the annalist's account of the frequent alternations of charge and counter-charge in the propaganda and actual war between Henry and his lay and ecclesiastical enemies, I shall quote his epilogue to the reign of Henry IV, inserted in the Annals under the year 1106:

> It is perfectly clear that Henry was a perverse man and excluded from the Church by a just judgment. For he sold all spiritualities, was disobedient to the apostolic see in advancing a usurper to it by substituting Wigbert for Gregory, in departing from his legitimate wife . . . and in holding at little the words of the Pope.

The result of this clash of authority between the pope and the emperor was civil war: 'since one took vengeance on another, brother spoke against brother, one supported the king and another the pope, so it happened many perished.' On the other hand, Henry is not depicted as entirely without merit, for the chronicler goes on to claim that he was a most merciful and forgiving man and a good friend to the poor.

The writer of the Annals devotes much space (in his entry for 1095) to matters connected with the First Crusade, generally thought to be one of the more positive manifestations of contemporary spiritual vigour. Once again, however, the issue is not as clear-cut as it might at first look. The start seems promising enough, when, in response to the message of Peter the Hermit (for some reason the pope's preaching the crusade at Clermont is not mentioned)

> kingdoms were left empty by their rulers, cities by their bishops, towns by their inhabitants and not only men and boys, but many women took part in the journey, for a marvellous spirit in those times impelled men to gather for the crusade.

This 'marvellous spirit' was somewhat marred by subsequent developments. The first of these was the massacres of the Jews, perpetrated by the crusaders in a number of Rhineland cities. What was first conceived of as an action of Christian zeal – forcible conversion or death – soon degenerated into all-out expropriation and murder, that is, of those who did not prefer to commit suicide. As the chronicler remarks with little hint of condemnation:

> some of them, although unwilling, took refuge in baptism lest they should lose both their lives and fortunes. However many were killed and their fortunes carried off by the Christians.

A laconic coda to this is found under the year 1097 where it is recorded that King Henry, returning from Italy, 'allowed the Jews baptised by force the previous year their law and Jewish rites'.

As well as this overzealous approach to the enemies of Christ within their midst, other aspects of the conduct of the crusaders left something to be desired. The chronicler remarks that a great number of the crusading army was killed near Mersberg in Pannonia; 'And deservedly, since men were travelling with women . . . and evil deeds of fornication and abomination were done between them.' Of such other testimonies to spiritual ferment as the founding of the new monastic orders, the chronicler has very little to say. Whether this is due to professional jealousy, or a lack of interest and information, is hard to determine. We read only under the year 1099, 'In these times an order of monks arose who wore not black, but grey clothes', together with the dubious information that their founder was said to have been Adam. The entry for 1098, the year of Hildegard's birth, reads simply:

> Ruthard Archbishop of Mainz would not support the excommunicated king [Henry IV]. He lost his grace and went into Thuringia and stayed there many years.

Even from this short selection of entries it can be seen that, as far as the Disibodenberg chronicler was concerned, contemporary events illustrated sudden reverses of fortune, shifting allegiances, and a world where the balance of good and evil was constantly fluctuating. In fact, he only seems to recognize unequivocal progress when his gaze is withdrawn from the wider world and concentrated on the establishment and growth of the monastery of Disibodenberg itself, culminating in the dedication of the chapel of St Mary by Henry of Mainz in 1146.

He does not mention the first abortive refoundation of the monastery by Archbishop Ruthard of Mainz, although he does record the probable reason for its failure in his note for the year 1098. The Archbishop returned from exile and was restored to his see in 1105 in time to witness the showdown between Henry IV and his son that Christmas. During this time he probably resumed his original project of establishing monks at Disibodenberg and restoring the site. Although the Annals state that the dedication stone for the new monastic church was laid in 1108, when an abbot from the archbishop's own foundation of St James at Mainz was installed, this does not rule out the possibility that monks were already there as early as 1105, a circumstance which becomes important when we turn to Hildegard's association with the place.[5]

What overall impression of the times do we receive from the

account of the Disibodenberg annalist? He describes a world in which physical conditions were harsh and social life was characterized by stark alternations of fortune. We find religious enthusiasm, and oppression in the name of religion, family and political allegiances which could as easily be repudiated as made, the enjoyment of high office dependent on the personal whim of the powerful, and the condition of the majority of people only to be inferred from their virtual omission from the story at all. But what of Hildegard?

II

On the subject of her family circumstances Hildegard is virtually silent. Godfrey, her first biographer, has little to add, although he does describe her as 'famed equally for the nobility of her birth and her sanctity'. He names her parents as Hildebert and Mechthilde and calls them 'wealthy and engaged in worldly affairs'. Comparison with the opening passages of other saints' lives indicates that this is an entirely conventional description of the subject's background.

Of course, such accounts may often reflect historical reality. The recruiting policies of most monasteries favoured the children of the well-born and, then as now, such a background was no disadvantage for worldly success. Recognition that it might not conduce to progression beyond this world was usually covered by a rider about the subject's equal or greater sanctity. Thus St Hugh of Lincoln († 1200), the third son of a knight, was described by his medieval biographer as 'a man of distinguished birth, but even more distinguished by reason of his sanctity'. Of course, the exact position and circumstances of the saint's family are hard to extract from such conventional descriptions. There was, on the part of biographers, an understandable tendency to exaggerate the worldly position of their subjects, considering the general regard in which noble status was held. Thus Eadmer describes the parents of St Anselm († 1109) as 'both of them of noble birth, so far as worldly dignity goes, and living spaciously in the city of Aosta'. This is rather too rosy a description, given that their condition was really one of 'decayed nobility', as Richard Southern has concluded from the little other evidence available.[6]

But what did it mean to say that Hildegard belonged to the nobility? In trying to locate Hildegard's social position it should be remembered that German society differed from the more highly feudalized societies of England and France at that time. The retention by free men of large amounts of allodial land (land held on one's own account and not from others) and the rise of the ministerial class (originally non-free men who rose to positions of power through personal service) complicate the picture. Hildegard's family, it seems, belonged to the free nobility as opposed to the unfree *ministeriales*. On the other hand, there is no evidence to suggest that her father enjoyed the status of the highest group of nobles, the *primores*, men who held titles and possessed the offices of duke, margrave, or count although, as we shall see, Hildegard was no stranger to such circles.

By an examination of charters and records of the donations of Hildegard's family to the convent of Rupertsberg, Marianna Schrader concluded that the family seat was at Bermersheim.[7] Presumably, then, the family lived (whether spaciously or not is hard to say, given the notorious variation of medieval land measures and descriptions) on these lands. No traces of the family dwelling have been found, although it has been suggested that they must have owned the surviving church at Bermersheim, and that their house would have been somewhere nearby. Clearly, however, since partible inheritance was customary, the next generation might have expected to live a more straitened existence, if indeed it is true that Hildebert and Mechthilde were the parents of ten children.

It is possible that the thought of providing for this tenth child caused Hildegard's parents to dedicate her 'with sighs' to religion as soon as she was born. Guibert of Gembloux's claim that she was dedicated 'as a tithe' (literally 'a tenth') is another possibility, although the dedication of children as tithes may be more a figure of speech than an actual practice. In other words, a child could be regarded as a tithe to the church even if it was not strictly tenth in a family. Moreover, some of Hildegard's older brothers and sisters may have already entered religious establishments by the time Hildegard was born and thus the 'tithe' would have been paid. Possibly some reference to Hildegard as a tithe was interpreted literally by Guibert to make her the tenth child in the family, a piece of information not recorded by anyone else. On the other hand, Hildegard certainly did come from a large family, as the names of seven of her brothers and sisters are known.[8]

The dedication of a child to religion at birth did not mean that he or she was irrevocably committed. It was in the nature of a private vow of intention on the part of the parents, rather than a public ceremony like oblation which indicated an actual change in status.

Guibert of Nogent, though dedicated to the religious life as an infant after his mother survived his difficult and premature birth, feared his father would make him follow the profession of arms. He was only relieved of this fear when his father died while he was still too young to start his military training. St Bernard of Clairvaux made the distinction between such a parental vow and formal oblation quite clear in several of his letters.[9] In Hildegard's case both spiritual and material considerations probably confirmed her parents' intention.

Almost nothing is known of Hildegard's infancy and early childhood before her entry into the anchorage at Disibodenberg. That she was breastfed by her mother for at least some time may be inferred from a stray remark she made many years later: 'from the time of my mother's milk' (that is, if it is not a conventional phrase used to refer to early infancy). Other evidence indicates that the use of wetnurses by the nobility was not universal at this stage. Several saints' lives, including that of St Bernard, suggest that noble and pious ladies made a point of nursing their own children, in the belief that the child imbibed the mother's good qualities along with the milk.

The image of the nurturing mother seems to come readily to Hildegard. We have, for example, a passage from the *Vita*, Bk 2 where she likens the granting of God's grace to her after the initial difficulties of the foundation of Rupertsberg, to those happy occasions when 'the sun breaks through as the clouds lift and when a mother gives her crying baby milk and he rejoices after weeping'. As a young child Hildegard would no doubt have spent most of her time in the company of servants, together with any of her brothers and sisters who were young enough to be under the care of a nurse. Indeed, the only surviving tale of Hildegard's childhood describes a prescient conversation she had about an unborn calf with her nurse, which serves to indicate the agricultural nature of her surroundings as well as her rank. The nurse, amazed at her description of the calf as 'white and marked with different coloured spots on its forehead, feet and back', told Hildegard's mother, and was rewarded in due course with the calf.[10]

It seems that Hildegard was not given any formal educational instruction while she was still at home. This is not surprising, since she would probably have been considered too young; formal teaching does not appear to have been started for either sex much before the age of about seven. Her informal education can only be guessed at. It must have included a certain amount of oral literature in the form of stories and songs, some basic religious instruction, and attendance at various celebrations and festivals.

One aspect of Hildegard's early life which does emerge from her reminiscences is that she seems usually to have been surrounded by other people. This accords well with what we know of the communal nature of medieval society and its general lack of privacy. Hildegard, in recalling these days, refers several times indirectly to the presence of others in such words as 'those who were about me' or 'those standing around'. The contrast between this crowded and busy household and the quiet and seclusion of the cell at Disibodenberg must have been very striking.

When writing about her early years Hildegard not unnaturally concentrates on the development of her spiritual being, rather than her material circumstances, although, as we shall see, her bodily states of sickness and health were ultimately connected with her visionary powers, a fact that Hildegard recognized herself. Hildegard places the first intimations of her extraordinary spiritual gifts at about the age of three when she 'saw such a great light that my soul quaked'.[11] However, at that age she was unable to communicate the nature of her experience to others. As her power to describe such experiences increased, so did her realization that she was in some way set apart from her fellows. The experience of the world that would allow her to distinguish what was normal from what was not may have been slow in coming to Hildegard because she was frequently ill. As she says, 'I was ignorant of many outside things because of the frequent illnesses I suffered . . . which wasted my body and depleted my strength' (*Vita*, Bk 2).

As time went on, she tried to conceal from others the nature and extent of her gifts. In her early years, however, she had not yet developed this facility, and she writes, 'when I was filled with this vision I said many things which were strange to the hearers' (ibid.). No doubt her frequent illnesses, as much as the evidence of spiritual gifts, strengthened Hildegard's parents in their resolve to deliver her over for the spiritual life as they had promised at her birth – both characteristics being more acceptable in a nun than in a wife. The question, then, was what form the fulfilment of their vow would take and when it might be implemented.

Although the practice of oblation, the rearing of children destined for a religious life in the cloister, was apparently losing popularity in the early years of the twelfth century, it was still sufficiently common to be an option open to Hildegard's parents, and seven was the usual age for such a step. The child oblate often entered an establishment close to home, so that some contact could be maintained with the family. The experience of Orderic Vitalis, who was sent, in 1085, from England to a monastery in France and never saw his parents again, was probably exceptional. There was no shortage of nunneries to choose from in the general vicinity of Bermersheim – there were at least two in Mainz, for instance, but it was not to these that Hildegard's parents applied.

The reasons may have been quite fortuitous. About the time that the question of Hildegard's placement would have arisen, the monastery of Disibodenberg was once more being refounded. The hill overlooking the junction of the rivers Nahe and Glan had long been the centre of a Christian cult, supposedly since the time of St Disibod, a wandering Irish bishop who settled there in the seventh century. A series of religious establishments had been located on or around the hill, sometimes housing monks and sometimes canons. Most seem to have had close connections with successive arch-bishops of Mainz. Around the time of Hildegard's birth, Archbishop Ruthard, in a spirit of reform, had decided to improve the monastery by expelling the incumbent canons (originally placed there by an earlier archbishop), in order to establish a stricter and more regular observance. As mentioned earlier, this plan was delayed when he was forced into exile in Thuringia by Henry IV in 1098. On his return in 1105 he was able to resume the project, and although the dating of the different stages of development is problematic it is clear that by 1108 arrangements at the hill were sufficiently advanced to warrant both an abbot and the laying of a new foundation stone for the church. It is probable that there were already some monks in residence several years earlier.

At about the same time a further development occurred at Disibodenberg. Jutta, the daughter of Count Stephan of Sponheim, rejecting all offers of marriage, had decided to dedicate herself to God. She chose the life of a recluse or anchoress, rather than that of a nun in a regular convent of women. In accordance with her wishes her father or possibly her brother, Meginhard, built her a cell at Disibodenberg. The location of Jutta's cell cannot now be established with any certainty. It would be usual to have it built adjacent to the church so that the recluse could observe the daily office. This is how Guibert of Gembloux describes the anchorage, when he says that Jutta was able to listen to the monks singing the *Opus Dei*. However, it is not clear whether Guibert is relying on what he was told about

3 Disibodenberg today.

specific arrangements at Disibodenberg or on his general knowledge of the layout of other anchorages.[12]

Since there are no detailed descriptions of Hildegard's first home at Disibodenberg, except for Guibert of Gembloux's mention of 'a small window through which they spoke to visitors at certain hours and through which the necessities of life were passed', some idea of what it might have been like can be gained from contemporary descriptions of other such houses for small groups of religious women. We may take as one example the establishment which St Gilbert of Sempringham organized some time in the 1130s, for the seven maidens who formed the first members of what became the only original English monastic order.

According to Gilbert's biographer the first house of his order was built 'by the wall of the Church of St Andrew on the north side'.[13] It was surrounded by a stout wall which had in it only one door and one window. At certain times of the day the window was opened to admit the passage of food for the nuns and to pass out refuse. The door was kept locked, with Gilbert, jealous guardian of the key and the nuns' chastity, being the only person who had access to them for the purposes of spiritual consolation, the teaching of religion, and the visiting of the sick. The addition of lay sisters and canons to the flock was made in a rather *ad hoc* manner, as Gilbert tried to work out the best way of meeting the needs of his nuns. As the numbers of both nuns and canons of the order grew, Gilbert drew up a more elaborate set of rules for the running of his establishments. The lengths to which he went in order to isolate the sisters from outside contact are vividly described: walls, ditches, barred windows, the *fenestra versitilis* (a revolving hatch so that the nuns did not see those who passed through the provisions), even the prohibition of singing for the nuns suggest a most zealous solicitude for the purity of the women under his care.

Guibert of Gembloux's description of the anchorage agrees in most details with Gilbert's and other accounts of this sort of building. He mentions the window, for instance, and as for the door, he suggests that Jutta and her companions were literally enclosed, with 'wood solidly wedged in by stone and all approaches blocked up'. On the other hand, there was a good deal of latitude allowed in such arrangements. Aelred, for instance, in his Rule for anchoresses, allows for a door which is to be tended by an old woman of exceptional probity.[14] Although the cell Christina of Markyate, a twelfth-century English anchoress, occupied for four years had a door, she was unable to open it by herself. She suffered a good deal as a result of being unable to leave her cell to satisfy the demands of nature until the hermit Roger paid his daily visit to her, especially since he 'usually did not come till late'.[15] Even if literal enclosure was the rule at Disibodenberg to start with, as the establishment grew there must have been some entrance for new members. Towards the end of Hildegard's stay there the abbot, at least, was able to enter, since we have an account of him visiting Hildegard on her sickbed.

When Count Stephan's plans for his daughter became known to Hildegard's family (the closeness of the relationship between the two cannot be discovered; Hildebert, however, is shown witnessing a charter with Stephan's son, Count Meginhard of Sponheim in 1127), the possibility of placing Hildegard with Jutta must have been canvassed. There were several apparent advantages, among them the proximity to home, a suitably aristocratic association, and perhaps the hope that a child of Hildegard's age and physical frailty might be better off in such surroundings than as one oblate among many in a larger, more impersonal community. On the other hand, it is difficult for parents today to understand the mentality of those who were willing not only to enlist their children as conscripts in the army of God (to paraphrase David Knowles), but to do so in such a strict and irrevocable form. There is no suggestion here that Hildegard was merely being educated by Jutta and that she might later choose a different course in life. She was enclosed on an equal footing with Jutta who, as an anchoress, was required to stay in her cell till death, with no hope of ever leaving it. The justification for committing a 7-year-old child to such a life (even if that is not how it turned out in Hildegard's case) may have rested on the assumption that the present was but a moment in eternity and that a life of such strict enclosure was the most certain way of attaining everlasting bliss.

Thus the scene from an altar in the Rochuskapelle in Bingen showing Hildegard's parents, sumptuously dressed in the styles of the fourteenth century, presenting their daughter to three Benedictine nuns who look no more formidable than the reception committee of a boarding school, suggests too optimistic a view of the matter. Nor does the fresco from the Abbey church at Eibingen, though considerably more austere and accurate as to clothes and general background, sufficiently convey the awesome nature of the transaction.

The enclosure of anchorites was a solemn liturgical rite, performed, where possible, by the bishop. Guibert of Gembloux gives a partial description of the rite which can be supplemented from an English pontifical of the twelfth century.[16] He writes:

4 Hildegard's entry to the anchorage. Her parents are shown presenting their daughter to three Benedictine nuns. Altar, Rochuskapelle, Bingen.

the day fixed for the induction came [1st November – All Souls' Day – according to the Annals] and with people of both high and low degree standing by, in the manner of those who are given over for the last offices of funeral rites . . . with lighted torches . . . they were buried by the abbot of the place and the brothers, as if truly dead to the world.

The comparison between entering the anchorage and burial was not idly made. As well as employing hymns and responses from the burial service, it was customary for the priest to rehearse the commendations of the soul made at the funeral 'as far as the placing of the deceased on the bier', in case the recluse died enclosed without benefit of this sacred service. After the main part of the service was over, the house had been blessed, and the choirs had withdrawn, the priest remained a little while to exhort the inmate to rise up in obedience and finish her life in the same way. Then he left, the door was blocked up, and the people departed.

III

What manner of life did the inmates of the cell lead? Judging by what happened later and because of the proximity of the monks, it seems likely that the Benedictine Rule was taken as their principal guide from the beginning. Once more our sources describe life in the anchorage only in the most conventional and general terms. Jutta, Godfrey writes,

carefully introduced her to the habit of humility and innocence. She taught her the psalms of David and showed her how to give praise on the ten-stringed psaltery. (*Vita*, Bk 1)

From this we should understand not that Hildegard merely learned the psalms by rote, but that she was taught to read by Jutta. The psalter was the universal primer of the Middle Ages. Psalters were often owned and read by laywomen. The English anchorite Christina of Markyate seems to have spent most of her time reading the psalter when not engaged in manual work such as embroidery. Hildegard, it seems, did more than read the psalms. If the reference to the psaltery is to a real instrument, rather than a biblical allusion to the psalms themselves, then music also formed part of her early education.[17] We should not forget the influence of the monks' services, which, according to Guibert, Jutta could hear by day and night. The Benedictine chant must have formed a background to Hildegard's life and thought, whether she took an active part in it or merely overheard it. She may, of course, have done both at different times.

Let us then suppose that Jutta and her companions followed, more or less closely, the order of the monks' day. This was structured around the regular performance of the eight offices of the *Opus Dei* (The Work of God), as originally prescribed in the Benedictine Rule, although variations had been introduced over the years and in different places. The original impulse for the ordering of monastic worship seems to have stemmed from two passages in Psalm 118 which read: 'Seven times a day do I praise thee because of thy righteous judgments' and 'At midnight will I rise to give thanks unto thee'. Since the timing of the offices depended on the Roman method of time-keeping, whereby the periods of daylight and darkness were each divided into twelve 'hours', the times at which the offices were held varied according to the season of the year, as indeed did the absolute length of each 'hour'.

A typical winter's day would begin at about 2 a.m. when all (monks and oblates alike) rose for the office of matins. This was the longest and most complicated of the offices and was meant to accommodate an entire repetition of the 150 psalms of the psalter each week. After matins there was a short interval before lauds, recited at first light, followed by prime at sunrise. The day offices were shorter than those of the night and were held at the first, third, sixth, and ninth hours, hence the names: prime, terce, sext, none. The evening office, vespers, was meant to be held while it was still light, and the day ended at sunset with compline.

Clearly, it would have been very difficult for an anchoress living in isolation to perform the full *Opus Dei* by herself because of the problems of time-keeping. Monasteries were accustomed to detail monks to stay awake to make sure that the night offices were held at the right time. On the other hand, if the cell were attached to a larger monastery, the bells sounded to wake the monks might have served the women as well.

Even if Jutta followed the full round of canonical hours there would have been some time left over. The Benedictine Rule prescribed both prayer and work for its followers. The interpretation of the work component changed over the centuries. Manual labour undertaken to support the monastery (which seems not to have been always envisaged even in Benedict's time – he found it necessary to include a warning to the monks about grumbling if they had to take in the harvest) had become increasingly attenuated as servants and tenants came to perform the necessary manual tasks. Intellectual and artistic work connected with the writing and production of books began quite early to play a larger part in the monk's day.

Instructions for those leading a solitary life pay particular attention to the necessity for keeping occupied – possibly because it was unrealistic to expect them to follow the complete Benedictine timetable of prayer on their own. Thus Peter the Venerable, Abbot of Cluny, wrote to advise a recluse against such dangers as pride and laziness and suggested that a suitable activity for the time not devoted to prayer might be copying the scriptures or, if this was too hard on the eyes (as well it might be in an ill-lit cell), making combs, boxes and wooden cups, rush mats, or osier baskets.[18] Aelred of Rievaulx, in the Rule that he wrote for his sister, also suggested what should be avoided and what practised by the anchoress. Interestingly enough, he decrees that the teaching of children, which would turn 'the cell into a school', is to be avoided, apparently because of the human interactions involved. It seems probable that he would also have disapproved of Jutta's reception and education of Hildegard in the cell at Disibodenberg. On the positive side, he advised his sister to vary her prayers and meditations with manual work, although he does not specify what kind. The only activity that the biographer of Christina of Markyate actually describes her engaged upon in her refuge is the reading of the psalter. However, it is also recorded in the *Gesta Abbatum* that she sent three mitres and a pair of sandals embroidered by her own hands to Pope Hadrian.[19]

Abelard, too, had some suggestions about the sort of work nuns might be expected to perform. The division was largely along traditional gender lines. Women might tend such animals as cows and poultry, and wash and mend the altar linen and monks' clothes. Obviously, some of these activities would be more appropriately performed in a convent of women rather than a narrowly-enclosed recluse's cell. Aelred, on the other hand, says that solitaries should not keep animals. Gilbert of Sempringham seems to have intended his nuns for a life of prayer and meditation, entirely free from manual work, except, possibly, for copying of manuscripts and some sewing, judging by the care he took to provide them with laysisters and laybrothers to look after the internal and external needs of the community and canons to see to their spiritual welfare.

Concerning the practical details of Hildegard's early religious life, we learn from Godfrey that she was raised on a frugal diet and simply clothed. Once more such a description accords with the spirit of the Benedictine Rule. Indeed, it seems likely that the cell was provisioned directly from the monastic kitchens. In that case the food supply would have been secure, if not particularly varied or exciting. This was no doubt preferable to having to rely on the possibly erratic generosity of the neighbouring populace. The biography of the English anchorite Wulfric of Haselbury has several rather unedifying episodes which seemingly arose from his anxiety to maintain his food sources.[20]

The Benedictine Rule provided for a single meal in winter and two in summer, consisting of two cooked dishes followed by vegetables or fruit and bread. No meat from four-footed animals was to be eaten, except by the sick or very weak. The cooked dishes were generally concocted from beans, eggs, fish, or cheese. The stringency of the diet differed according to the liturgical year. Once more, a good deal of discretion was allowed, or at least had become customary, to individual monasteries in dietary matters. At the monastery of Cluny, for instance, according to an eleventh-century account, the regime for summer would consist of two meals per day. At the first there would be a dish of dried beans, a course of cheese or eggs which was replaced by fish on Thursday, Sunday, and feast days, and a third course of whatever vegetables and fruit were available. On great feast days there were onions and little cakes instead of beans. An allowance of about a pound of bread a day was given, and more at supper if required. On fasting days (which included Wednesdays and Fridays, from Pentecost to 14 September, and every weekday thereafter till Lent) only one meal was served at about 3 p.m. On canonical fast days it was even later. Since the Rule took into account the special needs of the very young and the very old, it was usual for children to be given some sort of breakfast to get them through the long day, if only a drink and some bread. Aelred bases his description of the anchoress's food explicitly on the allowance of 'blessed Benedict'.

It is interesting to compare such a regime with what Hildegard wrote later in her medical works about dietary matters. On the whole her remarks agree with the Benedictine prescriptions. She suggests that for the sake of good digestion the first meal of the day should be taken around noon. Breakfast is only conceded to those who are weak, debilitated, or deficient in body so that they can obtain strength from the food. Supper, of the same kind of food which was eaten during the day, should be taken early in the evening, so that it is possible to go for a walk before bed (*Causae et curae*, Bk 2). This raises the question of what form of exercise was available to the inmates of the cell at Disibodenberg. It seems probable that there was little scope for walking there; such places were referred to as 'prisons' for good reasons. Hildegard, evidently, thought that women did not require as much physical exercise as men, but presumably a minimum was necessary even to them for good health.

Hildegard also has some interesting things to say about the relative merits of different beverages. Water, she suggests, is not to be taken in winter, and only in moderation and by healthy people in summer. Considering the dubious nature of most medieval water supplies this advice is probably quite sound. Beer and wine are her preferred drinks as she considers them better for weak constitutions. Beer, she claims, gives a lovely colour to the face and makes you fatter. Doubtless German monasteries brewed their own beer even in wine-growing districts. The Institutions of St Gilbert are very clear on the matter, having a special chapter to deal with the misfortune of the nuns being reduced to drinking water instead of beer.

On the matter of clothing, the Benedictine Rule, being written for monks, will not serve as a guide to Hildegard's practice, except in the spirit. The chief aim was to avoid ostentation and expensive materials. Clothes that could lead to vanity, thought to be an especial failing among women, were particularly to be avoided. Thus Aelred prescribes a veil of some dark colour to be worn, not of variegated or expensive material. Some rules also prescribed the number of each kind of garment which was allowed. Thus Aelred suggests that one tunic and two undergarments should be sufficient, while Gilbert of Sempringham shows himself quite prodigal by his allowance of five tunics, although he prescribes only one undergarment. Cloaks of wool, or sheepskin, were to be used instead of furs. There is a description in the biography of Christina of Markyate of how she put off the silks and furs of her former life when she donned the rough habit of a recluse.

Thus the kind of life Hildegard led at Disibodenberg during the first eight years of her vocation, her childhood, we might say, can only be reconstructed in the most conjectural manner. It could be seen as a series of contrasts or even paradoxes. On the one hand, it was a life of isolation and silence; on the other, a life lived in close proximity to a woman of some spiritual and worldly distinction, probably indeed, a closer relationship than she might have had growing up in an ordinary household. It was a life of physical austerity in terms of food and surroundings, yet one where the food supply was constant and the immediate environment secure. Finally, it was a life where intellectual horizons may have been limited, yet one which was potentially in touch with the entire tradition of Benedictine culture because of the physical proximity of the cell to the monastery. To what extent Hildegard was able to avail herself of this potential is another question.

For reasons which will be clear later, Hildegard tended to play down the human element in her educational formation. Yet it is hard to believe that there was no cultural interchange between the monastery and the anchorage. For one thing, spiritual direction would be needed, a confessor at least, presuming that it did not all devolve upon Jutta. We may recall Gilbert of Sempringham who visited his nuns for the purpose of religious instruction. Hildegard, indeed, mentions that she had chosen for herself a *magister* from among the monks, a title which presupposes some sort of instruction, and there is nothing to limit it to spiritual direction. Intellectual instruction, for spiritual ends, was no doubt also possible.

All the sources relate that as time went on (unfortunately none is more specific) the fame of Jutta and her pupil attracted other aspirants to the community. Thus the transformation of the cell into a small Benedictine nunnery was effected by degrees. Such growth no doubt had positive consequences for its members, not least Hildegard. Rather than being completely dependent upon the monks for food, liturgical services, and religious instruction, with a greater number of recruits more of these activities could be carried out by the nuns themselves. There would also be possibilities for increased leadership and responsibility. Living space may also have been enlarged although just where they could have expanded on the site is hard to determine.

Henceforth entrants to the convent would be admitted as nuns, rather than enclosed as anchoresses. The ceremony for the profession or veiling of nuns was also a solemn liturgical occasion, only to be undertaken at certain times of the year and requiring the participation of the bishop. (In this it differed from the ceremony for the clothing of a monk, which could be performed by the abbot.) At the mass, the habit and veil of the postulant were placed on the altar to be blessed by the bishop. Having retrieved the habit and put it on, the candidate approached the altar holding a lighted candle. The bishop then placed the veil on her head with an exhortation to virginity and continence. The prayers that follow are elaborations of this theme. Divine aid is invoked to ensure that the nun will become one of the wise virgins awaiting the arrival of the heavenly spouse and ultimately be numbered among the 144,000 following the Lamb.[21]

From the time of her adolescence, then, Hildegard was a member of what amounted to a double monastery, although it is probable that the women's community was much smaller than that of the men and therefore subordinate in ways additional to those usual for such institutions at the time. That the monks were prepared to countenance such a development may appear to conflict with the commonly held belief that association with women, even in the form of an enclosed convent, presented great dangers to monastic life.

Despite such notions, the needs of women religious did not go entirely unrecognized and there are many examples of double monasteries among the Benedictines, especially in Germany, not to mention new experiments elsewhere such as that of Robert of Arbrissel at Fontevrault. Such ambivalence towards monastic provision for women is succinctly illustrated by the *Annales Rodenses* which describe the founding of a double monastery at Rolduc. After some years the nuns were sent off to a place at a distance from the original house as it was thought unfitting for monks and nuns to inhabit the same site. However, this decision was reversed by the next abbot, who installed a smaller number of nuns on the original monastic site, with the explanation that the Bible enjoined the spiritual life on both sexes.[22]

Since Disibodenberg, when it was refounded at the turn of the twelfth century, was not intended as a double monastery, it is difficult to ascertain how things were arranged to accommodate both monks and nuns. Probably there was no provision made for dividing the church into two sides, as was done at Sempringham, or even for separate chapter houses, as seems to have been the case at Schönau. The buildings there must have been duplicated since Elisabeth of Schönau is often described as being alone in the chapter house. Presumably this was one set apart for the nuns' use and not frequented by the monks. It also seems that the nuns at Schönau used an oratory and not the monastic church of St Florian. However, when Jutta died it was in the chapter house of the monks that she was first buried, before her later promotion to the Chapel of St Mary.

Nor should it be forgotten that extensive renovations and rebuilding were carried out on the site during the time of Hildegard's residence there. The bald statements of the Disibodenberg chronicler announcing the dedication of the principal altars of the new church and other buildings such as the infirmary do not give an adequate idea of the disruption and confused activity which must have been experienced for years while the building work was in train. In such circumstances it is hard to see how strict enclosure and isolation from the male side of the community would have been possible. The way of life described in the custumals, such as that of Sempringham, must have been the ideal rather than the reality.

Indeed, details from the works of Elisabeth of Schönau suggest that a more relaxed form of association was common in German double monasteries.[23] We have, for example, a picture of Elisabeth leaning out of her window to talk to a monk and a description of a group of nuns standing in conversation around a priest on his way to bring the reserved elements to a sick nun. Elisabeth knows the names and recognizes the faces of certain members of the male community when she sees them in a vision. Such evidence suggests that the relationship between monks and nuns in a double monastery might be less than rigorously controlled. In Hildegard's case we have the example of her teacher and later, secretary, the monk Volmar. It is unlikely that Volmar was much older than Hildegard, since he died when she was over 70, or much younger, either, if their association began when Hildegard herself was quite young.

Some idea of the kinds of activities Hildegard might have been involved in during the early years of her profession can be inferred from her later achievements. One area of activity may well have been that of musical production. As the women's numbers increased it would have been possible for them to perform the *Opus Dei* themselves, rather than being passive spectators and auditors of the monks. Expertise in this area might easily have led Hildegard to try her hand at supplying the needs of her community in the same way that Abelard provided hymns for Heloise at the convent of the Paraclete.

A second activity in which Hildegard might well have been involved was medical practice. Medical skills were cultivated within the monastery for use on its inmates and reached such a high level that Benedictine monks became (in England, at least) royal physicians. A decree of Pope Alexander III, forbidding such outside practice, suggests it was widespread. Such a decree would not, however, have had much effect on the numbers of people who came to monasteries seeking cures, whether by natural or supernatural means. These circumstances may, for instance, explain Hildegard's acquaintance with certain gynaecological and obstetric matters that we might not otherwise expect her to have encountered within the convent.

In short, developments at Disibodenberg, in which the expansion of the cell played no little part, must have presented opportunities for the deployment of different skills and interests and given a sense of expanding vistas. While something could be seen from the window of an anchorite's cell, much more could be viewed from the gates of the enclosure where the sick were tended; a greater sense of one's own powers could be derived from writing and singing one's own praise to God than hearing it always sung by the monks, or by instructing new members of the community rather than being always the pupil.

Hildegard herself remarked on the fact that at this time her health seemed to have improved and she had reached vigorous maturity. This sense of vigour and maturity seems to have been linked in her thought with the progress and recognition of her visionary powers. Perhaps it is not surprising to find that in these years she was able to confide in Jutta and through her, in Volmar, and this degree of recognition, limited though it was, had something to do with her general well-being.

Also to this period of expansion belongs the death of Jutta in 1136, an event of which Hildegard makes surprisingly little. Although she describes her in glowing spiritual terms, the human element is somewhat lacking, in contrast to the account of her sorrow at the death of Volmar. Hildegard was the obvious successor to Jutta, and so she was elected by the community to be *magistra* or mistress of the nuns. What authority this position conferred on Hildegard is difficult to assess. It is clear that the nuns, including Hildegard, were subject to the authority of the abbot while they were at Disibodenberg, both with regard to financial affairs – the disposal of the nuns' dowries – and spiritual matters, including whether Hildegard was to commit her visions to writing. Thus Hildegard's sense of developing power and autonomy must have been somewhat tempered by the recognition that women were ever, in practical as well as other ways, dependent upon, and hence subject to, men.

3

OPPORTUNITIES AND CONSTRAINTS

But when I had passed my first youth and attained the age of perfect strength, I heard a voice from heaven saying . . . write what you see and hear. (*Scivias*, preface)

I

The third decade of the 1100s was, for Hildegard, a time of rising expectations. Instead of living the life of an anchoress, in the shadow of her holy mentor Jutta, and on the periphery of the dominant male religious culture represented daily to her consciousness by the monastery of Disibodenberg, she was now administrative head of a growing community of nuns and their recognized spiritual leader. Given such psychological conditions it would not be surprising to find that Hildegard was now ready to turn her attention to other fields of activity.

Indeed, it is at this stage in her life that Hildegard began to claim for herself the role of an authority on theological matters. This was not an unusual move, since spiritual authority of one sort or another was often accorded locally to revered figures, both male and female, who were consulted on a range of matters great and small. For instance, Jutta's *Vita* describes how she was considered as 'a heavenly oracle' by a variety of people from all walks of life who sought her advice. However, Hildegard's departure from the norm was her insistence on putting her ideas down in written form and in the Latin language, the medium of high culture. It seems likely that Hildegard experienced a certain amount of psychological conflict at this stage of her life. This supposition does not rest merely on the lateness of her decision to adopt such an unexpected course, given her sex and lack of education, but rather on her own descriptions of the accompanying events.

Hildegard's striking account of what happened when she was 'forty-two years and seven months old', which forms part of the preface to the *Scivias*, has already been cited in chapter 1. It was subsequently excerpted by Godfrey, her biographer, and incorporated in the first book of the *Vita*. Hildegard also describes this event in the context of the development of her visionary powers in one of the autobiographical passages from the *Vita*. About the first experience of her special gifts she writes that she saw 'such a great light that my soul quaked, but because I was an infant I could not reveal anything of it'. As she grew in years she astonished those around her by her prescience (though not her emotional maturity), unaware, at first, that she was specially favoured by having such inner vision as well as ordinary external sight.

By the time she was 15, however, she had become embarrassed and bewildered by her powers and sought to conceal them. This situation persisted for an unspecified time, until Hildegard found herself able to confide in Jutta. However, apart from 'disclosing this to a monk of her acquaintance', probably Volmar, Hildegard does not suggest that her mistress took any more positive steps. Still, as Peter Dronke points out, the mere fact of the acceptance of her visions by 'a loved woman teacher' may have been enough support at the time.[1] Reading between the lines, however, there may be a suggestion that Jutta was in some sense an inhibiting factor to Hildegard's self-expression. It is perhaps significant that the momentous events described only took place after her death. The two occurrences follow strikingly one upon the other in Hildegard's account of what happened:

> God infused this woman with his grace like a river of many waters so that she gave her body no respite, with vigils, fasts and other good works, until she crowned the present life with a good death. God indicated her merits by certain beautiful signs. After her death I continued to have visions till my fortieth year. Then in that same vision I was compelled by most painful pressure to reveal openly what I had seen and heard. (*Vita*, Bk 2)

We might also consider significant Hildegard's contrasting reactions to the deaths of Jutta and Volmar many years later. She saw herself as 'orphaned' by Volmar's death, but not by Jutta's. Was it because Jutta was less educated and her approval was worth less to Hildegard? Was it because Volmar was a man and thus his approval counted for more? Or was it because his approval was more active and had practical consequences? For whatever reason, the death of Jutta does not seem to evoke the warmth of feeling one might expect, given their close relationship.[2]

A further bar to Hildegard's making her visions public at this late stage was the very fact that she had kept quiet about them for so many years. As she wrote in connection with the *Scivias* vision, 'I was very fearful and ashamed to publish what I had kept silent for so long.' Thus several years passed until she felt so strongly compelled to act that she was able to overcome her diffidence.

But what was it that Hildegard now felt obliged to make public? We may conjecture, on the evidence of the vision which was subsequently given written form as the *Scivias*, that considerable development had taken place in the nature of Hildegard's visions over the years. What had first appeared as an inchoate light to her infant mind and subsequently manifested itself as an ability to predict the future ('I used to repeat much about the future in conversation . . . and said many things that were strange to the hearers') was now nothing less than the ability to 'understand, without any human teaching, the writings of the prophets, the evangelists and of other holy men and those of certain philosophers'. In short, her visions were to be her entrée into the world of the practising theologian.[3] Nevertheless, she does not seem to have abandoned all claims to more popular forms of prescience, as we will see from an examination of her correspondence in chapter 8.

Yet it was not simply subjective understanding that Hildegard gained by means of her vision. She also claimed for herself an educative mission. The possibilities for such instruction were either by writing or preaching.[4] Hildegard's mission, as she now conceived it, seems to have been chiefly concerned with setting her visions down in writing. Perhaps this was because while there were definite prohibitions against women preaching, the issue of their writing was less clear cut. Although her instructions in the vision ('write and say') could be applied to both writing and preaching, her main preaching activities belong to a later stage of her public career.

Thus Hildegard was to make her visions public for the edification of the Christian people. Even more remarkable was the fact that Hildegard undertook to write them down herself, using the learned language, Latin, rather than dictate them to a suitably qualified male intermediary, when she was, as she admits freely, only poorly educated. The choice of this medium effectively cut her off from the great majority of the population who had no access to, or means of understanding, Latin writings. It seems, then, that Hildegard must have intended her works for the religious élite, with at best an indirect effect on the masses. Thus, consciously or unconsciously, her undertaking to write her works in Latin, together with the nature of their content, places her squarely in the tradition of learned writing. However, the account she gives of her adopting this unusual course of action excludes any discussion of her own wishes or intentions. She is, from the beginning, merely the instrument of God, chosen more or less at random to deliver his words.

But can we discern behind all this a hidden agenda? By writing in Latin on theological subjects Hildegard identified herself with the male literary and theological élite. She only started to do so comparatively late in life and furthermore it took some kind of psychological crisis to get her going. Therefore, we may deduce that Hildegard had been for some time a frustrated writer. She even calls attention to the fact that she had suppressed the impulse to record her visions when she writes in the *Scivias* introduction: 'but till the time that God wished it to be made plain by his grace I had repressed [*depressi*] it in mute silence'.

Thus the event of 1141 marks Hildegard's entry on her career as a writer. 'Career' perhaps is not quite the right word, since her 'career' was that of an abbess even if that particular title was only infrequently used of her. However, it is her writing that her contemporaries remarked most of all, and which is still perhaps the most important and intriguing aspect of her life for us today. This is both because of the nature of what she wrote and the fact that she wrote at all.

II

The two main disqualifications Hildegard had to overcome in order to produce the works for which she is remembered were not unconnected. They were remarked upon both by Hildegard herself and her contemporaries. First, she was a woman, and second, she was unlearned. While her sex is hardly in dispute, the extent of her education is open to question.

Hildegard, as we saw in an earlier chapter, was taught the psalter by Jutta, as indeed repetition of the psalms formed the basis of the religious life she first undertook in the anchorage at Disibodenberg. From this we can assume that Hildegard learnt to read. Of course, being able to read does not entail a detailed knowledge of the language read (in this case Latin). However, it seems very likely that over the years of performance of the *Opus Dei*, Hildegard at least picked up what we might think of as a reading (or aural) knowledge of the language, although when it came to writing Latin she was less accomplished. Hildegard also seems to have been taught to write, that is, to form letters, at an early age, a skill not necessarily included in the process of learning to read.

Hildegard's claim in the *Scivias* preface that she did not know about the divisions of words, cases, and tenses need not mean that she lacked all knowledge of Latin syntax, but rather that she had no theoretical understanding of such categories. Such knowledge was one of the elements that went to make up the study of 'grammar', the first subject of the trivium, which together with rhetoric and dialectic formed the lower division of the seven liberal arts, the basis of the medieval curriculum.[5] Thus we may conclude that Hildegard was uneducated by twelfth-century standards rather than illiterate in the modern sense. But another distinction must be made. To say that Hildegard was uneducated according to twelfth-century standards means specifically that she had not followed the prescribed course of education, of which the first requirement was a thorough grounding in 'grammar'. This involved not only a practical and theoretical understanding of Latin syntax, but what amounted to a course in classical literature. Thus by degrees the student passed through the stages of the trivium to the quadrivium which included music, arithmetic, geometry, and astronomy, until he was competent to approach the crowning subject, theology, or engage in the more lucrative studies of canon law and medicine.

By the time Hildegard was writing, the monopoly on higher education had passed from monasteries, via cathedral schools to the shifting associations of masters and students from which the great medieval universities developed. A basic education along traditional lines might still be obtained in many monasteries. It is clear, though, that Hildegard's education was extremely rudimentary and thus her qualifications as a writer were slim. For someone to presume to write on theology who lacked such a background and was also a woman was a bold step indeed.

III

Why should this be so? To say that women were held in low esteem in all departments of life in the West during the Middle Ages is doubtless true, but perhaps not very helpful. Moreover, to cite the canons which prevented women from participating fully in church life and the laws which limited their participation in civil life always raises the suspicion that reality was perhaps less stringent. To repeat the fulminations of such church Fathers as Tertullian, Lactantius, or Jerome might be seen merely as giving space to crabbed misogynists. Instead let us take Abelard, a man far ahead of his times in many ways, and one who has been called, not without some justification, a 'feminist', and examine some of his pronouncements on women.[6]

Actually, when we come to examine it, Abelard's record on women is rather ambiguous, and if we depend on his own account of his relationship with Heloise, downright exploitative. He claims, for instance, in his *Historia calamitatum* (*Story of my Misfortunes*) that he insinuated himself into the position of Heloise's tutor in order to seduce her, even suggesting that if his well-known charms were to fail he would be in a position to satisfy his desires by force. On the other hand, there is no doubt about his genuine respect for Heloise's mind and learning. His description of her as 'standing supreme' in literary studies, while somewhat qualified by being limited to women, is to be all the more valued coming as it did from someone who tended to disparage other people's intellectual achievements. However, after suffering the revenge of her guardian Fulbert, Abelard forced Heloise to enter the convent of Argenteuil, doubting her ability to persevere in this intention if he should enter a monastery first.

Most aspects of Abelard's view of women can be attributed to his belief (outlined in his Letter 6 to Heloise) that men were naturally stronger than women both in mind and body ('Sunt et viri naturaliter tam mente quam corpore feminis fortiores'). That he believed they were also morally stronger is shown by his remark on the necessity for monasteries being set apart from other human habitations: 'Solitude is indeed all the more necessary for your woman's frailty, since for our part we (i.e. men) are less attacked by the conflicts of carnal temptations and less likely to stray towards bodily things through the senses.' For this reason Abelard envisaged a system of double monasteries, under the authority of an abbot, who was to act as a father to all, even to the extent of guaranteeing and safeguarding the nuns' chastity, like Gilbert of Sempringham. 'When the abbot himself is appointed he shall swear . . . that he will be to them a faithful steward in the Lord, and will carefully guard their bodies from carnal contact' (Letter 7).[7] Indeed, he seems to think that women should not even be abbesses of their own convents and the authority of women over men, as in the case of the Abbey of Fontevrault, is an overturning of the natural order.

Another specifically female frailty he refers to is the love of rich clothing. He applauds St Paul's strictures on the matter in I Peter 3: 1–4 with the following words: 'And he judged rightly that women rather than men should be dissuaded from this vanity, for their weak minds covet more strongly whatever can increase extravagance' (Letter 7). In real life the honours seem to have been pretty evenly divided, if we can believe, for example, Cistercian fulminations against the rich attire of the Cluniacs. It is important to note, however, that here, as in other cases, women were especially singled out for criticism on the basis of a biblical precept, whatever the realities of the situation might have been.

Examples of male imputations of women's inferiority, physical, mental, and moral, are thus easily assembled. A more difficult question to answer is how far this affected medieval woman's view of her powers and capacities, in short, her own self-image. The problem of evidence here becomes acute. Few women wrote anything directly on the subject, and to infer such attitudes from what they did, or more pointedly, from what they failed to do is a somewhat dangerous undertaking. Moreover, there would be variations among different classes and conditions of women. Some evidence suggests that certain noble and royal women, such as Eleanor of Aquitaine or Matilda of Tuscany, exercised a good deal of real power and need not have felt their world to be excessively circumscribed. At the other end of the scale some peasant women have been seen (if possibly through feminist glasses) as holding an honoured and honourable place within the domestic economy. It is quite likely, indeed, that misogynist attitudes weighed most heavily on women in religion, who were exposed to them more constantly, and where a set of special prohibitions – from assuming priestly office or from approaching the altar – were in force.

Thus, Heloise, on the evidence of her letters, seems to have internalized the male view of women's inferiority almost completely. The problem, of course, is to decide whether to take the views expressed there at face value. Peter Dronke, for instance, suggests that Heloise may be using such expressions of inferiority 'as a concession to Abelard . . . to provide an opening for him to say something opportune'. But such an optimistic view does not entirely square with how she seems to have conducted her life.[8]

Consider, for example, the opening of her letter to Abelard from the convent of the Paraclete (Letter 3) where she takes him to task for putting her name before his in the previous letter 'contrary to the conventions of letter writing, indeed to the natural order of things . . . a woman before a man, a wife before a husband, a servant before a master, a nun before a monk, a deaconess before a priest, an abbess before an abbot'. She goes on to suggest that it is the general lot of women to be the downfall of great men, citing Eve, Delilah, the cases of Solomon, and Job.

Later, in the letters of direction, she asks Abelard to send her a Rule for the convent of the Paraclete instead of their following the usual custom of women professing the Benedictine Rule where 'the same yoke of monastic institutions is placed on the weak sex as on the strong' (Letter 5). Noting the way in which St Benedict was prepared to make concessions in the Rule to the very young or old she asks: 'what would he provide for the weak sex whose frail and infirm nature is generally known?' In fact, her entire project, down to a reordering of the psalter, is predicated upon concessions to 'our weakness'. Such a low opinion of her own worth may partly explain why Heloise did not do more with her talents. Even with her acknowledged literary qualifications Heloise never seems to have essayed a large-scale composition. Was this because of her proximity to Abelard (admittedly psychological proximity rather than physical proximity in the latter part of her life)? The comparison with Jane Carlyle, busily writing her letters in the shadow of her husband Thomas, comes to mind.

Proximity to a great man was not a problem that Hildegard had to grapple with, although she had others, such as a lack of education. Nor, apparently, did Elisabeth of Schönau whose brother Eckbert, though educated and an author in his own right, was hardly of Abelard's stature. He claims that she knew hardly any Latin, and while Elisabeth describes herself on several occasions as reading the psalter, her visions show little evidence of wider reading. Although there is some suggestion that she kept notes, possibly dictated to one of the nuns, hidden under her bed, she was also content to let her brother commit her visions to writing and mediate between herself and her readership. Indeed, several of the visions are devoted to answering questions asked by her brother or other monks which she then conveys to her visionary mentors.

IV

What do these three examples indicate about educational opportunities for women in the twelfth century? Most striking, perhaps, is their range, although by all accounts Heloise was even then recognized as an exceptional case. There seems to have been no formal prohibition of women's learning: time and opportunity were another question. The provision of educational facilities for females was even more haphazard than for men. Some of the more elementary forms, such as instruction by the mother, may have been shared by both sexes. After that boys had tutors, especially if they were destined for a clerical career, as were Guibert of Nogent or St Anselm. Some went as oblates to monasteries and received there the full medieval education; some no doubt received much less. The question of the kind of education given to female religious is harder to answer and can only be approached obliquely. Thus we have the example of Elisabeth of Schönau who scarcely knew Latin and may not have been able to write, although other members of the convent could. Heloise, on the other hand, received her outstanding training in letters before she met Abelard, presumably from the nuns of Argenteuil, where she was not even an oblate.

The main difference in educational provision for men and women was, of course, that men could go from tutors, or from a monastic education to the schools (although this was discouraged for monks), the source of most educational innovation and ferment at the time. Women could only attend such places disguised as men and a very few perhaps did so.[9]

Just as the evidence about female education is contradictory and ambiguous, so are the consequences of such education. It might even be said that education for women tended to have a negative effect as far as their self-esteem was concerned, because educated women were then more exposed to prevalent male attitudes in their reading. Many of Heloise's arguments against marriage and for female inferiority depend on the written tradition. This may partly explain why the step from consumption of knowledge to production of it seems to have been more difficult for women to make than men, judging by the number of their works surviving from the period, even making allowance for a much smaller proportion of literate women than men. This also assumes that there was no wholesale interference with or destruction of women's works. But why was it that women were so reluctant to write?

V

To answer this question we might do worse than consider the reasons men gave for the writing of books, because most twelfth-century male writers seem to have thought it necessary to justify the activity in some way. While no doubt such justification is partly conventional, a modesty topos ultimately derived from classical authors, this is not the whole story. Actual cases show that some did write, and unwillingly too, at the request of a superior. Anyone who reads the exchange of letters between Aelred († 1167) and St Bernard († 1153), where the Abbot of Clairvaux asks Aelred to write the book on friendship which became the *Speculum caritatis* (*Mirror of Charity*) cannot doubt the sincerity on both sides.[10] There are many other cases in which knowledge of the circumstances of the writer indicates that more than a mere rhetorical convention is involved.

In the autobiography of Guibert of Nogent († 1124) there is an account of the impatience he felt as a young monk at Fly to be invited to put his literary talents to work. His chance finally came when the prior of a neighbouring monastery who had heard him preach suggested that he put his sermon down in writing. Guibert was careful to obtain his abbot's assent to the proposal, and having done so, used it as an excuse to embark on a long-held plan to write a commentary on the *Hexaemeron*, and more. The abbot, however, ordered him to stop after the first chapter of the *Hexaemeron*, and Guibert tells us, with scarcely a blush, that he was forced to complete the work in secret.[11] (Understandably, he dedicated the work to Bishop Bartholomew of Laon, rather than the hoodwinked Abbot Garnier.)

Some monastic writers took out a double form of insurance, not only making clear the fact that they had been told to write, but justifying the work according to the usefulness of its content. This, of course, differed according to the genre of the writing. The theological commentary or treatise was almost its own justification, and writers of history (loosely conceived) could point to the fallibility of human memory. Ortleib, the monastic chronicler of Zwiefalten, includes the following reasons in his acrostic preface to his history:

> For the ignorance of monks and canons or nuns is very great and abominable, when they do not know the beginnings of their monasteries, and they cannot even institute thanksgiving or sow words of prayer whose temporal benefits they are pleased to reap.[12]

Nevertheless, he claims that it took the combined pressure of his abbot Oudalric and the priest Bertulf, who in the end threatened excommunication, to make him agree to undertake the work.

A similarly circumstantial account of the genesis of a piece of writing is given by Rupert of Deutz († 1129) in his preface to *De victoria Dei (Concerning God's Victory)*. He recalls how, as a monk at Siegburg, he had been expounding the vision of Daniel in the presence of his abbot Kuno, who 'greatly delighted by this sort of reasoning, suddenly burst out with these words: "Write for me a book about the victory of the word of God".'[13]

Writers of saints' lives had a ready-made justification in the exemplary nature of their subject. Even so, the author was generally at pains to show that he had been requested to write by a third party. In the case of Hildegard's own biographer, Theodoric of Echternach, there were two such instigators, Ludwig of St Eucharius at Trier, a close friend of Hildegard's who afterwards became abbot of Echternach, and Abbot Godfrey of Echternach (who had previously visited Hildegard as a monk from St Eucharius and who later (1190–1210) served as abbot there). Even such an established figure as St Bernard of Clairvaux claimed that his life of Malachy, the Cistercian bishop of Armagh who died at Clairvaux on his way to Rome in 1148, was written at the urgent request of Abbot Congan of Innislonagh.[14]

Honorius of Regensberg († c. 1156), as befits his somewhat ambivalent status (his origins and institutional affiliations are unknown), employs a style of preface which sets him apart from the monks yet does not sufficiently identify him with anyone else. In his preface to the *Elucidarium*, a compendium of theological lore, he does not claim to be writing at the command of a superior but rather, having been 'often requested by my colleagues to explain certain problems', he decided to put down his answers in permanent form, thinking in this way to benefit posterity and also his own soul, by the prayers of his readers (a process he makes difficult by apparently concealing his own name). In his *Sacramentarium*, as well, he relies on the usefulness of the work as justification, remarking that his compendium will benefit those who do not have access to many books on the subject.

Not only monks, however, thought that the command of a superior was necessary for undertaking a literary work; the same device is found among canons who wrote. Thus Anselm of Havelburg († 1158) dedicates his *Dialogi*, on the differences between the Roman and Greek churches (a subject on which he was something of an expert, having been part of the imperial mission to Byzantium) to Eugenius III, and makes sure that his readers know that it was written specifically at the pope's request, in order to 'obey the sacred command of the apostolic beatitude'.[15]

It might be thought that outside the monasteries, in the more secular atmosphere of the schools or great episcopal households, different attitudes would be found. Yet John of Salisbury († 1180) gives two reasons for writing the *Metalogicon* in his dedicatory letter to Thomas Becket. In the first place, his friends urged him to write it, and on the other hand, as a refutation of the Cornificians, it is a reaction to provocation, rather than an independent initiative. It seems that even episcopal status was not sufficient to allow the writer to dispense with the notion of having been called upon by someone else to write. Thus Gilbert Foliot († 1181) dedicates his commentary on the Song of Songs to his friend and fellow bishop, Robert of Hereford who, having asked him to write it, was appropriately offered the first reading.[16]

On the other hand, those whose job it was to teach, whether as canons or clerks, show greater self-assurance. Confidence in his role as a teacher apparently allowed Hugh of St Victor († 1141) to dispense with a preface to his *Didascalicon*. Moreover, the tone is less personal than in the works of monastic writers. Hugh's opening statements have the generality of almost self-evident truths: 'Two things are above all necessary for whoever aspires to understanding, that is, reading and meditation'.[17] However, where his purpose is not so overtly pedagogical, as in the *Speculum de mysteriis ecclesiae* (*Mirror of the Mysteries of the Church*), his prologue mentions a request, although who asked him is not clearly stated.

The early writings of Abelard may conveniently be classed with those of other masters of the schools. At this stage of his life he shared the self-confidence of Hugh of St Victor, dispensing with prefaces for his *Ethics* and *Theologia Christiana* (*Christian Theology*). The *Sic et Non*, it is true, does have a preface, but one which underlines the unusual nature of the book. The preface to his *Theologia Scholarium* (*Scholars' Theology*), while bearing a superficial resemblance to those of his contemporaries in that he records how he was asked to write the work in question, uses his pupils rather than his superiors as the motivating cause and has a decidedly self-confident (not to say self-satisfied) tone.

In his last years, however, when Abelard had become a monk, we find him writing for a limited and particular audience. 'You ask by begging and beg by asking' reads the beginning of his preface to the *Expositio in Hexaemeron* (*Commentary on the Hexaemeron*). In this case we know from other sources that he is referring to an actual request and that Heloise had asked him for the work, as indeed she had for the *Rule for the Paraclete* and the *Hymns*.

VI

But Hildegard's position was even more difficult because of the subject on which she had chosen to write. While anyone (read man) with a basic education might essay a monastic history or saint's life, the study of theology, based as it was at this time on the explication of the Bible, or 'sacred page', was considered to be in a class by itself and not to be undertaken without a thorough grounding in the subjects of the trivium and quadrivium. There was also the problem of authority, the idea that once the Fathers of the church – such towering figures as Augustine, Jerome, and Gregory – had commented on a particular part of the Bible, there could be nothing left for lesser mortals to say on the subject.

Furthermore, there seems to have been a good deal of distrust of the unaided intellect and the assumption that a student would need to be initiated into the mysteries by a teacher in order to reach even a basic understanding. It should be remembered that the literal meaning of a text was only one, and often the least important of its meanings. Medieval readers had to take account of at least three others: the moral or tropological, the allegorical or mystical, and the anagogical.

This attitude is well illustrated by an anecdote Abelard tells in the *Historia calamitatum*. He relates how disappointed he was in the method of teaching theology practised by Anselm of Laon, which was based on an exposition of various older commentaries on the biblical text. Abelard 'was amazed that for educated men the writings or glosses of the Holy Fathers were not sufficient for interpreting their commentaries without further teaching'. He proved his point by taking an obscure prophecy of Ezekiel and returning next day to expound it to his fellow students, having used only a commentary and his own native wit to prepare his lecture. Not surprisingly this attracted the enmity of Anselm, who apparently forbade him to continue to teach at Laon.

Those who were less sure of their own intellectual powers, or indeed of their education (or perhaps just more modest) tended to allow a greater place for divine assistance, often thought of as an infusion of the Holy Spirit, in their understanding of scripture. Thus Rupert of Deutz, although he had been educated in the Benedictine Abbey of St Lawrence at Liège, the city then considered to be the chief educational centre in the German Empire, required a series of visions to set him on his writing career. As his modern biographer points out, 'it was not to his education but rather to a series of divinely inspired visions that Rupert ascribed the release of his prodigious talent.'[18] It seems then that most male writers did not consider inspiration to be a substitute for hard work and study. Thus Joachim of Fiore († 1202), the Calabrian abbot who was seen by later generations as the archetypal medieval prophet, did not even claim the same degree of illumination as Hildegard. He believed that the spirit of understanding was only to be gained by those who were prepared by years of study. As Marjorie Reeves puts it:

> Joachim would never have called himself a prophet in the sense of one who foretells the future according to revelations given directly and instantly to him. . . . The *spiritualis intellectus* or *intelligentia* with which he believed he had been endowed . . . was poured out only on those who wrestled and agonised over the hard, external realities of the Letter.[19]

It is in the light of such beliefs that we must attempt to see Hildegard's claims to have been suddenly empowered to interpret the Christian faith to her contemporaries. Since she was all too conscious of her lack of a conventional education, and also perhaps because she was more modest about her own intellectual powers (having internalized to a great extent the prevailing view of women's capacities), she tended to emphasize the part played by divine inspiration in her understanding. She does not, however, suggest that she had no acquaintance with what we might call the secondary sources – commentaries and possibly even glosses on biblical texts. She claims, rather, that she could understand these without the help of a human teacher much in the way Abelard did. But whereas Abelard rejected such teaching because he thought it was unnecessary, Hildegard made a virtue of rejecting what was unavailable to her anyway. Moreover, the fact that she perceived her own knowledge primarily as a series of visions, made such an interpretation of its source more compelling.

If, then, there were reasons for men to feel diffident about putting themselves forward as the writers of books, the situation of a woman writer would have been even more daunting, given the universally low esteem in which their sex was held. That women were responsible for only a tiny proportion of the literary output of the twelfth century (or any other, up to the present) was both a cause and a consequence of such attitudes. We have seen that Heloise, whose education and abilities went beyond those of many male writers, apparently produced nothing more ambitious than a few letters.

What then of Hildegard, whose own education could hardly compare with that of Heloise? It may have been because she lacked such qualifications for writing that she had to find a more radical authorization. We have seen how the command of a superior was frequently given as a reason for composition.[20] If the command of one's abbot was not to be gainsaid, then the order of the pope must have been even more compelling. Hildegard took this argument to its logical conclusion when she claimed to have been ordered by God to write down her visions.

Another advantage of such a prophetic claim was that God not only provided the authority to write, but also the knowledge of what was to be written. Indeed, a lack of formal education could be turned into an advantage (and even the extent of one's informal education might be somewhat played down), since this showed that what Hildegard had to impart, as in the case of the prophets of Old Testament and apostolic times, must have come directly from God. Finally, the role of prophet was available to women, both by biblical example and patristic approval – Hildegard's biographers cite Origen in this connection. Moreover, since the prophetess was merely God's mouthpiece, and he was known to use the weak to confound the strong, and fools to correct the wise, there were no upsetting consequences for the perceived natural order.

In this way, the experience that led to the writing of the *Scivias* served to validate, to Hildegard herself and to others, the mission she believed she had received from God to write down the contents of her visions. Hildegard was not unique in questioning her suitability for authorship – men too thought that some justification was necessary before putting pen to parchment. Such doubt was intensified in Hildegard because of her particular awareness of her unsuitability in being both a woman and uneducated. However, once she had overcome the initial hurdle and started to write, she went from strength to strength.

4

THE WAYS OF GOD

The word of God was given her not in a nocturnal vision, but by
an open infilling of her reason, instructing that she should declare
the things which were revealed to her from Heaven in writing and
give them to the Church to read. (Guibert's *Vita*)

I

Hildegard's three major visionary works, *Scivias, Liber vitae meritorum*
(*Book of Life's Merits*) and *Liber divinorum operum* (*Book of the Divine Works*)
stand apart from her other writings because of their length, their
shared visionary form, and their similar theological concerns. Indeed,
such considerations have led some commentators to see the books as
a trilogy. However, the works span Hildegard's entire writing life
(c. 1140–74 or 1175) and so while the *Scivias* and the *Liber vitae meritorum* may be conveniently described at this point, the *Liber divinorum
operum*, which was written towards the end of Hildegard's life and
represents her maturest thought on many of the subjects she treated
elsewhere, is best left till later. As a compromise between a chronological and a classificatory account of Hildegard's writings I have
decided to treat Hildegard's first two visionary works here and leave a
more detailed discussion of the *Liber divinorum operum* until chapter 8.
In this chapter I shall attempt to convey some idea of the scope and
nature of the works, rather than give an exhaustive analysis of their
theological content.[1]

The circumstances of the writing of the *Scivias* have already been
described in the previous chapter. Hildegard, at the age of 42, experienced a particularly striking vision in which she felt that she had
been instructed to make known that understanding of the basic
tenets and inner meaning of her religion which she had long been
accustomed to receive in visionary form. Such experiences and the
understanding she drew from them were not new, but the impulse,

55

or rather command, to record or write them down was. After some delay, due to her feelings of inadequacy for the task, Hildegard obeyed the command and started to write the *Scivias*. It took her ten years to complete.

This is not surprising, given Hildegard's other duties and the size of the work (something over 150,000 words or approximately 600 printed pages of text). The *Scivias* is divided into three books, or major parts, each consisting of a series of visions – six, seven, and thirteen, respectively. In each case Hildegard first describes what she sees and then records the explanations she understands to come from the 'voice from heaven'.

Significantly, Hildegard employs structural markers to indicate its prophetic nature at the beginning and end of each of the three divisions of the work. Furthermore, each separate vision is distinguished by the repetition of a concluding sentence which is different for each of the three books. Thus the visions of the third book conclude with the following words: 'Let whoever has sharp ears of interior understanding pant after my words in the burning love of my mirror and inscribe them in his soul's inner comprehension.'

Throughout the work the conclusion of Hildegard's description of each separate vision is also marked by a sentence which becomes stereotyped and differs for each of the three books. In the first book, after some initial experimentation, it is: 'I heard again the voice from heaven speaking to me.' In Book 2 we find the similar: 'And again I heard a voice from the heavenly heights speaking to me', while the last book favours the formulation: 'And I heard that light who sat on the throne speaking.' The cumulative effect of such repetitions is to emphasize the prophetic, God-given nature of Hildegard's writing and to distance it from the works of her contemporaries. It is a method that Hildegard employs for her three major theological works, as we shall see.

The length of the book, together with its rather rambling construction, makes its contents difficult to describe without going into great detail. The problem arises not so much on the level of the separate visions, which may be described individually, but when it comes to making sense of the larger divisions of the work. For one thing, the three parts differ markedly in length, the second being twice as long as the first and the third being equal to the first two put together. This may have something to do with what I will argue was the actual genesis of the work in separate visions experienced by Hildegard at different times.

Any description of the subject matter of the *Scivias* runs the risk of being unhelpfully broad. This even applies to Hildegard's own title 'Scivias', usually explained as a contraction of the phrase: 'Know the Ways (of God)'. Perhaps the difficulty is inevitable and arises from Hildegard's holistic approach to knowledge, life, the world, and religion. All is seen as grist to her mill, interdependent and worthy of consideration, an attitude we will encounter again in her scientific works.

The division of the *Scivias* into three major sections or 'books' reflects three different approaches to the same body of thought, rather than a logical or chronological progression, although elements of the latter are evident within the separate parts. Thus the first part, consisting of six apparently independent and formally unrelated visions opens with a relatively static picture of the eternal kingdom of God. This is contemplated by a figure representing 'the fear of God', which according to a well-known biblical text, is the beginning of wisdom. While this scene may suggest that the major subject of the *Scivias* is a certain kind of knowledge or understanding (as the title itself suggests), the most prominent initial theme is the entry of sin into the world with the fall of Lucifer and the subsequent fall of Adam. The consequences for humankind, and to a lesser extent for the world itself, are also examined.

From time to time the preordained remedy for the fallen world – the Incarnation – is mentioned or anticipated, but not described in its historical sequence. In fact, the fifth vision with its treatment of the synagogue (*Synagoga*) as a type of and contrast to the church (*Ecclesia*), looks forward to the Incarnation and New Dispensation, but the final vision in the first part comprises an account of the different orders of angels, possibly to be seen as an anticipation of the future state of the blessed. We might conclude, then, that many general themes are stated in the first part which are explored at greater length in subsequent books of the *Scivias*. Indeed, it is possible that Hildegard had not quite found her method at this stage.

The theme of the second part is more easily stated. It deals, as the voice of God announces in an early directive to Hildegard, with the 'fiery work of redemption'. Several subthemes go to make this up. Thus the first vision has to do with God, Christ, and the Incarnation. The second concentrates on the Trinity, and the remaining visions (now related to each other by a series of cross-references) are on ecclesiology. Here special reference is made to the sacraments, including baptism, confirmation, eucharist, holy orders, and penance – but not marriage, which is discussed in the first book as one of the consequences of the Fall. Thus the subject of this part can be seen as God's remedy for the world and man in the fallen state depicted in the first book of the *Scivias*.

The third part takes up the themes again and works them into a series of powerful visions in which architectural imagery is especially prominent. The entire third book has a somewhat theatrical cast and includes as its finale a version of Hildegard's musical play, the *Ordo virtutum*. In the last book Hildegard retraces the steps by which man will be saved, both in historical terms, by means of the Incarnation, passion, resurrection, and ascension, and in terms of the individual soul, where the virtues have a part to play. Here we get something approaching a complete salvation history and, in the eleventh and twelfth visions, Hildegard presents her well-known description of the end of the world and Last Judgement preceded by the persecutions of Antichrist. The thirteenth vision, consisting of a number of Hildegard's songs and observations on music, may be taken as a representation of the eternal blessedness of the citizens of heaven.

Such a bare account of the content of the *Scivias* gives little indication of the richness of the work as a whole and the strange power which it sometimes projects. At times, of course, the explications of the visions may seem somewhat trite or laboured, but at its best the method can be used to great effect.

In order to demonstrate Hildegard's method in the *Scivias*, let us look more closely at the fourth vision of Part 2, one of a series of interconnected visions about the church, *Ecclesia*, here represented as a beautiful and powerful woman. This particular vision is concerned specifically with confirmation:

And then I saw, as it were, a huge round tower entirely built of white stone, having three windows at its summit, from which such brightness shone forth that even the conical roof of the tower appeared very clearly in the brightness of this light. The windows themselves were decorated round about with most beautiful emeralds. And this tower was placed as it were in the middle of the back of the image of the woman mentioned above [*Ecclesia*], as a tower is placed in a city wall, so that the image could not in any way fall, because of its strength. And I saw those infants who had gone forth from the belly of the woman, as mentioned earlier, shining with great brightness; some of them were decorated from head to toe with a golden colour, others had the same brightness but lacked the colour. Some of these children were looking at a clear brightness, others towards a dull and reddish glow tending towards the East.

But of those who were looking at the clear brightness, some had clear eyes and sound feet and walked bravely in the belly of the image. Others having weak eyes and feet were blown hither and yon by the wind. But they, with crutches in their hands, were trying to fly to the image and from time to time they touched her faintly. Some who had good eyes but lame feet were cast around here and there in the air. Others who had weak eyes but strong feet walked wanly before the image. But of those who looked at the dull red glow, others walked bravely in the aforesaid image, well adorned; others, casting themselves from her, attacked her and impugned her decrees, others of them by the fruit of penitence were humbly returned to her, some however, in obdurate neglect, remained in the grip of death. And again I heard the voice from heaven speaking to me. (*Scivias* (*Sc.*), 2, vision 4)

The actual vision having been thus described, the rest of the section consists of fourteen chapters of explication, all understood as being delivered by the voice from heaven. (This vision is quite short and relatively uncomplicated; some continue for over a hundred chapters.) The method of explication can be seen from the second chapter, entitled: 'That the immense and unfailing sweetness of the Holy Spirit is given in confirmation'.

Now the reason why you see a huge round tower entirely built of white stone, is because the sweetness of the Holy Spirit is immense and entirely encircling all creatures in its grace, in such a way that no corruption in the integrity of the fullness of justice destroys it; since glowing, it points the way and sends forth all rivers of sanctity in the clarity of its strength, in which no spot of any foulness is found. Wherefore the Holy Spirit is ablaze and his burning serenity which strongly kindles the fiery virtues will never be destroyed and thus all darkness is put to flight by him. (*Sc.*, 2, vision 4, chapter 2)

In a similar fashion, the other details of the vision are explained, sometimes in fairly abstract terms, as above, and sometimes more concretely. Thus, for example, the three windows represent the Trinity and the emeralds surrounding them the 'most green virtues and pains of the apostles'. The children shining gold from head to

l. Quod omis baptizať p unchone
    epi ornari & ftabiliri deber.
ll. Quod uniufa & indeficienf dulcedo
    fpc fci daťur in 9 firmatione.
lll. Quod ineffabilif trinitaf is firma-
    tione manifeftať & uiridiffimif
    uirtutib' declaraťur. /-poteft.
llll. Q'd ecclia unchone fpc fci munita.
    nuiqm i errore pueritati deici _
v. Verba moyfi de eadem re.
vi. Q uod baptizati i unchone crifma
    tif apontifice decoranťur.
vu. Verba libri regu ad eande re.
vui. Q'd baptizať & n 9 firmať datur
    te baptifmati habeť f; ornatu
    7 fulgore unchoni fupio rd doc
    tori fui n habeť.
vuu. Q'd i honore fpc fci p folof epof con-
    firmatio querenda e.
x. Q ui 9 firmandu manib' tenet. ut
    carnali peritatione et n 9 uungať
xi. Q ui poft baptifmu ad diabolum re-
    uertit: n peruitat 9 dempnabit.
    qui aut baptifmu fidelit fatť ad
    fuicipiť. ecclia pftiif fuif din exoranr.
    T rei modi quib' ecclia refonar ut
    tuba.   / timoda.
xii. De diuerfitať baptizatoru mul
xiii. Verba ezechielif de eodem.
    Quarta Vifio Sede
    par tis.

5 Ecclesia and the Holy Spirit. *Scivias*, 2, 4, Eibingen MS.

foot are those who have been confirmed as well as baptized, and are distinguished from those who have merely been baptized by their golden colour. A further point is made here, apparently without reference to anything in the vision, about confirmation being an episcopal prerogative. Thus chapter 9 is entitled: 'That in honour of the Holy Spirit confirmation is to be practised only by bishops'.

Hildegard often goes beyond what is strictly mentioned in the vision in order to include all relevant material on the topic. There follows a digression about fulfilling the promises made in baptism and the three ways in which the church sounds like a trumpet, before Hildegard (or God) returns to the vision in order to describe the 'diverse kinds of the baptized'. Here an explanation is given of the children who were described as shining in different colours and those who were afflicted with blindness or lameness. The explanations are predictable enough for the shining figures but somewhat more complicated for the blind and lame – 'those who walked wanly before that image':

> they maintain a weak intention towards good works when they ought to advance bravely in deeds of righteousness and they do not run single-mindedly in the teachings of the Church because their minds concentrate on earthly rather than heavenly matters; and therefore they are foolish before God, because they wish to understand by secular wisdom what cannot be comprehended. (*Sc.*, 2, vis. 4, ch. 13)

These general explanations are sometimes backed up by direct reference to scripture. Thus Ezekiel 7: 27 ('The king shall mourn, and the prince shall be clothed with desolation . . . ') is cited to explain how those 'careless of life, with hard hearts on account of contumacious and impenitent folly receive the judgment of death, as Ezekiel says in his mystical vision'. This vision was a prophecy about the downfall of Israel but in commenting on the passage Hildegard confines herself to the moral or tropological level of explication. Here the king represents the soul and the prince the body weighed down by sin.

Having obtained some idea, then, of how the *Scivias* is constructed, let us now address the question of its content and purpose. Because Hildegard took pains to locate herself within the prophetic tradition of the Old Testament, as the opening formulae of her works indicate, we might expect to find in them more than just an explanation of the theology or history or ethics of the Christian religion.[2] Prophets were often politically and socially engaged and usually adopted a stance critical of the circumstances in which they found themselves. Hildegard, with her frequent moral exhortations and directives, is no exception to this rule. But what aspects of her society did she wish to castigate? Can any particular groups be singled out as receiving more blame and warnings than others? How does what she says relate to the preoccupations of the times in which she was writing, on the one hand in secular affairs, and on the other, in more particularly religious terms?

For instance, a great deal of emphasis is placed on right action and basic adherence to God's commandments. Much of her advice is directed to a general audience, the faithful (*fideles*), a term which is synonymous with practising Christians, both those living a secular life in the world and those who have dedicated themselves to religion in one form or another. However, Hildegard does at times make distinctions and address herself to specific groups. It is not surprising, given her own position, that she devotes more space to the life and duties of the religious than to those of laypeople. On the other hand, her treatment of the laity, whose chances of attaining the Heavenly City had long been considered rather slim (compare St Anselm's idea that few would be saved and they would practically all be monks), is relatively generous. She is at pains to assert that if they follow the ways of God, by adhering to his laws and struggling against sin and the Devil, they too may have eternal blessedness.

Hildegard has no illusions about the nature of some members of this estate (just as she has none about the clergy). She is quick to denounce those who 'pollute the church buildings with the blood of murders or semen brought forth in adultery or fornication' (*Sc.*, 3, vis. 5, ch. 25) as well as those who seize for themselves the tithes or other goods of the church. God is represented as saying to these people: 'O woe, wretched, O woe, wretched, O woe, wretched men who so foully cut themselves off and engage in such perversity before the eyes of my majesty.' This is not mere rhetoric – a notorious case of murder carried out in church was the slaying of Charles the Good, Count of Flanders in 1127. God, says Hildegard, will visit vengeance on them or on their children, unless they desist and repent. Hildegard thus typically holds out the option of repentance for even the most grievous sinners. Indeed, the only unpardonable sin is to believe that one's sins are too great for the mercy of God. (That, of course, pre-supposes some kind of basic acceptance of the faith. Non-believers who harden their hearts against God are to be cast into hell.)

Confession to a priest, preceded by true repentance, is the safest course, but in the case of imminent death, confession can be made to a layman or, failing that, to God himself. Likewise baptism can be performed in an emergency by laymen (possibly even laywomen, as in the case of midwives) so long as the correct formula, including the naming of the three persons of the Trinity, is employed.

The most important topic Hildegard deals with in connection with the laity is that of marriage. Hildegard had a generally positive attitude towards marriage and procreation in spite of the fact that its very institution was a result of the Fall. As a result of this transgression humankind and even the physical world were only imperfect versions of what God had originally planned for his creatures. The consequences of the Fall were thus far-reaching and account, among other things, for the Virgin Birth, as Hildegard writes in *Sc.*, 1, vis. 2, ch. 13 where the voice from heaven explains: 'For since the fall of Adam I have not found in human seed the righteousness which ought to be in it, since the Devil stole it away in the taste of the apple.'

A recognition, often somewhat grudging, of the place of marriage and the production of children within it was the current orthodoxy. However, a dissenting view was taken by various heretical sects such as the Cathars, who viewed the world and all its activities, especially procreation, as the Devil's work. Catharism, which had spread from Bulgaria to the Rhineland by the middle of the twelfth century, was particularly active in Cologne. Hildegard is known to have been interested in combating such dualist ideas (she urged the clergy of Cologne to preach against Cathars in the city) and it may be that her relatively enthusiastic view of matters sexual is, in part, polemical.

Most of her views on marriage seem to derive from, or at least be rationalized according to, the biblical creation story. Thus, since Adam and Eve are the model of a married couple, the wife must be subservient to the husband (*Sc.*, 1, vis. 2, ch. 11). And since they are one flesh, there can be no divorce unless decreed by the church, not even for adultery of either party. The only possible voluntary severance is if both parties agree to leave the world to enter religion.

Sexual intercourse among legally married couples, for the purpose of begetting children, is permissible since it was 'ordained through divine counsel for the multiplication of the sons of Adam by procreation' (*Sc.*, 3, vis. 10, ch. 3). To give it its most favourable construction, sometimes laypeople produce children who themselves undertake the better part – virginity. In *Sc.*, 2, vis. 5, ch. 37 the married are compared to fleshmeat or at best, that of birds, 'since those who live carnally in the world produce children, among whom can be found followers of chastity, that is to say widows, and the continent who fly to supernal desire through the taste for good works.' This sounds very like St Jerome's famous backhanded recommendation of marriage: 'I praise marriage and laud matrimony because it provides me with virgins.'[3]

By the twelfth century the church had an impressive array of prohibitions against even such divinely-sanctioned sex. Hildegard does not enlarge upon them except to rule out intercourse with pregnant and menstruating women. Hildegard often justifies such warnings by her own peculiar views of physiology, which are also used to explain prohibitions against adultery and homosexuality (*Sc.*, 1, vis. 2, chs 15–20). On the other hand, unlike Honorius of Regensberg, she allows women the privilege of attending church when menstruating (as did Gregory the Great when asked by Augustine of Canterbury) but she debars men, for the prescribed time, who have experienced nocturnal emissions, as well as those who have been wounded, not to mention both men and women after intercourse (*Sc.*, 1, vis. 2, ch. 21).

So although Hildegard sees a place in the church for the laity (a class or group almost coterminous with the married), it is definitely the lowest in the hierarchy. Hildegard's views on the relative position of laity, clergy, and the monastic order are set out most clearly in the fifth vision of the second book of the *Scivias*. Here she sees the figure of *Ecclesia* once more, bearing in her bosom 'a most beautiful image of a girl, bareheaded with dark hair and clad in a red tunic which flowed down to her feet'. She is surrounded by an admiring crowd dressed in ways which indicate their positions: some have mitres and bishop's stoles, others wear white veils and embossed circlets bearing various images. The maiden is addressed as *floriditas*, 'floweriness', and seems to represent both virginity in the abstract and its chief proponent, the Virgin Mary. The image of *Ecclesia* is surrounded by three waves of light, spreading far and wide, which stand for the three orders of the church, so numbered in honour of the Trinity. Within this brightness are many steps and ladders to show the interconnections of the three orders.

The three orders appear to be the seculars, 'the common worldly people' in *Sc.*, 2, vis. 5, ch. 3; that is, the laity living in the world; the priests and bishops, referred to here as *pigmentarii* or 'perfumers', who are the successors of the apostles; and finally, 'the living odour, vowing the way of secret regeneration', which represents the monastic order. Hildegard leaves no doubt as to the hierarchy of the orders, comparing them in *Sc.*, 2, vis. 5, ch. 37, first to the souls of the just, angels, and archangels, and then to flesh, apples, and grain. She makes it clear that people may aspire to a higher order, but not descend from a higher to a lower (*Sc.*, 2, vis. 5, ch. 35). This would mean that monks should not become bishops, as it is a lower order, although many did follow this course; some, like Eugenius III, even became popes. Possibly Hildegard would get around this by counting them still as monks, a practice encouraged by the behaviour of those such as Otto of Freising who continued to wear the habit of a Cistercian even when he was bishop.

Since she rates the monastic life so highly, it is not surprising to find various prohibitions and caveats against its too hasty assumption. These sections throw some interesting light on the conditions of the time, as the following chapter heading shows: 'That those who, not for the love of God, but constrained by some worldly trouble, falsely accept the sign of religion, are like Balaam' (*Sc.*, 2, vis. 5, ch. 41). Here she recognizes that some may enter religion through poverty, bodily weakness, or oppression by secular lords; such action is to be strongly discouraged.

Likewise, she objects to the indiscriminate oblation of children (*Sc.*, 2, vis. 5, chs 45–6). Children, she says, are not to be constrained to enter religion against their will but should be asked, on reaching the age of understanding, whether they wish to follow this course. Unfortunately, Hildegard does not suggest what age this might be, and it is quite likely that she was thinking of something like seven or eight (the age, in fact, at which she was dedicated to the religious life), rather than an age which would seem to us appropriate for such a binding decision.[4] In Hildegard's own case there is no suggestion that her views on the matter were ever canvassed. This is all the more important since once committed to the religious life there was no relinquishing it. Indeed, it was the duty of monastic superiors to pull back any waverers in their care, first with kind words or exhortations, and failing that, with blows and confinement on bread and water (*Sc.*, 2, vis. 5, ch. 49).

Turning to the other order of religious, the 'perfumers' or priests, which included bishops, we find a strange ambivalence. On the one hand, the priest has 'an honour . . . which is given . . . [to him] above all other men', that is, the power to bind and loose (*Sc.*, 2, vis. 6, ch. 95). However, there is plenty of contemporary evidence to suggest that parish priests, at least, were often scarcely able to perform their duties through lack of education and instruction. Moreover, living, as they did, among their flocks they tended to intermingle all too closely, taking concubines and fathering children. We can see, then, why Hildegard might rate them lower than pious monks or virgins on a scale of spirituality.

On the other hand, while Hildegard condemns sinful priests, her attitude here does not seem to be quite as uncompromising as that taken by some of her contemporaries (*Sc.*, 2, vis. 3, ch. 35). Their position was that such men should be rejected by their parishioners since the sacraments they dispensed would be invalid. Hildegard seeks to reform such priests by appealing to their sense of responsibility, their need to answer, in the future, for the souls entrusted to them, and the dignity of their position (*Sc.*, 2, vis. 6, chs 94–6).

Bishops presented a different kind of problem, especially in the Empire where they were so closely connected with secular government. Hildegard devotes a chapter to 'ministers of the church who do not enter by the gate but by the back door', that is, who are not canonically elected and consecrated, declaring that they 'lacerate Christ like those who crucified Him' (*Sc.*, 2, vis. 6, ch. 61). Once more, the sanctions against such behaviour are to be found in divine retribution, rather than human enforcement.

Hildegard goes thoroughly into the temptations experienced by the religious. Apart from sexual temptations, which they had in common with the laity, these included 'worldly sadness . . . and memory of earthly glory'. As well as these she mentions a concatenation of evils including 'bitterness and anxiety of heart' which leads to 'detraction, whispering and slander of neighbours' and finally (with special reference, perhaps, to bishops) the 'pretence of justice'. On the other hand if 'righteousness' in general, rather than 'justice' is implied, the description could apply to all religious. Indeed, it might be particularly directed at the newer orders, like the Cistercians, who were often accused by the Benedictines of being pharisees. Such vices are treated at much greater length in Hildegard's second visionary work, the *Liber vitae meritorum*. Suffice it to say for the present that Hildegard sees all these temptations, even if one falls from time to time, as surmountable: 'whoever, therefore, repelling the Devil, removes these vices from himself by penitence will arise to life' (*Sc.*, 2, vis. 7, ch. 23).

This is also true of the sexual vices which are given particularly comprehensive treatment in the *Scivias*; she claims:

> But there are many to be found both among the spirituals and the seculars, who pollute themselves not only in fornicating with women, but even place on themselves the most heavy burden of condign judgment, by contaminating themselves in perverse fornication. How? A man, who sins with another man according to the manner of women, sins bitterly against God and against

that conjunction by which God joined man and woman. (*Sc.*, 2, vis. 6, ch. 78)

Biblical authority for such condemnation (Lev. 18:22; 20:13; Rom. 1:27) is clear enough, but Hildegard adds her own characteristic reasons. Male homosexuality perverts the natural order, because God decreed that copulation should be between a stronger (man) and a weaker (woman), so that they might be mutually sustained.

> But these perverse adulterers, when they change their manly strength into the contrary weakness, casting aside the true nature of male and female, most foully imitate Satan in their perversity who wished to destroy and divide Him who is indivisible, in his pride.

The same, more or less, goes for female homosexuality, about which the Bible has less to say (cf. Rom. 1:26), although here it is a psychological, rather than a physical law which is being transgressed (*Sc.*, 2, vis. 6, ch. 78):

> And a woman who appropriates for herself these devilish arts, in that she simulates intercourse, taking the part of a man, with another woman, appears most vile in my sight . . . since she who should feel shame about her desire has impudently taken another law unto herself. And since such people have transformed themselves into a different mode they are contemptible to [God].

In much the same way masturbation is condemned for both sexes, as is bestiality. Certain penitential remedies are suggested such as lamentation, fasting, maceration of the flesh, and heavy beatings. Hildegard also outlines various dietary measures as a preventative against excessive libidinousness (*Sc.*, 2, vis. 6, ch. 79) in line with her medical views, to be examined further in connection with the *Causae et curae*. The meat of birds, rather than the flesh of animals should be taken, as it is less likely to be inflammatory. For similar reasons the consumption of wine is to be limited.

These examples should convey some idea of the nature of the *Scivias* as essentially a work of instruction and direction, a 'how to' book rather than an abstract meditation on theological questions. Of course, theological questions do arise and Hildegard has something to say on most of them, but her method of explaining the great mysteries of the Christian faith depends on analogy, often pictorial – they were visions after all. Hers is a very different methodology from that of Anselm or Abelard, who tried to explain the faith by logical or dialectical means. Indeed Hildegard, like St Bernard, often has recourse to the device of forbidding further prying into God's mysteries by asserting that they cannot be fully understood in this life:

> But if you, O man, in the instability of your heart say to yourself, how does the offering on the altar become the body and blood of my Son, then I shall reply to you: 'Why, O man, do you ask this, and why do you examine these things? Do I ask this of you – that you should pry into my secrets concerning the body and blood of my Son? These are not required of you but rather that you, receiving them in great fear and veneration, carefully conserve them and cease to worry any more about the mystery. (*Sc.*, 2, vis. 6, ch. 60)

Another very striking feature of the *Scivias* is the almost entire lack of emphasis on, or even mention of, the human nature of Christ. At a time when the Cistercian, Aelred of Rievaulx, could devote an entire treatise to 'Jesus at the age of twelve' and devise a series of meditations for his sister on the passion, in which each stage was imagined and suffered with Christ, Hildegard seems arrested at an earlier stage of spirituality, where Christ was viewed solely as a triumphal king and just judge. Abelard, too, suggested that Heloise should meditate on the passion in an intensely personal way: 'Gaze upon him on his way to be crucified for your sake, carrying his own cross. Be among the crowd, be one of the women who wept and sorrowed over him' (Letter 4). We may compare Hildegard's accounts of both the Son of God, and, perhaps even more surprisingly, His mother. For example, Hildegard does not seem to have seen Mary, in her human role as the mother of Jesus (or any other role), in the *Scivias* visions. When female figures appear in the visions they are of the virtues, or the church, or certain attributes of divinity, such as wisdom or charity. Some of these, notably the figure of *Ecclesia*, have more solidity and reality than any of the human figures in the *Scivias*. Barbara Newman, in her stimulating book, *Sister of Wisdom*, has argued that Hildegard's writing belongs to the tradition of sapiential theology. Her concentration on such 'female' aspects of the divine thus constitutes a 'theology of the feminine'.[5]

II

If the *Scivias* is basically a way of grappling with the problem of how people should best live their life in order to reach the Heavenly City, we might see Hildegard's second book, the *Liber vitae meritorum*, as a further and deeper exploration of the same theme. In it Hildegard deals at length and specifically with the vices that beset mankind on his journey. She also treats the corresponding virtues, but more as a way of defining and describing the vices themselves, than as a positive means of overcoming them. Indeed, the emphasis of the book is on future punishment and present penance, by means of which such pains may be avoided or at least mitigated.

The *Liber vitae meritorum* has, on the whole, a simpler structure and method than that of the *Scivias*. Instead of a series of apparently unrelated visions, the entire book consists of six visions, all variations on the same theme – that of the figure of a man superimposed on the world from the heavens to the abyss, who turns from one point of the compass to another, and observes various interactions between the powers of light and darkness. The same method, starting with a description of the vision, including words spoken by its various participants, and followed by a more detailed explication of what Hildegard sees, by the voice from heaven, is used in all six parts.

However, the methodology of the *Liber vitae meritorum* also resembles that of the later visions of the *Scivias*, where the vision is not fully described at the outset, since Hildegard sees more aspects as she goes along. Here, for instance, the punishments for the various sins do not form part of the scene described at the beginning of each book. Moreover, the line between the vision and its explication is not so strictly drawn as in the *Scivias*. There, all explanation was clearly marked as having come from the voice from heaven, but here the voice is sometimes Hildegard's, although she employs some such blanket justification as, 'I saw and understood all this' before continuing in what seem to be her own words.

As in the *Scivias*, where the separate visions were marked off from each other by the repetition of key sentences, here repetitions serve to give the work a formal, ritualistic cast, emphasizing the prophetic nature of the work. The frequency of such repetitions is, indeed, increased. Whereas the *Scivias* had them at the end of the vision proper to mark the transition to the heavenly gloss ('And I heard a voice from heaven saying to me . . . ') and also at the ends of the twenty-six visions, here they are also used to mark changes of course within the vision. For example, the change from general description of the vices to the section on punishments is usually marked by: 'And the things which you see are thus, and true and there are more . . . '. So too, the books conclude with a ritualistic formulation about taking what is said to heart. The first five books of the *Liber vitae meritorum* all follow the same order of arrangement and are similar in length. The last book replaces further descriptions of the vices with more general descriptions of the good and the wicked and a glimpse of the blessed in the Heavenly City.

For these reasons, and because the whole is concerned to enumerate and describe a total of thirty-five vices together with the punishment and penance for each, the *Liber vitae meritorum* can be rather tedious reading. This is partly due to the difficulty of making such a large number of vices sufficiently distinctive (for instance 'sadness' looks and sounds pretty much like 'despair'), and the problem is even more acute when it comes to the punishments.

Of course, there is more to the work than a mere catalogue of vices and punishments. Each vision includes a good deal of general information about the place of evil in the world, the actions of the Devil and his minions and God's redemption of man through His Son. Hildegard's views on bodily resurrection, the places of punishment, angels, and the fate of the unbaptized may also be discovered, especially in the last book.

The *Liber vitae meritorum* is not, however, a *psychomachia*, or series of physical combats between the vices and virtues in the tradition of Prudentius († c. 410), since here the virtues only play a very reduced part. Indeed, they are confined to speaking roles and their appearance is not described in detail. Their job is to answer the words of the vices, (usually, it must be said, in a rather *ad hominem* manner). Their battles here are verbal, not physical and, as a result, seem somewhat inconclusive. This gives Hildegard the opportunity to recommend a number of penitential activities (fasting, flagellation, and prayer, with the addition of hairshirts and isolation for particularly heinous crimes), to overcome the vices. These seem intended both as prophylactics and failing that, remedies for sin.

It may be that Hildegard thought she had treated the virtues at sufficient length in the latter part of the *Scivias* and did not want to repeat herself. Her tendency to treat the three visionary works as some kind of unity, indicated by what amounts to a series of cross-references from one to another, may have decided her to concentrate on a topic she had not already treated in detail before. Indeed in Book 3 of the *Scivias* Hildegard dealt quite fully with thirty of the virtues which make their brief appearances in the *Liber vitae meritorum*. In fact, it looks as if the selection of vices and their order of treatment in the latter work has been dictated by the *Scivias*, by the simple expedient of deciding which vice is the opposite of the virtues described there. On the whole the virtues depicted in the *Scivias* are not seen as combatting particular vices, being treated, rather, as *sui generis* or explicated in salvation-historical terms.

Thus the first seven virtues to answer the vices appearing in the *Liber vitae meritorum* are drawn from *Scivias*, 3, vis. 3; the next eight appear in 3, vis. 6; the next seven in 3, vis. 8; the next three in 3, vis. 9 and the next five in 3, vis. 10: they not only come from the *Scivias* but appear in exactly the same order.[6] The last five vices (scurrility, instability, black magic, avarice, and worldly sadness) cannot be matched with any group of virtues in *Scivias*, although the last appears in its own right, but not personified, in *Sc.*, 2, vis. 7.

Hildegard may also have had more personal reasons to treat this particular topic when she did. Her experiences of disaffection among the nuns at Rupertsberg, coupled with the loss of Richardis and financial and organizational problems, may have given Hildegard a rather jaded view of human nature. She might well have tended to accentuate the more negative side of humanity at such a time. Possibly the work was intended first of all for internal consumption at Rupertsberg. Were individual nuns meant to recognize in the hideous pictures of anger, love of the world, or despair, their own short-comings? We know, at least, that in Hildegard's lifetime the work was read with appreciation in the refectory among the Cistercians at Villers, and at the Benedictine monastery of Gembloux before retiring. No doubt hearing a short section or two at mealtimes would be a better way of tackling the work than attempting to absorb longer passages at a single sitting, given its repetitious structure and similar treatments of the vices and punishments. Here again the *Scivias* presents a contrast, since it does not easily divide into brief sections suitable for reading aloud. The close relationship of the *Scivias* illustrations to the text also suggests that the work was intended for individual perusal.

The fact that the vices do not seem to be confined to the experience of the nuns can be ascribed to Hildegard's penchant for covering every possibility. This encyclopedic tendency is especially noticeable in Hildegard's works on natural history, described below

71

in chapter 5. Besides, as we saw, the vices have been chosen to correspond to the virtues which appear in the *Scivias*. The proliferation of vices and virtues in Hildegard's works is in striking contrast to the original seven pairs in Prudentius' *Psychomachia*. Such a schema was adopted with minor variations by the sculptors of Romanesque churches in their depiction of the vices and virtues. Both Honorius of Regensberg and Herrade of Landsberg use fifteen virtues on their ladder to heaven, which is less than half the complement according to Hildegard's account. The vices of the *Liber vitae meritorum* do not appear to be ordered according to any recognizable scheme; Hildegard is usually content to say that some vice arises from, or is associated with, another. So much for the overall plan of the book. Now let us look more closely at some examples.

In the fifth vision of the *Liber vitae meritorum* we find a miscellaneous group of vices, not strictly tied to any virtues in the *Scivias*, among which is one called 'worldly sadness' (*tristitia saeculi*). Hildegard remarks that this often follows avarice because sadness arises from unfulfilled avaricious desires. This vice later appears in the *Vita*, Bk 2 as sometimes afflicting Hildegard's nuns. Hildegard describes its appearance as follows:

> I saw the fifth image in the form of a woman at whose back a tree was standing, wholly dried up and without leaves and by whose branches the woman was embraced. For one branch went around the top of her head, and another her neck and throat and one round her left arm and one to her right, her arms were not outstretched but held close to her body with her hands hanging down from the branches. . . . Her feet were of wood. She had no other clothes but the branches going around her. And wicked spirits coming with a very fetid black cloud swarmed over her, at which she lay back lamenting. (*Liber vitae meritorum* (*LVM*), 5, 9)

The explanation of the figure's attributes, which does not occur until chapter 35, serves to emphasize the paralysing effects of the vice. The sense of apathy and inability to turn either to the world or to God makes the condition sound like what might be called depression today. The dry and lifeless tree (the symbolic opposite of all natural and spiritual vitality and growth) oppresses the mind of the sufferer, preventing contrition. It constrains the neck and throat, thus preventing the assumption of the Lord's yoke or nourishment with the Food of Life. The branches hold the arms close to the body so that they cannot be extended in the performance of secular or spiritual works. The blocklike feet indicate that such people do not follow the path of faith or hope. There is 'no greenness in their ways', as Hildegard puts it. Finally, the figure is naked because it has no 'joy, honesty or happiness to adorn it' (a typical Hildegardian usage of clothing to indicate virtue). The evil spirits are to be taken literally, rather than symbolically, because Hildegard believed that they found the opportunity to enter such people and make them even worse, sometimes driving them into despair. I will have more to say on Hildegard's views of possession by demons in chapter 8.

For the words of Worldly Sadness we must go back to chapter 10:

Alas that I was born, alas that I live. Who will help me, who will free me? If God knew me he would not have sent me such perils. Although I trust in God, he does me no good, when I rejoice in him, he does not lift evil from me. I have heard a lot from philosophers who teach that there is much good in God, but in all this God has done me no good. If he is my God why has he taken all his grace from me? If he were to confer any good on me I would know him. But I know not what I am. I was conceived in unhappiness and in unhappiness born and I live without any consolation. Ah! what good is life without joy? And why was I created, since no good comes to me?

The reply of Heavenly Joy is twofold. First, Worldly Sadness does not know a good thing when she sees one, nor recognize that the good things she receives are from God:

Now observe the sun and the moon and stars and all the decoration of the greenness of the earth and consider how much prosperity God gives man with these things, although man sins with great temerity against God. . . . Who gives you a part in these bright and good things, if not God? When day comes to you, you call it night; and when your salvation is nigh, you call it damnation, and when all your occasions and things are good, you call them bad. So you are hellish! (*LVM*, 5, 11)

Then she contrasts her own behaviour with that of her antagonist:

I, on the other hand, possess heaven, since all that God created, and which you call noxious, I observe in its true light. I gently collect the blossoms of roses and lilies and all greenness in my lap since I praise all the works of God, while you attract the sorrow of sorrows to you since you are dolorous in all your works.

Heavenly Joy goes on to remark upon the inevitably mixed nature of life in the world, but finds good even in this, since the bad will be purged by the good, like gold in a furnace.

The punishment awaiting those afflicted by this particular vice is found in chapter 62. It reads in part:

> And I saw a dry and waterless place, full of worms, surrounded by darkness. . . . And wicked spirits drove the souls hither and thither through that place with fiery whips, shouting 'Why did you not place your faith in your God?'.

Then follows the penance enjoined on those who wish to avoid such punishments, introduced by several formulaic sentences:

> And through the living spirit I saw and understood these things. And again I heard from the aforesaid living light a voice saying to me: 'The things which you see are true, and are as you see them, and there are more. Wherefore, people piling up for themselves worldly sadness, if they wish to overcome the wicked spirits urging them to it, and if they desire to flee this torment, if they live in the world should devote themselves to the spiritual life; or if they are already living as religious, let them fulfil the common discipline more than is usual, and submit themselves frequently to humble obedience, and ponder on the Scriptures which put before them celestial joy, with frequent study, and do all these things not wantonly, but let them do it with the permission of the director appointed for them.' (*LVM*, 5, 63)

It is clear from these extracts that Hildegard advocates punishment and penitence in this world, so as to avoid punishment in the next. On the matter of purgation after death the seventy-seventh chapter of the first book sets out Hildegard's views, although brief summaries of the doctrine appear towards the close of the first five books as well. This is how she introduces the first of the punishments:

> And I heard a voice from the living light saying to me: 'The things that you see are true and are as you see them, and there are more. For the torments of these punishments purge the souls, who, living in the transitory world deserved there the purgation of their sins through punishment in the non-transitory [world]. They were not fully purged in the flesh, having been prevented by death, or even tried in the world by the divine flails of compassionate God. Therefore they will be purged by these punishments, unless they

are snatched from them by the labours of men and the virtues of the saints, which God worked in them through the invocation of the piety of divine grace.' (*LVM*, 1, 77)

The point is then made that the souls thus purged are those who will ultimately be among the blessed, for those who are consigned to oblivion will remain there experiencing other torments. That this purgation will take place in the interval between death and the Last Judgement can be inferred from the assertion that the works of the living can 'snatch' souls from their torments. Hildegard is not more specific at this point, although she devotes several chapters to the subject at the end of Book 5. Here such works include the recitation of psalms for the dead, almsgiving, prayers, and other holy works. Hildegard is perhaps unusual in not mentioning masses for the deceased (around which a whole chantry industry was later to grow up), although these may be covered by the category of other holy works. More is said about the location of purgatory in Hildegard's other writings. For instance, a passage in the *Causae et curae* suggests a naturalistic view of purgatorial fire, connecting it with thermal springs and volcanoes. On the question of the beneficiaries of purgatory Hildegard takes a latitudinarian line. Whereas in earlier times purgatorial fire was only invoked for the expiation of trifling and minor sins, Hildegard seems to apply it to all categories of wrongdoing, with the notable exception of suicide.

The role of the clergy in the administration of earthly penance is emphasized, as Hildegard writes: 'the priest is the judge in place of my Son' (*LVM*, 1, 79). The shift from public confession to private or auricular confession also seems to be suggested by Hildegard's description of the sinner manifesting his sin to God 'by the ear of the priest', a topic that has already been touched on in the *Scivias*.

Hildegard gives no very clear picture of the geography of the other world in the *Liber vitae meritorum*. She seems to suggest that purgatorial punishments took place in an upper division of hell. The place of consignment of the damned is represented as a vast lake or pit of fire in the same general area. The souls undergoing purgation are usually subjected to some form of trial by fire, in places variously represented as pits, lakes, or in one case a hollow mountain. Fire is not always present, sometimes being replaced by a stinking marsh or lake (as in the purgation for inept levity, vainglory, and instability). Toads, worms, vipers, and scorpions complete the catalogue of horrors. Hildegard no doubt owes something in her description of purgatorial punishments to a tradition of visionary literature which depicted the torments of hell, such as the vision of Drythelm in Bede.[7] However, her torments have what might be seen as an academic dimension, rather than being chosen simply for their shock value. No detail is gratuitously included, each aspect of the punishment having a further referent or going to point a moral. Here is how she describes the purgation of the unjust:

> And I saw a horrendous place, full of fiery thorns and spikes and horrible worms, through which wicked spirits harried with fiery whips the souls of those who while they were in their bodies in the world stood for all kinds of injustice. And because they upheld injustice in word and deed, they are punished with thorns and spikes; and since they preserved bitterness in it, they are tortured by worms; and since they were merciful to no one through injustice they are afflicted by the wicked spirits with fiery whips. And I saw and understood these things. (*LVM*, 4, 43)

While the suffering of the souls is clearly not metaphorical, Hildegard does not dwell overmuch on it or try to demonstrate that it would be like the suffering of bodies on earth, but much worse. This may be because she had a very clear notion of the separation of the soul from the body at death and of the fact that they would only be reunited at the Last Judgement. In most sections of the *Liber vitae meritorum* she returns to the idea that final blessedness can only be attained when the soul is reunited with the body after the destruction of the world.[8] Her insistence on the partnership and equal dignity of soul and body (albeit transformed at the resurrection) may once more be directed against Catharist doctrines. In practical terms, Hildegard's view of what happened after death, and the part played by the efforts of the living in lightening the soul's torments, explains why she could be consulted by people wishing to help their deceased relatives (see pp. 158–9).

In the *Scivias* and *Liber vitae meritorum* Hildegard provides, by describing her visions and their meaning, a comprehensive guide to Christian faith and action. While she does not neglect such mysteries as the creation of the world, the fall of man, the Incarnation and the sacraments, she lays particular stress on the proper course of action for humankind, fallen from its original condition, and existing in a flawed world.

5

THE SUBTLETIES OF NATURE

She elucidated the nature of man, the elements and different creatures and told how humankind is to be served by them. (*Vita*, Bk 2)

I

In chapter 3 I outlined the mechanism by which Hildegard was empowered to start writing and suggested that her adoption of the role of prophetess was the crucial factor. However, the case of her medical and scientific writings is somewhat anomalous, because she seems not to have depended on prophecy for their production. On the other hand, there is a sense in which their subject matter, the '*secreta Dei*' or 'secrets of God' pertaining to the natural world, could be seen as examples of prophetic knowledge. For this reason, Hildegard and her contemporaries were able to describe such works as prophecy, even though they may not have been presented in visionary form.

When talking of Hildegard's medical and scientific works (as distinct from her medical and scientific ideas, which are to be found here and there in the theological works and the letters) we are referring to two sets of writings. These are confusingly known under a variety of names, but most commonly called the *Physica* (*Natural History*) and *Causae et curae* (*Causes and Cures*). Collectively this body of work is also referred to as the *Liber subtilitatum*, an abbreviation of *Subtilitates diversarum naturarum creaturarum* (*The Subtleties of the Diverse Natures of Created Things*).[1]

These works are the most problematic of Hildegard's *oeuvre* for reasons of form, content, and manuscript transmission. Indeed, Charles Singer, the historian of science who studied Hildegard at the beginning of this century, refused to accept that they were hers at all.[2]

Other scholars, while rejecting this extreme position, have suspected major interpolations in *Causae et curae*. Even those who do not doubt Hildegard's ultimate authorship, acknowledge that the form in which the material survives may well be far removed from that in which it was originally written.[3]

The *Physica* and *Causae et curae* are also distinguished from Hildegard's other works by not being presented in visionary form or containing any reference to a divine source for their contents. Nowhere does she attribute her knowledge of these matters to any kind of revelation. While Hildegard does not claim the information presented as entirely her own, neither is it said to be the word of God. Of course, there may once have been some sort of general introduction where Hildegard acknowledged God's direction of her thought but even this would not explain why she does not present any of the information in visionary form.[4]

Were the works, then, based on actual observation and experience? We learn from other sources that Hildegard was well known for the cures she performed at Rupertsberg, even though Theodoric says it was her 'blessings' rather than medical treatments which produced them. This need not rule out the possibility that Hildegard actually practised medicine, since the hand of God was always to some extent involved in such cures. *Causae et curae* suggests in several places that cures will only be effective with God's co-operation, and several passages in the *Physica* require quasi-liturgical invocations to be performed as part of the suggested remedy, notably in the curative use of precious stones. Unfortunately, it is not clear whether what she says reveals a practical knowledge and interest rather than a mere educated acquaintance with the received authorities.[5]

One way of tackling the problem is to look at the contents of the works themselves and try to separate what might have come straight from an ancient authority, from what could be seen as local medical lore or the result of actual experiment and practice. Of course, the most that could be said here is that Hildegard takes over something directly from Pliny or Isidore or Galen or Soranus. She might still have made whatever she took over from these authorities part of her own practice; conversely, if we do not know of a direct source, it hardly follows that the idea or information necessarily originated with her and represents the fruits of practical knowledge rather than speculation. Indeed, much of her medical lore may well have resulted from deductions made from a set of first (medical) principles.

For the sake of inclusiveness, and because I cannot see compelling enough reasons to reject them out of hand, I will treat both *Causae et curae* and the *Physica* as if they were genuine (and separate) works by Hildegard, reserving for the moment any judgement on the authenticity or degree of corruption of the texts.

II

The *Physica* consists of nine books or sections, the first and most bulky of which is a collection of over 200 short chapters on plants. There follow books devoted to the elements (earth, water, and air, but not fire), trees, jewels and precious stones, fish, birds, animals, reptiles, and metals. There is a definite bias in the descriptions of all the subjects under investigation towards their medical uses. On the other hand, in contrast to many medieval herbals, little attempt is made to describe the plants for purposes of identification, which must presumably have reduced the book's practical utility. In contrast to Hildegard's other works, many German words (apart from the vernacular names of some of the objects under discussion) are interspersed through the Latin text. This is partly why Singer doubted Hildegard's authorship.

The comprehensiveness of the section on plants in the *Physica* suggests that it was a topic in which she took a particular interest. If Hildegard were indeed practising medicine, this would hardly be surprising. We may speculate that the other sections, dealing with the rest of creation, perhaps arose from a characteristically medieval desire for completeness – so that what started out as a herbal ended up as an encyclopedia of natural history.[6]

The medical and physiological theories behind the use of plants in the *Physica* are assumed, rather than spelt out. Briefly, the traditional view of created things consisting of mixtures of four elemental qualities – hot/cold/wet/dry – in which one or two qualities predominate, is combined with a theological notion ultimately derived from Genesis according to which everything on earth was put there for man's use. Since the balance of elements and their corresponding humours was what determined good or bad health in man, it was important to know the elemental qualities of plants. One could then determine their effect on the persons who ate or used them, according to whether they were themselves in or out of humour – that is, in a balanced or unbalanced state.[7]

Thus the most important fact Hildegard has to give about the plants is whether they are considered hot, cold, dry, or moist. It should be said here that the information is often only given in terms of hot and cold, the oppositional qualities which seem to assume most significance for medical purposes. After conveying this information Hildegard usually goes on to indicate what medicinal purposes the plant in question serves. Sometimes this follows fairly obviously from its qualities; at other times the connections are more tenuous and less convincing.

Some examples may serve to illustrate her method. Chapter 158 concerns a plant called '*Juncus*', a kind of reed of which we are told only, '*Juncus* is not rightly hot and not rightly cold, and therefore is not useful as a medicine'. On the other hand, in chapter 160 we find the following:

> *Dornella* (tormentil) is cold, and that coldness is good and healthy and useful against fever that arises from bad food. Take tormentil therefore, and cook it in wine with a little honey added . . . and drink it fasting at night and you will be cured of the fever.

It seems clear from this that the coldness of the plant counteracts the fever, although we find in chapter 124 that aloe is hot and is also good for fevers. The apparent contradiction might be explained by the fact that aloe was to be applied externally rather than taken as a medicine.

These are relatively simple examples; more complicated is the following:

> *Reynfan* (tansy) is hot and a little damp and is good against all superfluous and flowing humours. And whoever suffers from catarrh and has a cough, let him eat tansy, either in . . . cakes, or with meat or any other way. It will bind the humours so they do not overflow and thus will lessen. (*Physica*, Bk 1, ch. 111)

Tansy is also good for a dry cough and those suffering from 'heaviness and ponderousness of the stomach', not to mention strangury due to the stone. In this case the plant is apparently able to treat opposite conditions – superfluous humours and their lack.

Other plants must be combined to produce the remedy as in the following case:

> *Cranchsnabel* (common storksbill) is very hot and a little damp. . . . Take storksbill therefore and a bit less of *bertram* [?pyrethrum] than storksbill, and a bit less of nutmeg than *bertram* and pound them up and mix them together, and let whoever suffers a disease of the heart eat the powder, with or without bread. (*Physica*, Bk 1, ch. 144)

From such examples of Hildegard's use of herbs it is not really possible to decide whether she is relying on her own experience, traditional lore, or written authorities, although she does not seem to depend much on either Pliny or Isidore. On the other hand, the plants she uses, many of which she refers to by their vernacular names, such as *Woulfesgelegena*, *Sonwirbel*, or *Sichterwurz* are generally those which could be collected from the woods and fields or grown in the monastery garden. More exotic ingredients, like ginger, pepper, incense, and sugar no doubt had to be purchased for the infirmary, as Abelard advised in his letters of direction to Heloise. The range of plants used in the remedies in *Causae et curae* is more restricted than that of the *Physica* and may thus argue actual usage, while the catalogue in the *Physica* aims for comprehensiveness.

It is harder to make a case for the rest of the *Physica* being a guide to Hildegard's practice. There are, however, certain recurrent themes and preoccupations, which, together with bits of local colour or knowledge place Hildegard's stamp on the material. The section on the elements, for instance, contains descriptions of the rivers with which Hildegard would have been particularly familiar – the Rhine, Main, and Nahe.

Trees, the subject of the third book of the *Physica*, present a rather more complicated picture than plants in general because of the obvious seasonal transformations of trees and their capacity to bear fruit. Hildegard relates their hotness or coldness to the size and quantity of fruit produced. Thus trees that produce abundant large fruit are hotter than those that yield small and sparse fruit, although on the whole, fruitbearing trees are cold rather than hot. Apart from the fruit, which may or may not be good to eat, other parts of the tree may have medicinal uses. Some of her cures seem to derive their effectiveness by association from other qualities of the tree, such as its vigour or *viriditas*, freshness, or tenderness. As she explains in her section on the walnut tree, the leaves are only good for medicine before the fruit matures, because after that their vital fluid (*succus*) goes into the fruit.

Thus a cure for 'dimness of the eyes' depends on a salve made from apple leaves taken in spring when they are fresh and healthy 'like young girls before they have borne children'. As for the fruit, they are good eaten raw by the healthy but should be cooked for the sick. Pears on the other hand should always be cooked. The quince depends for its medicinal effects on the fact that it is dry, rather than on its relative heat or cold (like other fruit trees it is cold rather than hot) and can be eaten raw, although it is better cooked. Its intrinsic dryness will help those suffering from excessive saliva, and will likewise dry up an ulcer when externally applied. The peach tree, like the cherry, is considered more useful for medicine than food, its bark, leaves, and kernels figuring in various remedies for skin infections, bad breath, and headaches. Cherry seeds, pounded and mixed with bear fat, are good for skin disorders, while taken internally (minus the bear fat), kill intestinal worms. Hildegard completes her account of the fruit trees with the uses of different varieties of plum, rowan, and mulberry before turning to a description of nut trees, among which she holds the chestnut pre-eminent.

From such familiar trees Hildegard turns to a consideration of the more exotic fig and laurel or bay. The fruit of the fig should not be eaten by the healthy, as it gives them ideas above themselves, making them seek for honours and become avaricious and unstable, but it is beneficial when taken by those in a weakened condition. The laurel, being hot and dry, has many medicinal uses, both internal and external. So too have the olive, datepalm, citron, cedar, and cypress.

Of the forest trees Hildegard particularly esteems evergreens such as the box and the fir, because of their exceptional heat. The latter has the power to keep evil spirits away. The oak, on the other hand, is seen as bitter and tough, without any softness and not fit food for humans, although pigs fatten well on it. Ash leaves are good applied externally and if used in the preparation of beer, instead of hops, will have a cleansing effect on the stomach. Aspen leaves have a special role in the treatment of skin conditions to which babies are subject. She writes:

> If any baby lying in its cradle is suffused and vexed with blood between the skin and the flesh so that it is greatly troubled, take new and recent leaves from the aspen and put them on a simple linen cloth and wrap the baby in the leaves and cloth and put him down to sleep, wrapping him up so that he will sweat and extract the virtue from the leaves; and he will get well. (*Physica*, Bk 3, ch. 28)

Hildegard continues to list forest trees and describe their uses, including the pine (poisonous to cattle), the spindle tree (used for treatment of dropsy and diseases of the spleen), juniper, and elder (for chest, lungs, and liver). She includes some trees which cannot now be positively identified under their German names, such as *Folbaum*, *Felbaum*, and *Schulbaum*. On the whole these are useless, if not actually dangerous. Heather, on the other hand, is good for skin afflictions and the eyes. The ashes of blackthorn mixed with honey and certain other ingredients are good for bodily and mental weakness, while sloes are excellent eaten raw with sugar or cooked for the sick.

Vines, as well as their obvious role in winemaking, have medicinal uses. The ashes of vine wood mixed with wine heal the gums and make teeth firm, while wine mixed with olive oil is used to treat ulcers and wounds. The last tree considered by Hildegard is the *Gichtbaum* which apparently acts as a kind of catalyst or enhancer rather than having any virtue of its own even though it is said to be very hot. Henceforth the book seems to degenerate into a series of miscellaneous jottings, on smoke, moss, and 'St Hilary's ointment', which are possibly not Hildegard's work.

Passing on to her account of precious stones, we find that her catalogue of jewels is rather selective and consists principally of those that are mentioned in the Bible, with the addition of a few others. Similar principles of the combination of hot and cold operate here, although some complications are introduced because of her theory of their genesis. Precious stones, she asserts in her prologue, have their origins in the east where the heat of the sun is greatest and causes mountains to heat up inside. When, as they do from time to time, rivers flood and rise to the heights of the mountains, the reaction of the heated mountains with the water causes a foam which hardens into precious stones. The varieties of precious stones with their different qualities are formed by their hardening out at various times of the day under different ambient conditions. Thus, although all are a combination of fire and water they have different powers.

Emerald was commonly held to be the chief of jewels. Hildegard puts this down to its pre-eminent *viriditas* or greenness. Isidore mentions this too, in the context of explaining the Latin name, *smaragdus*. He says it is bitter (*amarus*) because of its 'excessive greenness' (*nimia viriditate*). For Hildegard this is its chief virtue – she describes it as having sucked up all the greenness like a lamb sucking up milk. It is a specific for pain in the heart, stomach, or side, epilepsy, headache, colds, and sores. The cure is effected by external application in most cases, although sometimes just looking at the jewel while repeating a religious charm will produce the desired effect; alternatively, it can be placed in wine which is then drunk.

While Pliny describes where the different stones are to be found, mostly in the east – India, Egypt, Ethiopia – but at least one in Germany, Isidore classifies the stones by colour, not by the supposed hour of the day at which they solidified. In contrast to the matter-of-fact catalogue of jewels found in Isidore and the exhaustive information given by Pliny, Hildegard's account is heavily biassed towards their magical qualities. Thus the sapphire can be used to improve intellectual powers if held in the mouth for a short while on rising in the morning, or used to free those possessed by malignant spirits if hung in a bag round the neck. Topaz indicates the presence of poison in food, and so should be worn in a ring and frequently inspected. However, even these virtues are somehow connected with the amount of heat or cold possessed by the stone, thus 'Alabaster is not rightly hot or cold, but is lukewarm and so it is that there is almost no medical use for it.'

It seems unlikely that jewel therapy was much practised at Rupertsberg or other monasteries, particularly on outpatients. However, other sections of the *Physica* seem more in keeping with everyday employment and experience. The large and detailed section on fish doubtless reflects the prime importance of this food in medieval diets, especially that of the religious. Possibly in the interests of maintaining supplies, Hildegard pays great attention to the reproductive habits of fish. With the exception of such 'classical' fish as the whale and porpoise, most of the fish described could be found in European rivers and many of them are referred to by their German names. Apart from dealing with fish in terms of their four qualities, Hildegard appears here to be engaged in rationalizing and explaining known facts and preferences. Take, for example, her account in chapter 22 of the herring. Hildegard's acquaintance with herrings would have been predominantly in their salted form, since they are ocean fish. Possibly taking a hint from Isidore, who derives the Latin name for herring from 'brine', she asserts:

> A freshly caught herring is no good for man to eat since it may easily make him swell up. . . . But when it has been soaked in much salt the foulness in it is lessened by the salt so that it will hurt him less.

It is still dangerous for someone in poor health to eat too many herrings, and on the whole they are better baked than boiled. If a fresh one has been procured by some means, the danger of eating it can be lessened by sousing it in wine and vinegar and letting it stand for some time. There also seems to be good sense in her prescription for skin infections where she suggests taking a herring that has long been soaking in brine, washing it in water and applying the water to the affected parts. Of course, the antiseptic virtues of the original brine might have proved superior to that procured at one remove by soaking the fish, but possibly the first solution would have been too strong.

The dietary suitability of different kinds of fish seems to depend upon the sort of food they eat, rather than their being hot or cold. It is not clear whether Hildegard is here relying on actual observation of the feeding habits of fish or rationalizing contemporary tastes. Thus the trout can be safely eaten because it does not feed on filthy matter. The pike, although it eats other fish, Hildegard also considered safe. Indeed, its flesh was thought to be strengthening for the eater, a belief which seems to owe something to sympathetic magic, given the pike's extreme aggressiveness. However, even on these grounds the outcome is not predictable, although on the whole, fish that eat plants are considered more suitable for human consumption.

Thus the gudgeon is hot rather than cold and eats clean food and so is good eating for people whether sick or well. The greyling, although cold, feeds on grass and little plants which make its flesh suitable for human consumption. Its skin also features in a cure for sore eyes. A fish referred to by Hildegard as the *monuwa* on the other hand, is cold and sometimes eats filthy little worms (*immundis vermiculis*) and so its flesh should be avoided. For similar reasons the flesh of the eel is tolerable, but that of the sea lamprey harmful, 'exciting a tempest in all the veins'.

The seventy-two birds and assorted insects treated by Hildegard include such exotics as the griffin and the ostrich. The griffin (a cross between a lion and an eagle, according to Isidore), is hot and partakes of the nature of the wild beast and the bird. The former quality is enough to rule it out as food for man. The ostrich, on the other hand, is so hot that it cannot sit on its eggs without boiling them and so incubates them in the sand. Doubtless this is the reason that Hildegard recommends it in cases of epilepsy and for those suffering from melancholy, although her instructions that they should eat often of its flesh and liver seem rather impractical. From such creatures the account moves via the peacock (with comment on its promiscuous habits) to the more familiar herons, swans, and other water birds (with a passing glance at the eagle whose flesh is too hot for man to eat because of its affinity with the sun). The farmyard duck, although it eats filthy food, is cleansed by the water in which it swims and so can be eaten by those who are in good health.[8] Next various sorts of poultry are described, from the domestic hen to the black grouse (*birckhun*); then varieties of hawks, which on the whole are not considered good to eat since they eat other birds.

The sparrowhawk, however, figures in a complicated recipe for counteracting libidinousness in man or woman:

Take a sparrowhawk, pluck it, then having discarded the head and entrails put the rest of the body in a new pot perforated with small holes and put it on the fire without water and put another pot under it to catch the drippings. Pound some *calandria* and a little camphor and mix with the drippings and heat it on the fire again and thus make an ointment, and a man should anoint his genitals with this for five days and then his libidinous cravings will be gone in a month. The woman should put it around her waist and in the navel and her ardour will cease in a month. (*Physica*, Bk 6, ch. 20)

Next Hildegard considers the crow family, all members of which she considers inedible with the exception of the *musar* (?hooded crow), because of their supposed bad characters. The raven or jackdaw, for instance, is said to have the nature of a robber and thief. Nevertheless, some crows may be used to make ointments for external application. Hildegard then suggests that doves and pigeons are not good to eat either, because they are too dry, although they can be tolerated. The parrot, likewise, is considered and found wanting.

Owls are hot, but not good to eat because of their furtive and lugubrious natures. However, like crows, their flesh may be reduced and made into ointments. Next follows a miscellaneous collection, including cuckoos (no good), snipe (excellent), and woodpeckers (the green variety being useful for skin diseases). Small birds such as sparrows, tits, blackbirds, thrushes, and larks are on the whole edible and healthful, especially the thrush in the case of sore throats. Quail, nightingales, goldfinches (*distelwincke*, i.e. 'thistlefinch'), the chaffinch, bunting, and wagtails of various sorts are mentioned, as is the swallow which is no good to eat because of the unclean food it feeds upon.

There follows a rather macabre remedy for jaundice, using a stunned bat which is tied to the back of the sufferer before being transferred to the stomach and worn there until it expires. Hildegard then passes on to a consideration of insects, including bees, flies, cicadas, and wasps. Few of these are considered good to eat – a fly inadvertently swallowed being particularly dangerous. Glowworms, on the other hand, are cold and should be gathered and tied live in a cloth which is placed on the stomach of anyone suffering an epileptic seizure.

The seventh book, on animals, treats such creatures as the elephant, lion, leopard, camel, and unicorn as well as the more familiar wolf, fox, bear, otter, rabbit, the domestic animals, and insect pests. Yet even here the theme of their utility (or otherwise) to man is maintained, whereas Isidore makes no attempt to take this into account. Thus we learn that, because of its heat, a lion's ear is a remedy in cases of deafness, if it is cut off and placed on the afflicted part. On the other hand, the leopard seems to have no medicinal uses at all.

Turning to domestic animals, Hildegard writes that the sheep is cold, but hotter than cattle and moist where they are dry; thus mutton is better eaten in summer than in winter. Woollen clothes and sheep skins are better than other furs (partly, it seems, since they were recommended to Adam in Genesis 3:21). The use of woollen night caps for various afflictions of the head is recommended in *Causae et curae*, which is rather puzzling since in other cases it is the supposed warmth of the animal that makes it good for clothing. Thus in describing the stoat, Hildegard remarks: 'their skins are no good for human's clothes, because the animal is cold', while the red squirrel, being hot, has a pelt which is good for clothing. On the whole, animals do not have a great deal of medicinal utility. Sometimes other qualities, for instance the fact that they are carnivores, even makes their meat unsuitable for human consumption.

In the case of the dog, however, it may be its privileged position as friend to man that rules out such exploitation. Hildegard, after describing the dog's fidelity and usefulness goes on to say: 'But their flesh is of no use to man, and the liver and innards are rather poisonous and their breath is noxious'. Whether it was indeed simply the smell of the dog's breath which led to such conclusions is hard to decide, but it might be noted that eating the liver of dogs has been known to lead to severe vitamin A poisoning. Pliny does not include this information in his comments on dogs, but then, like Isidore, neither does he suggest eating them.

Other glimpses of medieval mores appear in Hildegard's notes on insect pests. The same principles of hot/cold and wet/dry are applied to get rid of fleas. This creature, Hildegard remarks, is hot and so hides in the earth during the winter. But in summer, when the earth warms up, it becomes too hot for the fleas which emerge from the ground to plague humans. The remedy is to get some earth and dry it completely by heating in a vessel on the fire, then to 'sprinkle the earth in your bed, and when the fleas sense the dryness they cannot stand it and depart and perish, and thus one can have peace from them'. Here perhaps Hildegard is expanding a hint from Isidore, who says that fleas get their name '*pules*' because they are largely nourished on dust, '*pulvere*'.

The eighth book, on reptiles, covers a selection of the noxious creatures later to be depicted with such gusto by Breughel and Bosch. These range from the dragon and basilisk to the humble earthworm, slugs, and snails. In the preface it is explained that such creatures arose after the original creation; indeed some of them owe their origin to the corruption of animals exterminated in the Flood, and this is the reason for their being exceptions to the rule that God made everything for man's use. Even so, some are less dangerous than others, surely a reflection of common knowledge. For instance, the slow worm is not to be shunned like the viper, and lizards and frogs, while contributing little to the pharmacopoeia, are not themselves poisonous.

Once again, the creatures under investigation are classified according to whether they are hot or cold. Reptiles are not all cold, as might be expected. Most of the poisonous ones seem to be hot, as is the earthworm, while slugs and snails are cold. In this case it is hard to explain why the slug figures as a substitute for the earthworm in some recipes.

Once more, there are a few entries which are hard to identify, such as the *Harumna*, possibly a kind of toad, of which Hildegard writes:

> *Harumna* is cold and the heat which it has in it is poison. But the venom is not so strong as to hurt man very much. And there is no medicine in it. (*Physica*, Bk 8, ch. 7)

A practical note is introduced in the section on the earthworm where Hildegard remarks:

> If you cannot find earthworms easily when you want them and it is not raining so they do not come out of the ground, then dig the earth in a damp place and search for them, and make the medicines described with them, but they are better for such medicines when they come out of the ground when it rains. (*Physica*, Bk 8, ch. 17)

The last and shortest book in the work briefly treats eight metals, the origins of which are traced to the time when the Spirit of God moved upon the waters. The metals are classified as either hot (gold and copper) or cold (silver, lead, tin), apparently on the basis of their colour. Iron and steel are the exceptions to this rule, both being very hot. Lead is known to be poisonous and Hildegard advises against putting food or drink in leaden vessels. However, her cure for fevers using copper boiled in wine sounds rather dangerous, especially if the wine were acidic Since many of the prescriptions involve ingestion of powdered metal, they seem unlikely to have been employed on a large scale. Steel, which 'signifies the divinity of God' is reckoned most powerful against the Devil who flees its presence, and placed in food or drink suspected of being poisoned will attenuate the poison, although the person who eats it may still fall ill.

III

What are we to make of all this? The *Physica* gives some impression of the medicinal resources at Hildegard's disposal, whether actual or potential. Because she suggests lions' ears as a cure for deafness it does not mean that she failed to use the things which were more readily available, such as bats or moles. The collection also serves to indicate the natural and ecological background to her existence, provided some of its more far-fetched denizens are disregarded. The question of Hildegard's dependence on earlier authorities, such as Pliny and Isidore, and anonymous herbals and bestiaries is harder to settle. It seems likely that Hildegard used these as starting points in some cases, but then expanded upon them according to her particular preoccupations and interests.

The subtitles of the two works (*The Book of Simple Medicine* and the *Book of Compound Medicine*) suggest that the *Physica* should describe the simples or single ingredients that are used to make up the complex prescriptions of the *Causae et curae*. However, the *Physica* clearly does more than this since it also contains quite complex remedies, although its aim is inclusiveness, rather than theoretical refinement. The *Causae et curae*, on the other hand, while still extremely comprehensive, especially in its catalogue of diseases and cures, gives more space to medical and physiological theory. The first section of the book is thus devoted to an account of man and his relationship with the cosmos and the world of created things.

The structure of the *Physica* is fairly straightforward, depending simply on enumeration within nine general classes. That of *Causae et curae* is less obvious, with passages treating the same or allied subjects often found at widely separated intervals or scattered throughout the work. This is true even of what might be called the theoretical or cosmological framework, since not until the second major section, for instance, do we read of the interdependence of the elements, which goes some way to explaining otherwise anomalous features of the theory, such as that water consists partly of fire. Since this is so, I shall treat the contents of the work under thematic headings, which may or may not follow the arrangement of the book itself. Whether this merely reflects the corrupt state of the manuscript or was intentional on Hildegard's part cannot be decided from the evidence at our disposal.

IV

Causae et curae consists of five sections, which like those of the *Physica* are of very different lengths. The first starts with the creation of the world and includes both cosmology and cosmography. The second section sets man within this context, and having expounded a version of the humoral theory, begins to introduce a series of illnesses and disorders to which humans are subject. Here the illnesses are named, rather than described – the names ranging from vernacular German to ones derived from the Greek. This section is by far the longest, consisting of 296 chapters. The following two sections (3 and 4 in Kaiser's edition) present remedies or cures for the conditions previously described or listed. The remedies are mostly herbal and comparisons may be made here with the *Physica* and its suggestions about the medicinal uses of the plants and other natural products. On the other hand, it should be said that the *Causae et curae* employs more detailed and complicated prescriptions with due attention being given to the proportions of the ingredients to be used.[9] The fifth and final section is rather a mixed bag, containing chapters on general medical questions such as the signs of life and death, uroscopy, hot baths, cherries, and a long list of astrological prognostications (*lunaria*) according to the state of the moon at the time of conception. Here a prediction is given for each day of the month.

Causae et curae, then, like several other works by Hildegard, starts with a description of the creation of the world and the heavenly bodies. In the course of this she introduces the theory of the four primary elements, which underlies her account of the physical world. These four elements have particular relevance to the dispositions and illnesses of mankind. Her cosmological explanations rely partly on a scientific or naturalistic tradition ultimately derived from Greek cosmology and partly on a Christian tradition which depended upon the account of creation in Genesis. Later Christian sources, such as the works of Isidore, may also have provided Hildegard with material for elaboration.

As in her later theological opus, the *Liber divinorum operum*, a belief in the close relationship between the cosmos and its parts and humans and their parts underlies much of the *Causae et curae*. Hildegard makes this clear early in the work (Bk 1, 4) when she writes:

> O man, look to man. For man has the heavens and earth and other created things within him. He is one, and all things are hidden within him.

In the *Liber divinorum operum* this assumption is used for erecting an extremely comprehensive set of correspondences, but here attention is focused on more strictly physiological and medical matters. For this reason, certain elements, like the winds and the waters of the earth, are emphasized.

When it comes to specifying the nature of the relationship between mankind and the cosmos Hildegard is often hard to pin down. Sometimes the supposed relationship seems little more than an explanation by analogy, using either human physiology to illustrate a feature of the cosmos or vice versa. For example, light rain is said to help plants grow; it is likened to someone weeping for joy, as opposed to heavy downpours which are like storms of grief. Again, the following explanation is given for the red appearance of the sun at dawn and dusk:

> That the sun is red when it rises comes from the fact that the air is cold and damp, because the cold and damp then present, makes men's eyes red. In the same way, late in the evening when the sun turns red, this is from the coldness of the air, because then it is about to set. (*Causae et curae*, Bk 2, 18)

Since the first book is mostly about the macrocosm, this kind of explanation abounds. For instance, we are told that the winds hold the firmament together, just as the soul stops the body from disintegrating, and further, that the stars perform the same office for the firmament as the veins do for the body. The five planets are said to be the ornaments of the firmament, like the five senses in man, and so on.

Such explanation is carried on at quite a high level of abstraction. In the long section describing different kinds of water found on earth,

91

we are told a good deal about the sources of salt springs, rivers, and freshwater springs and their differing properties. These properties are derived from their supposed source in one of the four directional divisions of the world. However, there is no attempt to bring the theory into line with actual geography and named rivers or for Hildegard to situate herself in the picture. Moreover, lacking such a reference point it is also hard to see what practical purpose such watery typology is meant to serve. We do find, however, that Hildegard recommended boiling river water before drinking it, which seems prudent enough, though why she should think water from a well preferable to spring water is puzzling – on empirical grounds, that is; her theoretical grounds are unassailable, once her premises are granted.[10]

In a similar manner the various geographical regions of the world are described as having differing agricultural capacities. The traditional idea that paradise is located in the east (and thus represented at the top of the map in medieval times) no doubt has something to do with Hildegard's belief that the plants which grow there are good for medical purposes. Northern crops, although subject to weeds, are strong, but other plants grown in the north are not much use for medicine. It might be noted that such considerations do not figure at all in the *Physica*.

There are further references to cosmology in the rest of the work, mostly in the second book where the origin of stones and the nature of the rainbow are mentioned in passing. Unexpected windows are occasionally opened on medieval perceptions of the natural world, as when Hildegard remarks that in contrast to her own times, before the Deluge rivers were small and easily crossed, and there were no vast impenetrable forests, merely pleasant woods.

Hildegard's idea of physiology is predicated upon her cosmology. The belief that man is constituted of the same (or similar) elements as those which constitute the world goes back to early Greek scientific speculation.[11] Schemes linking the four qualities, hot, cold, moist, and dry, to the four elements and to the four ages of man, the four seasons and the four humours in man, varied somewhat over the millennia, but by the twelfth century had settled down to the following schema:

hot	fire	choler [yellow bile]
dry	air	blood
moist	water	phlegm
cold	earth	melancholy [black bile]

Illnesses were thought to arise from an acute imbalance of these four humours, while certain characteristic types of personality (the choleric, sanguine, phlegmatic, and melancholic) were thought to be attributable to a chronic, constitutional imbalance of the humours.

Judging by the chapter headings of the *Causae et curae*, such as 'About the sanguine woman', Hildegard appears to be writing in accordance with this tradition. However, there is some doubt about the authenticity of these headings, which may not have been part of Hildegard's original work, but the addition of a later copyist who described her ideas using a more up-to-date terminology. In point of fact, the chapter headings in the manuscript are in a different hand from that of the main text. However, it is not simply a question of terminology which sets Hildegard's physiology apart from that of her contemporaries, but also a difference in assigning the correspondences between the elements and the humours.

The first difference arises from her identification of the four elements of the macrocosm with those in man. She says, for instance, that fire is represented by heat, air by breath, water by blood, and earth by man's flesh. The humours get their characteristics and the names peculiar to Hildegard from these four components of the body. Thus the burning heat in the human body gives rise to the dry humour (*siccum*), the warm dampness of breath to the damp humour (*humidum*), the watery blood to foamy humours (*spumaticum*), and the earthy flesh to the cool humour (*tepidum*). To complicate matters, Hildegard does not always refer to these as 'humours' but also uses the (virtually untranslatable) terms '*flegmata*' and '*livores*'. While 'humours' appears to be the most general term, the latter two are used in a relational sense according to the relative strengths of the humours in the body. Thus any of the four humours can be referred to at different times as either '*flegmata*' or '*livores*'. At any particular time the dominant two humours are called '*flegmata*' and the subordinate ones '*livores*'. Finally, it appears that a state of balance in Hildegard's scheme is not one of strict equality, but one where the superior humours maintain the right measure of dominance over their inferiors (an idea Hildegard would no doubt have found congenial given her known social views).[12] For example she writes:

> Whence if in any man the dry humour [*flegma*] outweighs the damp and the damp outweighs the foamy and cool, here the dry

humour [*flegma*] is like the mistress, and the damp is like the maid, and foamy and cool like lesser and inferior and envious servants, and these last two, are according to their strengths the complement [*livor*] of those superior ones. (*Causae et curae*, Bk 2, 44)

Most trouble seems to arise when the *livores* strive for dominance with the *flegmata*. Thus Hildegard writes:

If the damp and the cool [humours] which are the complement [*livor*] of the foamy and the dry were to change their mode, soon the damp would turn like a wheel and will sometimes cast the person into the water, sometimes into the fire, and the cool makes him mindless. (*Causae et curae*, Bk 2, 50)

Thus physical and mental disturbances are attributed to the '*livores*' when they depart from their subordinate position and struggle for precedence with the other two dominant humours, the '*flegmata*'.

Turning to the humours themselves, we find Hildegard's scheme differs further from the traditional one. Thus while the dry humour (*siccum*) can be located in the sequence fire/summer/hot-and-dry/yellow bile/choleric person, and the cool humour (*tepidum*) with the sequence earth/autumn/cold-and-dry/melancholic person, Hildegard's two remaining humours present some problems of identification. In Hildegard's scheme, blood is linked to water, and its humour is called 'foamy' (*spumaticum*), while in the more usual schemes the humour associated with water is the phlegm. Moreover, blood, in the traditional schemes, is linked with the element air. For Hildegard, air is represented in the body by air itself, and the associated humour she calls 'damp' (*humidum*) (since air is warm and moist).

In Hildegard's account of the humours, therefore, they not only have different names from the traditional ones, but some of then have different correspondences and ultimately, different qualities. This is no doubt why her classification of men and women according to humoral type or temperaments found later in the work shows such anomalous features, including a mixture of the traditional terminology and her own more specialized uses of '*flegmata*' and '*livores*'. Whether Hildegard recognized that her theory was incompatible with the more generally held humoral account is hard to say. It should also be noted that this carefully worked out theory of the proportional interaction of the humours is not applied in other sections of the book; there, in her accounts of various diseases, Hildegard contents herself with vague reference to 'noxious humours' without trying to quantify them too closely.

It is now time to look at some of the themes on which Hildegard concentrates in the earlier, non-therapeutic sections of the *Causae et curae*. Of particular interest is her treatment of the differences between the sexes and her understanding of what is generally known today as sexuality. What Hildegard has to say about women in general and their relationship to men is an important indicator of how she viewed her own capacities and abilities. In addressing these topics Hildegard attempts to synthesize the biblical account of the creation of man and woman and the first couple's fall from grace with her naturalistic humoral understanding of human physiology. The resulting account involves a more detailed and comprehensive coverage of the field than anything to be found in contemporary writings. As in the case of the *Physica*, it is very difficult to tell how much of her knowledge comes from experience or observation, and how much she deduces from her first principles and various authorities. If direct knowledge of some elements of her descriptions must be ruled out for obvious reasons, it is still possible that experience as a confidante and adviser to laywomen might have provided her with much of her material.

Hildegard usually writes as if sexual intercourse takes place between husband and wife for the purposes of procreation (which was, of course, the preferred understanding of the church). However, in her accounts of the different temperaments, other forms of sexual expression and behaviour are recognized, usually without either commendation or condemnation. She has several different accounts of what determines the characteristics of the offspring conceived in different circumstances. In one instance she writes as if the sex of the child depends upon the strength of the man's semen (strong semen produces boys, weak semen girls), while the disposition of the child depends upon the amount of love the man and woman bring to the transaction. The worst case envisaged is that where the seed is weak and neither parent feels love towards the other – the result in this case is the birth of a bitter daughter.

In the last book of the *Causae et curae* a much more elaborately deterministic view of conception is put forward, depending on the phases of the moon at which it takes place. Hildegard had earlier made the point that conception was most favourable when the moon was waxing, because of its effects on the blood of both men and women. Briefly, the blood increases when the moon is waxing and decreases when it is waning, and since semen is a product of the blood (Hildegard was not alone in thinking of it as a sort of foam whipped up by sexual desire), the state of the moon could be thought to exert an indirect influence. The same may have been true for women, since Hildegard sometimes writes as if women also contributed something in the way of seed to the conception.[13] Since she believed the foetus to be nourished by menstrual blood, the moon's influence was felt here as well. However, a different character for every day of the month seems harder to justify in naturalistic terms, and not easily applicable in retrospect, since although it may have been possible to note the state of the moon on the day a child was born (and indeed most *lunaria* take this as the important time), there would have been great practical difficulties in determining the state of the moon at the child's conception. The only practical use this might be put to would be in a kind of sexual, pre-natal counselling, rather than as an aid to predicting the characters or lifespans of those already living (as some commentators have suggested). The other problem is how all this is meant to be reconciled with Hildegard's other determining factors.

Hildegard's account of the place of sex in the earthly realm is, on the whole, remarkably optimistic, although Peter Dronke detects what he calls 'the Manichean shadow' falling across her descriptions from time to time. But while she seems to find the idea life-affirming rather than the reverse, Hildegard makes it clear that sexual intercourse has been greatly changed as a result of the Fall. The exact nature of what has been lost is not fully described, although it involved a loss of man's 'immutable and perfect state' and the transformation of his pure blood 'into another mode, so that . . . instead of purity it threw off the spume of semen'. So too, his heavenly voice was changed into one which was typified by coarse laughter.[14]

Optimistic though her view might be, it is also fairly mechanistic. In her discussion of sexual desire Hildegard writes in a mixture of metaphorical and direct language which at times defies translation. Her description of man being tossed by the winds of desire is not just a metaphor, since this 'wind' arises in the marrow, sweeps down to the loins, and is constricted there within a narrow space. In fact, finding its way into the testicles, the wind is concentrated as in a bellows, inflating the penis. Woman's desire is also a wind, but in her case it finds its way to the umbilicus and is able to spread itself there, and is thus less importunate, though more constant. In another metaphor, the man's desire is likened to a brush fire, the woman's to the warming sun. There is a practical reason for the difference in strength and frequency of male and female sexual desire; for one thing, if man was constantly in a state of arousal it would be too much for him to bear, while woman must be less ardent in order to nurture the foetus. It has been noted by several writers that in this account Hildegard goes against the generally accepted idea that women were more lustful than men, although even here Hildegard's view is complex. According to her descriptions of the temperaments, the degree of sexual desire varies in both men and women according to their humoral composition and probably other factors as well.

Apart from her description of sexual desire Hildegard has an even more unexpected account of the nature of sexual pleasure. Other medieval writings, such as the *Salernitan Questions*, are known to have treated this topic, usually from the male point of view.[15] Sometimes it is suggested that the woman, being more passionate, also got twice the pleasure, by the emission of her own seed and the reception of the man's. Hildegard, however, has a description of the sexual act from the woman's point of view, which even if it does not describe vaginal contractions (as has been suggested), is still remarkable:

> When a woman is making love with a man, a sense of heat in her brain, which brings with it sensual delight, communicates the taste of that delight during the act and summons forth the emission of the man's seed. And when the seed has fallen into its place, that vehement heat descending from her brain draws the seed to itself and holds it, and soon the woman's sexual organs contract, and all the parts that are ready to open up during the time of menstruation now close, in the same way as a strong man can hold something enclosed in his fist.[16]

It seems, however, that Hildegard may have been led to this description more by her notions of the mechanics of conception than by a knowledge of the physiology of coitus. Why, otherwise should the woman's orgasm take place only when the seed has been emitted by the man?

Hildegard's other images of coitus carry a lesser degree of 'enraptured feeling for the beauty of the sexual act'. In one case the woman is seen as the threshing floor pounded by many strokes, and in another as land under the plough. In the descriptions of men and women according to humoral type, we encounter once more some enduring sexual prejudices or stereotypes: that men have uncontrollable urges but women do not; that men are ruled by their sexual appetites and women by their wombs, and the thwarting of either leads to trouble. Some women, according to Hildegard, suffer if they do not have children, though not, apparently, if they do not have sex.

Thus the sexual relationship between men and women is unequal, although not in the simple sense of the Aristotelian opposites. Behind her theories, however, is the basic notion that woman is weaker than man, because he was made from earth, and she from flesh. There are some compensations for the woman in this, for instance that she is more nurturing (also, no doubt, a compensation for man), and less subject to gout and hernias; women are also more able to control their weaker and more diffuse sexual appetites.

Fascinating as such questions may be, when the humoral typologies are considered as a proportion of the whole work, they are found to be something of an aside. The largest part of the work is devoted to a series of brief descriptions of diseases and afflictions which are associated with different parts of the body, starting at the head and working down, with occasional digressions when some aspect of what she has been talking about suggests another line of thought. Thus Hildegard mentions a range of illnesses and con-ditions, including migraine (called '*emigranea*' in the text), asthma, urinary incontinence, and recurrent fevers. Along the way she throws in additional information, for instance the fact that the age of menopause is 40 to 50 but in some women about 70 (possibly an allowance made for some notable biblical exceptions to the general rule). Hildegard comments on diet, which is to be different in summer and winter because of the necessity of balancing heat and cold according to the changed conditions, and bloodletting, including its veterinary applications. She also covers laughter and tears, sneezing and nosebleeds, and a variety of rashes and infestations including lice and several different kinds of intestinal worms.

The third and fourth books contain between them some 107 chapters (as opposed to the second section's 296) and provide the medical remedies for the diseases and conditions described therein, although the correspondence is not exact. It looks as if Hildegard may have intended to supply a remedy for each condition, but some-times got carried away or sidetracked. The first prescription, however, is a cure for baldness, which was the first condition described in Book 2: the cure includes bear's grease (recommended for the same purpose in Pliny) and ashes of wheaten straw mixed into a paste and smeared on the head, to be left on as long as possible. Hildegard explains that the heat of the bear fat is the active ingredient, while the vegetable products help to strengthen the hair. We might also suspect that there was some sort of sympathetic magic involved arising from the shagginess of the bear.

The same principle seems to be at work in her cures for sterility, where as well as using vegetable products (hazelnuts, convolvulus, water pepper) the ingredients include, for men, the liver of a young male goat, and for women, the uterus of a sheep or cow. On the other hand, the rationale for dunking a little bitch in water as a remedy for drunkenness, and using the water to bathe the head, depends on the combined coldness of the bitch and the water minimizing the heat of the veins in the forehead (*Causae et curae*, Bk 4, 23). Another remedy for epilepsy seems to combine folk medicine ingredients, such as moles and ducks' beaks, with recommendations for the diet to be followed in this illness (*Causae et curae*, Bk 4, 37).

The question of the availability of the ingredients for the cures leads us back to the *Physica* and the problem of whether this was a handbook or a general encyclopedia. On the whole, it seems that the remedies used in *Causae et curae* are mostly vegetable, or to a lesser extent, animal, and hardly ever employ jewels or minerals, although Book 4, 56 uses '*creta*', a kind of white clay, against worms.

So, for example, the prescription for headache arising from melancholia includes such ingredients as mallow, sage, and olive oil (or failing that, vinegar) used as a compress on the head. The migraine, however, perhaps because it is more intractable, requires more exotic remedies such as aloe, myrrh, and poppy oil mixed with flour. The combination of their heat (aloe), dryness (myrrh), the blandness of the flour and coldness of the poppy oil (all qualities attributed to these plants in the *Physica*) combine to allay the headache. On the whole, it seems as if the ingredients for the most commonly prescribed remedies would have been available locally, although such products as pepper, nutmeg, ginger, cloves, and sugar which are also used would presumably have had to be bought in.

Other remedies seem not only practicable but practical. The idea of rinsing the mouth and teeth on rising with pure cold water while no doubt less efficient than a toothbrush may have done some good for those who wished to have 'healthy and firm teeth'. Still others make use of herbs identified by their German names, which suggests that they were common and readily available, such as '*Wullena*' (woolly) mullein, '*Heiternezzele*' nettle, and '*Dille*' dill, all of which were employed in a prescription for diseases of the lungs. Hildegard recommends hot baths containing herbs such as feverfew, tansy, and mullein for women who fail to menstruate, a procedure which may suggest abortion to us, but is more likely to be a treatment for amenorrhea brought on by malnutrition. Here her suggestions for strengthening diets may have been more effective.

While most of the cures are of a fairly straightforward pharmacological kind, depending on the combination of qualities derived from plants (or occasionally animal products), to counteract similar (or opposite) qualities which are causing the illness, a few entries reflect more magical and superstitious practices. This is especially true where poison and witchcraft, rather than naturally occurring diseases, are to be dealt with. In Book 4, 16, Hildegard outlines an elaborate procedure against poison, involving plantain, geranium, and mallow plants, to be picked in the middle of April and kept alive by sprinkling with water at certain specified times of the day or night, placed to dry at a high window, and then made into a sort of potpourri to be smelled every day. The mixture can also serve as an anaphrodisiac, tied in a cloth around the loins of a man, or the woman's waist. The reason for the particular virtue of the recipe depends on the 'tempering' of the ingredients by the sun, moon, and air at all hours of the day and night.

The fifth book contains a miscellaneous collection of information. Some of this is of an overtly medical sort, such as the signs of life and death and uroscopy. There follow comments on the use of bathing, where frequent baths are only recommended for those who are thin and dry, or in the case of hot or steam baths, for those with the opposite humours. Even the types of stone best suited for heating such baths are specified according to their predominant qualities of heat or cold.

The last part of the *Causae et curae* is devoted to the *lunaria* mentioned earlier. It is perhaps better to see these as an exercise in the description of various types of men and women rather than the working out of a particular theory. There is, for instance, some difficulty in trying to accommodate Hildegard's earlier investigations of male and female temperaments to this later account. For example, a woman conceived on the second day after the new moon is subject to melancholy but not, apparently, a man conceived at this time. Once more we are faced in the *Causae et curae* with an embarrassment of theories, not all of which seem to be fully integrated with each other. However, the presence of many of Hildegard's typical preoccupations, her style and vocabulary throughout the work make it inadvisable to discard any particular sections of it.

How then are the *Physica* and *Causae et curae* to be summed up? There is little doubt that the material bears Hildegard's own stamp, although it is hard to conceive of the original form of her medical and scientific work. The *Physica* seems to reflect an overall encyclopedic purpose, arising, perhaps, from Hildegard's special knowledge of herbs. On the whole the strictly medical parts of the *Causae et curae* appear to follow the principles assumed in the *Physica*. The theoretical parts of the former work, however, are more complicated and in some senses peculiar to Hildegard and not readily assimilated to what seems to have been contemporary scientific thought. The particular attention paid to women and the sexual dimension of life also sets Hildegard's work apart from other medieval writings with which it might be compared. Finally, Hildegard seems to have used much of her scientific writing as raw material, which later reappears, often in rather different forms, in her theological writings, especially the *Liber divinorum operum*.

6

CELESTIAL HARMONIES

Who would not marvel that she wrote a song cycle with sweetest melody? (*Vita*, Bk 2)

During the time Hildegard was working on her books of natural history and medicine, she was also engaged in a project of an apparently quite different nature: composing her cycle of over seventy songs which, together with her musical play, the *Ordo virtutum* (*Play of the Virtues*), forms what she called the 'symphony of the harmony of heavenly revelations'. For many years a neglected aspect of Hildegard's work, recent records and performances of her music have made Hildegard's name, if not a household word, increasingly familiar.

While there is no debate about the authorship of the musical works, there is some question about when they were composed. We know from a letter of Odo of Soissons that Hildegard was already recognized for her musical compositions as early as 1148, but to confine her musical activity to her youth and middle age is somewhat arbitrary and surely unlikely for one who attributed such a high place to music.[1] The structure of the *Symphonia* would allow for works to be added or deleted over the years. There is evidence to suggest that the *Ordo virtutum* was in existence in something like its present form as early as 1151, since the final sections of the *Scivias* seem to contain adaptions from it. On the other hand, some of the sequences, especially those connected with the saints of Trier, may well belong to the works of Hildegard's last years. The earliest surviving manuscript of Hildegard's music (Dendermonde) was written in the 1170s and could thus contain songs which span Hildegard's entire musical career, although a version of the *Symphonia* was completed in the 1150s.

102

The existence of several pieces on the same subject – the Virgin Mary, St Ursula and the 11,000 virgins, and St Disibod – might suggest that she had favourite topics to which she returned from time to time, although the pieces on particular saints could also have been composed as a set for the liturgy of a particular feast day.

To speak of Hildegard's musical works as 'songs' (L. *carmina*, Gm *Lieder*) may give the wrong initial impression, for all her compositions were conceived of in a strictly religious mode. Perhaps a better description might be 'liturgical songs', since they were almost all composed in forms – antiphons, responsories, sequences, hymns – which were used in the performance of the *Opus Dei* or the celebration of the mass.[2] Thus it is clear that her compositions arose directly from the needs of the monastic life and, unlike the writing of a theological treatise, required little apology or justification. During the Middle Ages many availed themselves of the remarkable freedom to add to the liturgy (as witness the fifty-five volumes of the *Analecta Hymnica*), although very little of their work has found a place in today's official liturgy.[3] Sometimes this involved writing pieces for the feasts of saints of local interest not previously celebrated, or not celebrated in fitting style, but traditional themes, such as that of the Holy Spirit or the Virgin, also lent themselves to reworking and elaboration.

The idea of combining what might otherwise have been a series of *ad hoc* compositions into a cycle had several precedents, notably the *Liber Hymnorum* by Notker of St Gall (composed between 860 and 870).[4] Hildegard's work, however, is not so obviously ordered according to the liturgical year. In many cases the pieces are not specified for any particular day, even if the part of the office for which they were intended, matins, lauds, and so on, is noted. The original arrangement of the *Symphonia* is problematic, and the order of the pieces in the two manuscripts (Riesenkodex and Dendermonde) is not the same. The earlier manuscript is fragmentary and lacks nineteen of the songs found in the Riesenkodex, as well as the *Ordo virtutum*.

The arrangement in the Barth/Ritscher edition follows that of the Dendermonde manuscript up to no. 57, with the remainder taken from the Riesenkodex, more or less in the order in which they occur there. This obscures the fact that in both manuscripts the songs are arranged according to their subjects, in hierarchical order with God at the apex. In the Riesenkodex there are traces of a second arrangement according to liturgical type. For instance, the antiphons and responsories for the 11,000 virgins occur together but the sequence for St Ursula (*O Ecclesia*), comes towards the end of the collection with other sequences to Eucharius and Maximin.

Because any description of the original, or indeed, final arrangement of the *Symphonia* is conjectural in many of its details, it seems best to consider the songs separately. The analogy here is to studying individual poems from an author's collected works rather than separate sections of a single work. Such an approach is also justified by a consideration of the nature of the pieces and their relationship to the context in which they were performed. Of course, it should not be forgotten that we are dealing with songs, rather than poems, and ideally they should be discussed in connection with their music. However, I intend to make only a few very basic remarks about the nature of Hildegard's music and its relationship to the tradition of Gregorian or plainchant in which she was writing.[5]

To say that Hildegard's musical compositions are examples of plainchant implies first, that her songs consist of a single melodic line without harmony or polyphony and second, that they are not characterized by regular rhythm. The musical styles of the different liturgical categories for chant melodies in office and mass varied from the predominantly syllabic and recitation style for office antiphons, office responsories, and psalm verses and doxologies within mass introits and communions, to the neumatic style for processional and Marian antiphons of the office, and mass introit and communion antiphons – where a syllable may be sung to a group of notes ('neumes', in medieval notation). Melismatic melodies (where many notes are sung to one syllable) were used for mass kyries, graduals, alleluias, offertories, and the great responsories of the office of matins. While the resources at the disposal of the composer of plainchant might seem somewhat limited to a twentieth-century listener, subtle effects of emphasis, and, for example, the use of parallelism in text and music, were exploited to great effect by Hildegard.[6]

When the collection is viewed as a whole, it is found that the greater part of it consists of relatively short pieces in the form of responsories (18) and antiphons (43). The longer pieces – sequences, hymns and the three unclassified songs – together number fourteen. The total is brought to seventy-seven by the addition of a kyrie and an alleluia.

Office antiphons originally consisted of short biblical texts sung before and after the psalms and canticles. Since the psalms are repeated throughout the year, the antiphon is used as a kind of commentary which indicates the mood of the psalm, according to the liturgical season. During the Middle Ages new antiphons were freely composed in language approximating that of the scriptural antiphons, although they were often more elaborate. The best known of these are the so-called greater or O-antiphons, which were already in use in the eighth century. They were sung before and after the magnificat at vespers for the week before Christmas Eve, and take their name from the initial invocations: *O Sapientia, O Adonai, O Radix Jesse, O Clavis David, O Oriens, O Rex Gentium,* and *O Emmanuel.* In the present liturgy the number of antiphons following this pattern is virtually limited to these and four others, but it will be noted that a large proportion of Hildegard's antiphons begin with an invocation and are also longer than most antiphons in the Gregorian repertory, which suggests that Hildegard's antiphons were modelled on the great antiphons.

If we divide Hildegard's poetry thematically we find antiphons on almost all the subjects covered in the *Symphonia*: God, Christ, the Holy Ghost, the Trinity, Mary, angels, patriarchs, apostles, John the Evangelist, St Disibod, martyrs, confessors, St Rupert, virgins (including St Ursula and the 11,000), the dedication of a church, and St Boniface.[7] Probably not much will be gained by trying to match the antiphons to the specific feast to which they were attached, although this is easy enough in the case of the named saints. (As we just saw in the case of the O-antiphons belonging to Advent, such topics as the persons of the Trinity or Mary were not necessarily confined to particular days.) Rather, I will look at some of the antiphons themselves as pieces in their own right.

I have chosen four antiphons to illustrate the type and scope of the form as handled by Hildegard. They range from a simple six-line description of the vivifying force of the Holy Spirit (Newman, 24) to a twelve-line meditation on the wonder of the Incarnation and its power to reverse the consequences of the Fall. Although some of Hildegard's antiphons are invocations followed by petitions (as in the great antiphons), the examples chosen here do not exemplify this form. Here is her antiphon about the Holy Spirit:

The Holy Spirit, lifegiving life
is the prime mover and root stock of every creature,
washing all from stain,
wiping away sin and salving wounds.
It is lambent and laudable life,
all rousing and reviving.[8]

The description of the Holy Spirit as the root, which washes away sin and salves wounds, may at first look like a rather mixed metaphor, but if we recall Hildegard's medical works it does not seem so inept. It is perhaps an example of association of words, '*radix*' in the first sense being metaphorical (basis, foundation), but suggesting also the connection of actual roots with healing, examples of which are found in her medical writings. The therapeutic imagery is extended to the triumphant affirmation of the last line. The musical style of the piece is neumatic, which is appropriate for Marian and processional antiphons.

One of Hildegard's many antiphons about Mary (Newman, 16) neatly sums up a good deal of spiritual history, in a brief meditation on the Incarnation:

O great the wonder
that in a hidden female body
a king entered.
God did this
as humility rises above all.
And O great the happiness
in that woman,
because the evil that came from woman,
this one then swept away.
She built up sweet-smelling virtues
and adorned Heaven yet more than
she had first marred earth.

The poem as a whole depends on a series of contrasts, bordering, in the sentence about humility, on paradox. This line of thought, which is often given expression in the New Testament, was familiar to Hildegard and used by her to justify her own activity as writer and prophet. The particular lowliness of womankind is implied in the 'wonder' of the first line, where Hildegard goes even further than Anselm when he asked 'Why did God become man?' Hildegard's answer to the implied question, 'How could he have stooped to enter the womb of a woman?' is the paradoxical justification already noted: humility rises above all. The choice of Mary is also warranted by the appositeness of a second woman overturning the evil done by the first. This was a theme that appeared early in Christian writings, and lent itself to a number of more or less ingenious parallels and echoes, one such being the palindromic significance of the angel's salutation '*Ave*' to Mary, as a reversal of '*Eva*'. Hildegard goes even further here in an apparent identification of Eve with Mary: the ambiguity in the last sentence of the antiphon, in the use of 'she' for both Eve and Mary, is in the original. The connection of virtue with sweet smells, sometimes represented as incense, will be encountered in other poems and here functions as a kind of shorthand for such associations. The cosmic consequences of the Fall, in perverting the true nature of creation, have already been explored and explained by Hildegard in several sections of her medical/scientific works, especially the *Causae et curae*. It is interesting that the antiphon does not call upon Mary directly, but the salvific function to which she lent herself, and more especially, her rehabilitation of womankind is briefly evoked.

Slightly more complex in its theology is her antiphon '*O quam mirabilis*' (Newman, 3), which hymns the divine foreknowledge. This was also a favourite theme with Hildegard, as was her notion that man was the peak of God's creation in which all things were somehow implicit and complete. Hildegard's idea of the relationship between man and the universe as microcosm and macrocosm has been noted in connection with the *Causae et curae* and it receives its most extended treatment in the *Liber divinorum operum*. This is how the idea is given expression in the antiphon:

O how wonderful is the prescience of the divine heart,
who foreknew every creature.
For when God looked on the face of man,
whom He had made,
all his works
He saw completed in his form.
O how wonderful is the breath
which brought man to life.

In this antiphon some of the wonder seems to be transferred from God to his final creation, man. Here Hildegard expresses one of the most striking features of what we might call her spiritual anthropology: the paramount place occupied by mankind in creation. There is, perhaps, some question of whether woman could also be said to share this exalted position, since the event celebrated in the antiphon is actually the creation of Adam. On the other hand, the creation of Eve and the subsequent history of humankind was implicit in the creation of Adam, and thus it might be allowed that woman also shared, albeit at one remove, in the high esteem accorded to man. We find, then, in this antiphon a density of meaning scarcely indicated by its apparent simplicity.

The fourth antiphon (Newman, 51) does not concern a member of the Trinity or Mary, but an eighth-century Anglo-Saxon missionary, Wynfrith, known to Hildegard as St Boniface, first Archbishop of Mainz and a martyr for the faith in what is now Holland. Whether this antiphon was destined for the monastery of Fulda, where he was buried, or for local use at Rupertsberg, which was in the diocese of Mainz, cannot now be ascertained. What is clear, however, is that Hildegard uses some of her favourite images to suggest rather than describe explicitly the saint's life and death:

> O Boniface
> the living light saw you
> like a wise man
> who returned to their source
> the pure waters flowing from God
> when you watered the greenness of the flowers.
> So you are the friend of the living God
> and the true crystal shining
> in the benevolence of the straight way
> where you ran wisely.

The central, horticultural image refers to the blood shed by Boniface at his martyrdom. In several other poems, notably those on Ursula, Hildegard connects blood with flowers and jewels. Here Boniface's death is seen as a repayment in kind for the grace of knowledge and evangelization he received from above, represented by the water flowing from God. The connection between blood and water is, of course, a venerable one in the Christian tradition, epitomized by the blood and water that flowed from Christ's side on the cross. Hildegard also laid special emphasis on their relationship in her theory of human physiology.

The picturing of human life as a journey towards God, run at different rates and by different paths, recurs in much of Hildegard's work and was central to her thought, witness the explanation of *Scivias* as 'Know the ways of the Lord'. The accelerated progress of the martyr is also alluded to in the Ursula poems, together with motifs of blood, water, and jewels. The use of the crystal with reference to Boniface sets up the same kinds of resonances and harks back to the mention of water earlier in the poem, thus tying the whole together. The music for this antiphon, generally neumatic in style, has a striking example of melisma on the last word *'cucurristi'* ('you ran'), suggesting by its reiterated arches the action of running, or possibly, hurdling.

So much for office antiphons. The other short liturgical pieces found in the *Symphonia* belong to the class of office responsories. These responsories perform a similar function to the office antiphons in modifying or commenting on another part of the liturgy. They can be divided into two categories, the great responsories which follow the readings of the lessons at matins and the short responsories which follow the chapters, read within the day hours, from prime to compline. Two performance schemes are indicated for the majority of Hildegard's responsories: (i) respond, verse, partial respond, Gloria Patri, partial respond; and (ii) respond, verse, partial respond. These schemes also correspond to many responsories in the Gregorian repertory. In contrast to the office antiphons, many responsory texts are neither psalmodic nor even biblical. Hildegard's responsories, judged by their length, seem to be more like the great responsories, and would thus be intended for use at matins. The following (Newman, 56), taken from a group of songs about virgins, is one of the shorter ones:

R: O most noble greenness, rooted in the Sun
and shining in bright serenity
in the wheel
which no earthly excellence
understands,
you are encompassed by the embrace of the divine mysteries.
V: You glow like the dawn
and shine like sunbeams.

Once again we have Hildegard's familiar association of ideas: greenness, '*viriditas*', which we saw as one of the first principles in her scientific works, and its connection with the vivifying sun and other images of light. As for the versicle, the Virgin Mary is often celebrated in such terms, which makes the connection with other virgins implicit. In fact, there is nothing in the responsory to mark off this particular virgin – presumably Ursula or one of her band – from the archetypal Virgin. Or should we say that it is not a particular virgin, but rather the concept of virginity which is being celebrated?

The second responsory (Newman, 22) is more particularly about the Virgin Mary and her special place in the divine plan:

R: O how precious is
the maidenhood of this Virgin,
she of the shut door
whose womb the holy Godhead

filled with His fire
so that a flower bloomed in her
and the Son of God
from that secret place
went forth like the dawn.
V: Thus the sweet seed, who was that Son,
through the shut door of her womb
unlocked paradise.
R: And the Son of God
from that secret place
went forth like the dawn.

The images of shut doors, enclosed gardens, and budding flowers are entirely traditional but Hildegard's repetition of the dawn motif is significant. As one of the longer responsories, it would have been sung at matins when the coming of the dawn was no doubt anticipated, and thus the central idea is conveyed by timely and appropriate imagery. The precious virginity of Mary is an attribute which might also be thought of as particularly esteemed by nuns as a validation of their own virginal status.

The responsories and antiphons, then, depend for some of their force on the liturgical context in which they are embedded. This, together with their relative brevity, may explain why they have not received as much attention as Hildegard's longer and more auton-omous pieces, the hymns and sequences. These two forms also have their place in the liturgy. The sequences, for example, occur in masses performed on the saints' days, but are freestanding and of sufficient length for quite sophisticated development of thought and imagery. Because Hildegard's compositions generally approximate the older type of sequence which lacks regular repetition, and because she does not make use of rhyme or regular rhythm, some earlier com-mentators dismissed her sequences as mere prose. It is largely due to the efforts of Peter Dronke that Hildegard's sequences have received the acclaim they deserve, and my account owes much to his pioneering work.[9]

The subjects of the longer pieces are somewhat more circum-scribed than those of the collection as a whole. The Holy Spirit is the only member of the Trinity to whom an entire piece is devoted (with a hymn and a sequence, perhaps an indication of Hildegard's partiality), although Christ is invoked in the *Symphonia Virginum* (Song of the Virgins), and possibly all three persons are addressed in the

Symphonia Viduarum (Song of the Widows). Three pieces – a sequence, a hymn, and one unclassified (Newman, 19) – are on the subject of the Virgin Mary, while St Ursula and the 11,000 virgins are represented by a sequence, a hymn, and possibly also the unclassified piece on virgins. The remaining songs are devoted to St Disibod, St Rupert, St Eucharius, St Maximin, and St Matthias, all of which are sequences except the last, which is a hymn. Since Hildegard's sequences are not in the usual sequence form, they are hard to distinguish from the hymns, especially since these also are not in the conventional hymn form of the period. However, the sequence had a particular place in the mass, between the allelulia and the gradual, while hymns might be accommodated in the mass or, more usually, in the office hours.

It is in the sequences and hymns that startling poetic effects, particularly the use of unexpected combinations of images, occur most frequently. That is not, of course, to say that all are equally dependent on spectacular imagery for their effects. Some, for example, are more straightforward, developing a discursive line of thought or argument, rather than relying on densely packed imagery for their meaning. An example of this type is the Hymn to St Matthias, the disciple who was chosen after the Ascension to replace Judas among the twelve. This hymn was no doubt intended for Hildegard's friends at the monastery of St Eucharius in Trier, which underwent a change of patron in 1148, with the deposition there of relics of St Matthias. In the hymn (Newman, 50) the events of his life are only briefly indicated, more prominence being given to the unlooked-for operation of divine grace in choosing the instruments to carry out its purpose. Hildegard may well have recognized the similarity between her own case and that of Matthias.

1 Matthias, holy by election,
made a champion through his victory,
before the sacrifice of the lamb he was not chosen,
but came late to understanding
like a man not properly awake.

2 The gift of God awoke him,
when he for joy
like a giant put on his strength
since God foreknew him
like the man
whom He made from earth

when the first angel fell
who denied God.

3 The man who saw the election
alas, alas, he fell.
He had cattle and sheep
but he turned his face from them
and sent them away.

4 Whence he entered the pit of coals,
kissed his heart's desires,
by his own efforts
raised them like Olympus.

5 Then Matthias by divine election
rose up like a giant
because God put him in the place
which the lost man did not want.
O wonderful miracle
that shone so in him!

6 For God foresaw him
in his miracles,
when he did not have merit through works,
but the mystery of God had joy in him
which he did not have of his own making.

7 O joy of joys
that God works so
when He lays his grace on the unsuspecting;
thus when small he cannot know
where fledged he flies up
on wings God gave to the child.

8 God then savours those
who do not know themselves,
whose voices call to God
as Matthias did who said:
'O God, my God, and my Creator,
all my works are thine.'

9 So now let all the Church rejoice in Matthias,
whom God, in the lattice of the dove
thus chose. Amen.

Perhaps the most striking aspect of this hymn is the strong sense of direction imposed by its progressive structure, rather than the imagery which is rather spare and seems, with its giants and references to Olympus, classical rather than biblical. Indeed at some points, especially the third and fourth stanzas, the imagery and even the meaning is hard to interpret. Who, for instance, had the cattle and sheep? Do they perhaps represent Jewish sacrifices? Is the fourth stanza a reference to the harrowing of hell? And why Olympus? We are on firmer ground towards the end of the poem with the pinions of divine contemplation and the evocative 'lattice of the dove', a reference to the action of the Holy Spirit which recalls or anticipates the famous opening image of the sequence for St Maximin, '*Columba aspexit*'.

Each stanza in the hymn is linked to the next by a semantic echo or sometimes actual repetition of a word, except for the problematical fourth stanza which is shorter than all the rest and might once have been intended as part of stanza 3. Thus stanzas 1 and 2 are linked by awake/awoke (*vigilat/excitavit*), stanzas 2 and 3 by the repetition of fell (*cecidit*), the fourth and fifth stanzas are linked by rose/arose (*erexit/surrexit*), the next pair by the repetition of 'miracles', the seventh and eighth by 'joys', the penultimate two by repetition of the word 'know' (actually *nescit*), and the last two by the repetition of 'Matthias'. Thus a chain of thought is forged which reflects and exemplifies the central theme of the inevitability and inscrutability of God's grace. Here then, it is the form of the poem itself, rather than a particular use of imagery, which is employed to great effect. The music of the piece also reflects the movement of the thought. Unlike many contemporary hymns which display regularity of verse form and metre, allowing each verse to be sung to the same melody, the Hymn to St Matthias has no such regular returns to a set pattern, although it must be admitted that some phrasal repetitions can be seen, notably between stanzas 3 and 4.

Somewhat similar in style is the *Symphonia Virginum* (Song of the Virgins), an invocation to Christ which also depends on a controlled progression of thought rather than elaborate imagery, and moves from lamentation and despair to hope, with the turning point coming, once more, in the middle of the poem (Newman, 57):

1 O sweetest lover!
O sweetest enfolder!
help us to guard
our virginity.

2 We were born in dust
alas, alas, and in Adam's crime.

3 It is very hard to resist
what tastes of the apple.
Set us upright Saviour, Christ.

4 Our burning desire is to follow you.
O how heavy it is for our wretched selves
the spotless and innocent King of Angels
to follow!

5 Yet we trust in you
and your desire
to seek a gem in the dust.

6 Now we call on you, husband and consoler,
who redeemed us on the cross.
We are joined to you in a marriage of your blood
rejecting men
and choosing you, Son of God.

7 O most beautiful form!
O most sweet savour of desirable delight!
We ever sigh after you
in fearful exile,
when will we see you and dwell with you?

8 We are in the world
and you in our minds
and we embrace you in our hearts, as if we had you here.

9 You, the prepotent lion broke through the heavens
descending into the chamber of the Virgin
and overcame death
building life in the Golden City.

10 Grant us citizenship in it
and to remain in you, O most sweet Spouse,
who has wrested us from the jaws of the Devil,
who seduced our first parent.

The central image of the virgins as jewels derives from the idea of
the heavenly Jerusalem being made of living stones. The saving will
of Christ involves looking for such jewels in the dust of the world and

helping them to achieve their desire, by means of the 'marriage of blood' on the cross. This seems to be a specialized case of the marriage of *Ecclesia*, or the church as a whole, to the crucified Christ which is described in the *Scivias*. The virgins, although knowing themselves to be already married in this way, are yet separated from Christ as exiles in the world. Stanzas 7 and 8 give poignant expression to their feelings of separation and longing. This leads to a consideration of the Incarnation as a prerequisite for any such marriage. The description of Christ breaking through the heavens like a lion (Rev. 5:5) marks a change in the tone of the poem from one of longing to one of triumphant affirmation, in which the desires of the virgins for their spouse are generalized as the hope of all Christians.

As a transitional type between the poems which depend on narrative or logical progression and those where imagery is the principal means of expression, let us now consider the hymn to the Holy Ghost (Newman, 27) '*O ignee spiritus, laus tibi sit*':

1 O fiery spirit, praise be to you
who works in tympana and lutes!

2 The minds of men take fire from you
and the tabernacles of their souls contain their strength.

3 Whence will ascends and imparts a taste to the soul
and his light is desire.

4 Understanding calls to you with sweetest sound,
and prepares buildings for you with reason
which distils golden deeds.

5 You always hold the sword to sever
what the poisoned apple brought through the blackest killer,
when will and desire are clouded
and the soul flaps and circles.
But the mind is the bridle of will and desire.

6 Now when the spirit raises itself as it seeks
to see the pupil of evil and jawbone of wickedness
you swiftly burn it in fire
when you wish.

7 But when reason through ill deeds lies prone
you strain and beat upon it with force
and restore it by the infusion of experience.

8 When evil draws a sword against you
you strike it to the heart
just as you did with the first fallen angel
when you cast the tower of his pride into hell.

9 And here you raised another tower
of publicans and sinners
who confessed their sins and deeds to you.

10 Whence all creatures which have their life from you
praise you,
for you are the most precious ointment
for broken and stinking wounds
when you convert them into most precious jewels.

11 Now deign to gather us to you
and show us the right paths. Amen.

The opening images of fire and sound are balanced at the close of
the poem by another set of arresting images where the Holy Spirit is
seen as changing the wounds of the sinners into jewels. The
intermediate stanzas explore the nature of moral choice and outline
the part the Holy Spirit plays in strengthening the soul. The manner
in which this is done is vigorous, if not violent – the sword to cut off
evil, burning, and the strengthening of reason (which has been laid
low by wicked deeds), by pulverization and infusion.[10]

Hildegard has several sequences and hymns devoted to the Virgin
Mary. In terms of imagery these are perhaps the most stereotyped,
simply because the liturgy itself was a storehouse of Marian imagery.
Thus we find the white lily in '*Ave generosa*' (Newman, 17), but the rod
of Jesse in no. 19 has been given a typically Hildegardian epithet
when it is described as 'most green' (*viridissima*), and extended to
become a tree full of birds, 'since her womb brought forth corn/and
the birds of the air/have their nests in her'.

I have chosen to look more closely at '*O virga ac diadema*' (Newman,
20) since it receives a tantalizing mention in the *Acta*, where
Hildegard is described as singing this sequence as she walked through
the cloister.[11] The meaning of the passage is not entirely clear, but it
does seem to suggest that this song was a particular favourite of
Hildegard's.

1a O rod and diadem of royal purple,
you are like a breastplate unbroached.

1b Your branching flowered in contradiction
to the way Adam brought forth all mankind.

2a Hail! Hail! From your womb
a different life came forth
from the life that Adam denied his sons.

2b O flower, you were not budded by the dew
nor drops of rain, nor the circumambient air,
but divine light brought you out
from this most noble stem.

3a O stem, your flowering
God foresaw on the first day of his creation.

3b And from his Word made you the golden matter,
O praiseworthy virgin.

4a O great is the strength of man's side,
from which God took the form of woman,
and made her the mirror of all adornments,
the clasp of his entire creation.

4b Then the celestial harmony sounded
and all earth marvelled,
O praiseworthy Mary,
because God loved you so.

5a O plangent and doleful it is
that sadness and crime at the serpent's word
flowed into woman.

5b For that woman, whom God placed as mother of all,
ruined her womb with the wounds of ignorance
and brought great sorrow on her children.

6a Yet, O dawn, from your womb
a new sun came forth, who cleaned away all Eve's sin
and through you brought a greater blessing
to mankind than all Eve's harm.

6b Whence O saving lady, who brought a new light
to human kind
unite the members of your Son
in celestial harmony.

The regal and martial imagery in the first stanza is soon abandoned in favour of developing the other side of the double meaning of '*virga*' – 'branch', rather than 'rod' or 'sceptre' – in a series of contrasts between natural and supernatural generation. The ideas in stanza 2b are paralleled in Hildegard's scientific works, where the production of flowers is said to depend on dew, raindrops, and the right atmospheric conditions. Here the flower which was the result of this unique and unnatural process is Christ. By a familiar association of ideas, Hildegard turns her attention from the Incarnation to what it was supposed to rectify, the fall from grace of the first couple, especially, in Marian contexts, that of Eve. Indeed, it goes further than that since the whole course of events was foreseen by God on the first day of creation. Thus the contemplation of Mary brings in its train an evocation of the entire salvation history. This is achieved by a familiar series of contrasts between Eve and Mary, including metaphors of sun, dawn, light, and music, as well as some less usual ones, such as that where Mary is described as the 'golden matter, or matrix' and the mirror and clasp of creation.

As already suggested, the most spectacular examples of Hildegard's poetry are found in the sequences devoted to local saints at Disibodenberg, Rupertsberg, and Trier – St Disibod, St Rupert, St Ursula and the 11,000 virgins, St Eucharius, and St Maximin. It is in these compositions that she allowed her visionary imagination full reign and the imagery, while still largely traditional, is deployed in novel ways.

The sequence about St Disibod (Newman, 45) was probably composed in response to a request by Abbot Kuno. Hildegard was later to write the *Life of St Disibod* for his successor, Helenger. During her time at Disibodenberg, she had no doubt absorbed whatever was known about the patron of the monastery. Legend has it that he was an Irish bishop who came to the Rhineland in the seventh century and founded the monastery where Hildegard was to grow up. In the sequence, Hildegard merely alludes to his earthly life, while emphasizing his role as symbolic founder of the monastery. Even more important in her eyes is his ultimate destination and role as intercessor for his monastic family on earth.

1   O bishop of the true city
who in the temple of the corner stone
reaching towards heaven
bowed down on earth
for God.

2   A pilgrim from the seed of the world,
you longed to be an exile
for the love of Christ.

3   O mount of secret thought,
you took care to present a beautiful face
in the mirror of the dove.

4   You hid yourself out of sight
drunk with the smell of flowers in the windows of the saints
reaching towards God.

5   O shaft of the keys of heaven
because you exchanged the world for
a cloudless life,
this prize, sweet witness,
will ever be yours in the Lord.

6   For in your mind
the living fountain in brightest light
leads forth the purest streams
by the way of salvation.

7   You are a great tower
before the altar of the highest God
obscuring the shaft of this tower
with clouds of perfume.

8   Disibod, through your light
and the agency of pure sound
you have raised aisles of wondrous praise
on two sides through the Son of Man.

9   You stand on high, unashamed before the living God
and you protect with vivifying dew
those praising God with these words:

10   O sweet the life and holy the determination
which in this blessed Disibod
ever built the glorious life
in heavenly Jerusalem.

11   Now let there be praise to God
from those who wear the beautiful tonsure
striving manfully.

12　And let the heavenly citizens rejoice in those
who imitate them in this way.

The first stanza introduces the notion of paradoxical reversal
which is central to much Christian thought: the elevation of the
humble. This idea was also a favourite with Hildegard, who applied it
not only in her writings, in the *Ordo virtutum*, for example, but also
to her own life. Thus Disibod is now a member of the true city, the
heavenly Jerusalem (or, even more strikingly, a leader or bishop there)
because he humbled himself on earth. The mention of the finial
stone (*angularis lapidis*) refers to a passage in Matt. 21:42 which is
another statement of the theme: the stone which the builders rejected
(Christ) has come to crown the building. In the second stanza St
Disibod, in leaving Ireland literally became an exile for the love of
God. Such exile was referred to in Irish as 'the white martyrdom' to
distinguish it from literal martyrdom, 'the red martyrdom'. Thus he
doubled the burden of exile, in the sense that all mankind can be seen
as pilgrims journeying to the heavenly homeland.

The third and fourth stanzas which picture the end of Disibod's
wanderings and settlement at Disibodenberg are more difficult. At
times the meaning of the evocative images Hildegard employs can
be discerned by reference to her other works, especially the *Scivias*.
Thus the mirror of the dove suggests both contemplation of the Holy
Spirit and the ascription of the qualities of the dove – 'simplicity
and sincerity' (according to *Scivias*, 2, vis. 3, ch. 26) – to St Disibod.
However, Hildegard may have had another more specific use of the
mirror in mind. In the third book of the *Scivias*, in a chapter about
men who choose celibacy, she writes that they will be secured from
attacks of the Devil by being made consorts of Christ, who will be
placed before them like a mirror. So too, the intoxicating smells of the
flowers may suggest inebriation with the virtues, as well as being an
allusion to the fertile and pleasant surroundings of Disibodenberg
itself. Disibod's longing for the divine is further expressed in the lines
' . . . in the windows of the saints reaching towards God'. '*Cancellos*',
which I have translated here as 'windows' appear in the illustration to
Scivias, 3, 6 as blind arcades which are pierced at various times by
God's mercy, thus letting in knowledge of the divine.

In the next stanzas the theme of exile is extended to one of
rejection of the world which Disibod has exchanged for a heavenly
reward. Because his mind is filled with grace and knowledge of the
Holy Spirit, expressed by Hildegard's favourite images of light and

running water, he becomes a channel for the salvation of others. The invocation of the fifth stanza suggests an interesting play on words. The word that I have translated as 'shaft' also means the stalk of a plant, and 'keys of heaven' is the Latin equivalent of the German name for cowslip, *Hymelsloszel* in the *Physica*. Is Hildegard carrying on the flower imagery here by a kind of pun? If so, the cowslip is a particularly appropriate choice, since she claims in the *Physica* that it obtains all its heat and *viriditas* or vigour directly from the sun.

In the next stanza the imagery becomes architectural. Disibod is a tower, censed with perfumes used in the celebration of mass – no doubt an allusion to his founding Disibodenberg, a place dedicated to the work of prayer and praise. The specifically monastic element is emphasized with the reference to the pure sound and the two aisles, suggesting the antiphonal chant of the monks.

Disibod's role as mediator between God and man is expressed in the next stanza, the refreshing dew recalling the living fountain of a few stanzas earlier. The last two stanzas emphasize the unique worth of monastic praise, and affirm that the life of the monk is an earthly imitation of the life to come, which, with its mention once more of the Heavenly City brings the poem back to where it started.

While the progression of thought in the sequence just described is relatively direct, Hildegard's long sequence for St Rupert (Newman, 49) is more complicated and elaborate. Most of the stanzas in the sequence for St Disibod were either addressed to, or descriptions of, the saint. In this sequence, however, as the opening address indicates, there is no simple concentration on the saint himself. Indeed, aspects of the saint's biography are even less evident than in the Disibod sequence. In fact, to borrow the words of Peter Dronke, 'images of the saint are set against images of the heavenly Jerusalem, the unity is that of a collage.' Since this is the case I will comment on the stanzas in turn.

1 O Jerusalem, golden city
adorned with kingly purple,
O building of highest goodness,
a light never darkened.
You are decorated
with the dawn and heat of the sun.

Dronke notes here that the association of dawn and sunlight with the Heavenly City is unusual since its illumination is said to come from God and the Lamb. Hildegard might, however, have intended a

6 The virtues. The illustration shows blind arcades pierced at various
times by God's mercy, allowing in knowledge of the divine. *Scivias*, 3, 6,
Eibingen MS.

less literal meaning and could be alluding to the Incarnation, which
she often describes in terms of dawn and the sun's heat. The mention
of dawn and sun may then arise from a verbal coincidence, although
other resonances (such as a growth in spiritual understanding) need
not be ruled out.

2 O blessed boyhood
shining in the dawn

and O praiseworthy youth
flaming in the sun.
For you, O noble Rupert,
shine like a jewel in them
whence you cannot be hidden by fools
just as the valley cannot hide the mountain.

These stanzas are the only concession to a description of Rupert's
life and subsequent cult in the poem. The fools is probably a reference
to the Vikings who sacked Bingen and destroyed the shrine of St
Rupert in the ninth century. The mountains and valleys could, as
Dronke suggests, be a play on words – Rupertsberg being identified in
a direct way with Rupert. We may recall that St Disibod was also
apostrophized as a mountain. The next stanza returns to the heavenly
Jerusalem with which Rupert is linked, by describing him as shining
in its windows. Whether at this stage Hildegard is referring to St
Rupert as he was on earth or in his present sanctified state is unclear.
If the latter, being reflected in the windows would seem to put him
outside the heavenly Jerusalem, but perhaps too much can be made
of the distinction between this life and the next. Hildegard emphasizes that St Rupert's earthly life was nothing if not an anticipation
of his ultimate state.

3 Your windows, Jerusalem
with topaz and sapphire are excellently adorned.
You shine in them, O Rupert, and cannot be hidden
from those of little faith –
like the valley and the mountain,
crowned with roses, lilies and purple
in a true showing.

This stanza may also allude to Hildegard's re-establishment of
worship at Rupertsberg by founding her monastery there, the plan for
which she attributed to 'a true showing'. We may recall that she was
hindered for a time in this by people, including the monks at
Disibodenberg, who had little faith in her plans. The mention of
flowers, referring both to Rupert and Rupertsberg leads on to an
apostrophe of him in terms ultimately derived from the Song of
Songs, and also as a perfect and unsullied urn:

4 O tender flower of the meadow
and O sweet sap of the apple
and O harvest without pith

which does not divert hearts to sin.
O noble vessel which is not defiled
or consumed in the dance
of the ancient cave, and which is not oozing
with wounds of the ancient destroyer.

The juxtaposition of two images here, one positive and one negative, with its apparent reference to pagan ritual, serves to reinforce the description of Rupert's excellence in an unexpected manner. It is extended in the next stanzas, where the dance becomes angelic and the vessel one of purity, accompanied by the spiritualized smells of good works:

5 In you the Holy Spirit makes music
because you are numbered in the angelic chorus
and shine in the Son of God
since you have no stain.

6 What a seemly vessel you are O Rupert,
who in your childhood and youth
sighed for God in the fear of God
in the embrace of love
and the most sweet odour of good works.

The concluding four stanzas of the sequence return to the vision of Jerusalem, built of the living stones of the blessed, among whom Rupert has a place. The poem ends with a plea for him to help his servants, the nuns of Rupertsberg, attain the Heavenly City.

7 O Jerusalem your foundation is laid
with scorching stones,
that is with publicans and sinners
who were the lost sheep
but found by the Son of God.
They ran to you and were placed in you.

8 Then your walls flash
with living stones
which by greatest effort of good will
have flown like clouds in heaven.

9 And so your towers, O Jerusalem,
glow and blaze in the dawn
and heat of the saints

and through all the ornaments of God
which you do not lack, O Jerusalem.

10 Whence you, O decorated
and O crowned ones
who dwell in Jerusalem
and you, O Rupert,
who are their fellow in that dwelling
help us, your servants,
labouring in exile.

Compared to the sequence just discussed, Hildegard's treatment of
the theme of St Eucharius (Newman, 53) is relatively simple,
although once more the emphasis is on the universal meaning of
sanctity, rather than the saint's own particular history. Eucharius was
supposedly a third-century missionary, who, together with his
companions Valerius and Maternus, converted the citizens of Trier
from paganism. This sequence was undoubtedly directed to the same
recipients as the hymn for St Matthias:

1   O Eucharius
you walked in the joyful path
where you dwelt with the Son of God
touching Him
and seeing the miracle He wrought.

2   You loved Him fully
when your companions were sore afraid
because they were but men
and were not able
fully to comprehend the good.

3   But you
in the burning love of full charity
embraced Him
when the bundles of His commands
you gathered to yourself.

4   O Eucharius
you were much blessed
when the word of God
tried you in the fire of the dove
when you were made to shine like the dawn
and thus fashioned the foundation of the Church.

5   And in your breast
the day shines forth
in which three shrines
stand on a marble pillar
in the city of God.

6   Through your mouth the Church savours
the old and the new wine
which is the draught of holiness.

7   And in your teaching
the Church reaches understanding
so that she has proclaimed on the mountains
that the hills and woods should bow down
and take suck from her.

8   Now in your clear voice
beseech the Son of God for this crowd
lest they fail in God's rites
but ever perform the living sacrifice
before the altar of God.

For some reason, St Eucharius does not seem to have evoked such
an imaginative response from Hildegard as did some other saints.
Was it because she thought of him as a bishop rather than a monk
and thus somehow tainted by secularism? Or was she fitting her style
to her subject – the 'clear voice' of the evangelist, rather than the
mystical intoxication of the contemplative? The sequence is notable
for the directness of its imagery, although it does become rather more
allusive in the second half. Do the three shrines on the marble pillar
denote the Trinity, or some combination of the virtues, or something
else again? The following stanzas appear to refer more particularly to
the situation at Trier, as I take the Church, in this context, to refer
especially to the converts made by Eucharius, when he filled them
with the wine of the Old and New Testaments. The next stanza, then,
might allude to the spread of his teachings to surrounding districts, in
the bowing down of the hills and woods. Finally, the last stanza asks
Eucharius to continue his work by keeping the faith alive among the
people of Trier.

While the last sequence was concerned, in a sense, with
worshipping God by means of the celebration of the mass, through
its introduction at Trier by St Eucharius, the tone of the poem is low-
key, its ideas conveyed by external description or statement. In the

sequence (Newman, 54) for St Maximin (the disciple said to have sailed with the three Marys and Lazarus to Provence) and patron saint of yet another monastery at Trier, we have a different and more compelling statement of a similar theme. Here, according to Christopher Page, the entire sequence is presented as a vision of St Maximin as mystical celebrant of the mass. In the words of Peter Dronke, Hildegard gives 'lyrical expression to the relation between mankind, the saint and God'.[12]

1 The dove looked in
through the window grates
where before its face
balm was crystallizing
from shining Maximin.

2 The heat of the sun blazed
and shone in the darkness
whence a gem budded
in the building of the temple
of the purest loving heart.

3 He, the highest tower
of the tree of Lebanon
and cypress made
has been adorned with jacinth and sardonyx,
a city outshining the artifice
of all other builders.

4 He, the swift hart, ran
to the fount of purest water
flowing from the mightiest stone
which runs over with sweet perfumes.

5 O perfumers
who are in the sweetest greenness
of the king's gardens
mounting on high
when the holy sacrifices
have been fulfilled with the rams.

6 Among you shines this architect,
the wall of the temple
who desired the wings of the eagle
kissing his nurse Wisdom
in the glorious fecundity of the Church.

7 O Maximin,
you are the mountain and the valley,
and a high building in both
where the goat walked with the elephant
and Wisdom knew delight.

8 You are strong
and gentle
in the rites and glittering of the altar,
mounting up like the smoke of incense
to the column of praise.

9 Where you intercede for the people
who reach towards the mirror of light
for which there is praise on high.

While much of the imagery of this sequence is taken from the Song of Songs and other parts of the Old Testament, notably the description of Simon as High Priest in Ecclesiastes, Hildegard here puts it to new uses. Of course aspects of the Old Testament were routinely seen as prefigurings of the New. Hildegard, in applying such imagery to St Maximin, seems to take the process one step further. By this means she is able to maintain a constant interplay between the personal and universal aspects of salvation. This can be seen in the first stanzas where the temple is both a church and the inner temple of Maximin's pure heart. The reference to budding gems and heat is reminiscent of Hildegard's poems about the Incarnation and may suggest that Maximin has somehow conceived Christ in a mystical relationship, or may merely represent a divine parallel to his own formation.

The imagery becomes less ambiguous from stanza 4, where the hart runs to the stone, which Page suggests represents the altar. Hildegard may well have been familiar with such imagery from the liturgy used in the dedication of a church. The perfumers here, as in the *Scivias*, would then be priests or bishops, and the rams (a less fortunate metaphor, but one also drawn from the *Scivias*), the child oblates. Maximin is outstanding among these people because of his ability to communicate with Wisdom in contemplation and yet return to walk among men, as the references to eagles, goats, elephants, mountains, and valleys proclaim. We might note that Hildegard, too, was praised in the *Vita*, Bk 2, for being concerned with the affairs of mortals despite her contemplative gifts. The reciprocal relationship between earth and heaven exemplified in Maximin's life is suggested throughout the poem by ascending and descending movements, including that of perfumes from earth to heaven and of light from above. For a final comment on this poem, the imagery of which is both allusive and elusive, I return to Dronke, who concludes that it 'produces a poetic effect profounder than any explication can hope to suggest'.

No account of Hildegard's poetry would be complete without a consideration of her sequence about St Ursula, '*O Ecclesia*', which has been extensively discussed by Dronke, Martin, and Newman.[13] In other sequences, biographical details (even of the saints whose lives Hildegard had written or was to write), were of less moment than the symbolic importance of the saint as missionary, founder of a see, founder of a monastery, or celebrant of the divine office. However, with the sequence for St Ursula, the saint as martyr, her story or supposed history assumes greater importance. According to the tradition current at the time Hildegard was writing, St Ursula was a British princess who had repudiated her marriage, and with a company of 11,000 like-minded maidens (the large number apparently arose from a copyist's error) made a journey to Rome. On the way back the entire company was martyred by the Huns at Cologne. The discovery there of an old Christian cemetery early in the twelfth century which was thought to be the burial place of the martyrs led to a great traffic in their supposed relics, a few of which were acquired by Disibodenberg. Later, Elisabeth of Schönau provided visionary authentication for some of the relics, but that may have been after Hildegard wrote – at least Hildegard does not seem to owe anything to this source. Here is the sequence in its entirety:

1 O Ecclesia
your eyes are like sapphire
and your ears like the Mount of Bethel
and your nose is
like a mountain of myrrh and incense
and your mouth like the sound
of many waters.

2 In a true vision of faith
Ursula loved the Son of God
and turned away from her husband and this world
and gazed on the sun
and called to the most beauteous youth
saying:

3   With great longing
have I desired to come to you
and abide with you in celestial marriage,
running to you by a strange path
like the clouds which fly in pure air
like sapphire.

4   And after Ursula had spoken thus
news of it spread among the people
And they said:
In the innocence of girlish ignorance
she does not know what she is saying.

5   And they began to mock at her
with great music
until the fiery burden
fell upon her.

6   Then they all understood
because rejection of the world is like the Mount of Bethel
and knew the odour of myrrh and incense
because rejection of the world
rises above all things.

7   Then the Devil
entered his minions
who the most noble lives
in those bodies
killed.

8   And this, with a loud cry,
all the Elements heard
and before the throne of God
they said:

9   Woe! the red blood of the innocent Lamb
in its coupling
has streamed out.

10 Let all the Heavens hear this.
And in highest music
praise the Lamb of God!
Because the throat of the ancient serpent
in these pearls
of the material of God's word
has been choked.

This sequence, like that for St Rupert, does not begin with an apostrophe to the saint herself, but to the entity in which she is subsumed, *Ecclesia*, the church as a whole. In the first stanza various biblical allusions are introduced: sapphires, the Mountain of Bethel, myrrh and incense, and the sound of many waters; these recur later in the sequence, thus incorporating Ursula into the divine scheme in a most striking manner.

The next five stanzas swiftly sketch the salient points of her story: her rejection of marriage and the world and her longing to be united with Christ, immediately followed by the reaction of her worldly contemporaries to such unwonted behaviour. We might note here that the details of the story have been reduced to the bone, the only residual reference to the journey being that of the music, possibly recalling the games the maidens played on board ship.

In the next stanza a check in the narrative occurs when a reference is made back to the opening of the poem. We are told that those who were trying to amuse or tease Ursula finally recognized her contempt of the world for what it was 'when the fiery burden fell upon her'. After this comment on the central meaning of the poem the narrative is resumed when the Huns, as limbs of the Devil, massacre Ursula and the 11,000. The action is made to sound curiously impersonal as the Huns strike at 'the most noble lives/in those bodies'.

At this point the virgins are assumed into the celestial embrace and the Elements, in a deliberately ambiguous comment, declare the marriage consummated in the red blood of the Lamb. The Lamb, of course, usually refers to Christ, and the blood, that which issued from his side on the cross, but the virgins could also be seen as lambs and the blood of their martyrdom assimilated to the blood shed at the consummation of their heavenly marriage.

The closing image, where the martyred virgins become pearls (through the action of Christ) in a necklace which throttles the Devil, is justly famous. It shows how Hildegard can, at her best, completely transform and transcend the materials at her disposal. Finally, it should be noted that the dramatic possibilities of the story are exploited to some extent by the use of dialogue at important points in the narrative.

The mention of dialogue brings us to what is perhaps the most remarkable portion of the *Symphonia*, Hildegard's musical drama, the *Ordo virtutum* (*Play of the Virtues*), which has rightly been called the 'earliest surviving morality play'.[14] Where Hildegard got the idea for her work is impossible to say. (Dronke suggests she knew Prudentius'

Psychomachia, a rather predictable contest between the vices and virtues; Hozeski, less persuasively, suggests the plays of Hrotswitha of Gandersheim.) I have already pointed to the use of dialogue in some of the other poems, admittedly on a much smaller scale, and it should not be forgotten that the *Scivias* contains a good deal of direct speech, including, of course, God's commentary on the visions.

The characters in the play are all personifications except for the patriarchs and prophets of the prologue and the Devil. They include sixteen virtues led by their queen, Humility, and Anima, a soul, referred to as happy or unfortunate as the play proceeds. There is no evidence to suggest that the play was ever performed, but it is quite possible that Hildegard did have it staged, and if it was costumed according to the illustrations of the virtues in the *Scivias*, it would indeed have looked spectacular. The letter of Tengswich of Andernach about the dress of her nuns suggests that Hildegard was not afraid to put the ideas she received in her visions into practice.[15]

The play opens with a brief exchange between the prophets and patriarchs and the virtues. This serves to identify the latter as the fruit of the tree that the wise men of old themselves constitute. The imagery suggests a dynamic process: the virtues are still building up the limbs of the Word of God, which was foreshadowed in the Old Testament.

> *Patriarchs and Prophets*: Who are they, who are like clouds?
> *Virtues*: O saints of old, why do you marvel at us? The Word of God shines forth in the form of man, and we shine with him, building up the members of his beautiful body.
> *Patriarchs and Prophets*: We are the roots and you the branches, the apple of the living eye, and we were in its shadow.

The chorus of prophets then gives place to a chorus of souls, still bound to their bodies in the world. They lament their exile from the heavenly kingdom and in a memorable image plead: 'O living sun, carry us on your shoulders to our most rightful inheritance which we lost through Adam.' The request is echoed by one soul in particular, called here in the rubrics 'Happy Soul' (*Felix Anima*), but shortly to be called 'Unhappy Soul' (*Infelix Anima*), who wishes to come directly to the kingdom and receive the kiss of the heart. When told by the virtues that this cannot be done without struggling against the world, the flesh, and the Devil, she capitulates almost at once and goes off to enjoy their enticements. Her attitude is commended by the Devil, who says, or shouts (there is no music for his words in the manuscript, which is hardly surprising, since Hildegard considered the ability to make music a divine attribute): 'What good is struggling, foolishly, foolishly. Look to the world, it will embrace you with great honour.' The soul goes off to enjoy the world, perhaps running through the audience and out of the door of the church, while the virtues lament the fact that her celestial longing concealed a worldly longing for pleasure.

The virtues and the Devil indulge in a series of exchanges, the virtues identifying themselves in a similar manner to that found in the *Liber vitae meritorum.* To their rather complacent speeches the Devil gives various retorts, indicating that he is not impressed.

After all this, the soul returns from her encounter with the world, beaten into submission, but too weak to approach the virtues unaided. She appeals to Humility to lift her up. This is about to be done when the Devil rises and grabs her. There is a struggle and Humility sends the virtues to assist her. They bind the Devil in chains and Chastity places her heel upon his neck with a speech identifying this moment with that of the Virgin's triumph at the Incarnation:

In the mind of the highest, O Satan, I placed my heel on your head,
and I nurtured a sweet miracle in virgin form,
when the Son of God came into the world.
So you are laid low with all your spoils,
and now let all the inhabitants of heaven rejoice,
because your belly has been confounded.

The Devil's reply to her is perhaps most noteworthy of all. He claims that Chastity does not know what she is talking about because she has not known sexual love or motherhood. The 'sweet miracle' does not come from human copulation, which God had prescribed for mankind. He suggests indeed, that there is something unnatural about the Virgin Birth and therefore it has no particular relevance for humankind.

Chastity's answer is that the Virgin Birth was not unnatural but supernatural, greater than nature, and thus drew all humanity to itself. This is apparently meant to be the last word on the subject and the play ends with a kind of epilogue, sung, according to Dronke, by the virtues and the chorus of souls which appeared at the beginning. The theme is one of reintegration, in which some of Hildegard's most characteristic images reappear: light, flowing waters, burning love, greenness. Their speech includes an address by Christ to God, which indicates that the body of the church is still being formed:

> *Virtues and Souls*: In the beginning all creatures were green,
> flowers bloomed in their midst,
> afterwards greenness diminished.
> And the victorious one saw it and said:
> 'This I know, but the golden number is not yet full.
> You then, look in the mirror of your father:
> in my body I bear hurts,
> even my little ones fail me.
> Now remember that the fullness first made
> should not dry up, and you have in yourself
> what your eye shall never surrender
> until you see my body full of gems,
> for it pains me that all my members have become scoffers.
> See Father, I display my wounds to you.'
> So now, all people
> bend your knees to your Father
> that He might stretch out His hand to you.

I will conclude the section on Hildegard's play with a very brief comment on its music. On the whole it seems to be written in a simpler and more syllabic style than some of the liturgical songs. No doubt this would have been an advantage if, indeed, it was intended for performance before an audience. There is, however, a notable use of melisma on the last word of the play '*porrigat*' ('he may stretch out'). The action of this word, which encapsulates the theme of reintegration of God and his creatures, is admirably suggested by the music.

7

MAN AND THE COSMOS

Man, too, is God's handiwork, like every other creature. But man is also God's journeyman and the foreshadowing of the mysteries of God. (*Vita*, Bk 2)

In the years between 1163 and 1174 Hildegard was engaged on the creation of her third and greatest visionary composition, the *Liber divinorum operum* (*Book of the Divine Works*). That she considered it her most important work is suggested by the way she describes its genesis in the *Vita*:

> At a later time I saw a mysterious and wonderful vision so that my inmost core was convulsed and I lost all bodily sensation, as my knowledge was altered to another mode, unknown to myself. And by the inspiration of God, drops, as it were, of sweet rain were sprinkled on my soul's understanding as the Holy Spirit filled John the Evangelist when he sucked the most profound revelations from the breast of Jesus. . . . Thus the vision taught me and allowed me to explain all the words and teachings of the Evangelist which concern the beginning of God's works. And I saw that this explanation should form the beginning of another work which had not yet been revealed to me, in which many investigations of the divine mysteries of created things would be sought.

How this particular vision differed from Hildegard's other experiences will be discussed in more detail later. For the moment we shall concentrate on its exceptional force, and note how its working out was to proceed in stages.[1] It should also be remembered that work on the vision was interrupted by illness, preaching tours, the composition of smaller pieces such as the *Vita Sancti Disibodi* (*Life of St Disibod*), and finally the death of Volmar, the monk from Disibodenberg who had been Hildegard's faithful helper since she first began to write the *Scivias*.

Despite this, the *Liber divinorum operum* can be seen as a triumph of synthesis in which Hildegard brings together her theological beliefs, her physiological understanding, her speculations on the working of the human mind and of the structure of the universe, into a unified whole.[2] The simplifying idea by which she binds the diverse elements together is that of the relationship of man and universe as microcosm and macrocosm. Her method is to make a *rapprochement* between the opening of St John's Gospel, and the account of the creation of the universe in the first chapter of Genesis.

Many of the themes have been touched on (or even explored in detail) in her earlier works. We may recall the description of the earth with its concentric shells in the *Scivias*, and the investigation of the moral economy and the doctrine of penance in the *Liber vitae meritorum*, as well as the central place of the Incarnation in both. Much is predicated upon the physiological theories explored in her medical and scientific works. In the *Liber divinorum operum* such themes are taken up and refined (as in the case of the structure of the universe), in the light of Hildegard's further understanding, or sometimes simplified (as with the humoral theories), but always made subject to her overall theme and grand conception.

If this leads on occasion to what we might see as rather strained analogies and relationships, we may still admire Hildegard's attempt to demonstrate sense and regularity in the life of humankind and the cosmos in accordance with her theological beliefs. A final element which deserves mention here is the burning visionary imagination, seen already in her poetry, which can give forceful expression to such abstract concepts as that of love animating and vivifying all creation. (Indeed, we might wish in some cases that Hildegard had confined herself to describing the visions, when her explications become a little tedious or tendentious.)

The *Liber divinorum operum* consists of ten visions, divided into three books of somewhat differing lengths. The lengths of the individual visions are also quite unequal, the fourth consisting of over 100 chapters, and the sixth less than ten. The first five visions (which comprise Books 1 and 2) are chiefly concerned with tracing the relationship between man and the natural order; the last five introduce the notion of time into the essentially timeless description of the created universe and thus deal with the history of the world as the history of salvation, culminating in the Last Days and Final

Judgement. The virtual absence of descriptions of the joys of heaven may once more be attributed to Hildegard's concern not to repeat herself, as this topic had been extensively covered in the *Scivias*.

Although Hildegard seems to say in the autobiographical fragment quoted above, that the *Liber divinorum operum* is to start from an explication of the beginning of St John's Gospel, it is first necessary to go through a good deal of preliminary matter. Book 1 opens with a vision of a shining four-winged figure, surmounted by a venerable bearded head, holding the Lamb of God and trampling beneath its feet a monster and a hideous writhing serpent. The only illustrated manuscript of the work, which came originally from Rupertsberg and is now at Lucca, captures these details wonderfully.

Charles Singer, much influenced by the idea that Hildegard was borrowing from Bernard Sylvestris' *De Universo* (*About the Universe*), sees in this figure 'Nous pervaded by the Godhead'. But, although the figure describes itself in the text in various ways, this particularly neoplatonic formulation is not used.[3] What it does say recalls strongly the description of the Holy Spirit in Hildegard's poetry:

I am the supreme and fiery force who has kindled all sparks of life and breathed forth none of death and I judge them as they are. Tracing the revolving orbits with my upper wings, that is, with Wisdom, I have established true order there. I, the fiery life of the divine substance, blaze above the beauty of the fields, shine in the waters, and burn in the sun, moon and stars. And with the all-sustaining invisible force of the aerial wind, I bring all things to life. . . . I am also Reason, having the wind of the sounding word by which all things were created, and I breathe in them all, so that none may die, because I am Life. (*Liber divinorum operum* (*LDO*), Bk 1, vis. 1, ch. 2)

Chapter 3 of the vision introduces the definitive explanation with the now familiar words: 'And again I heard a voice from heaven speaking to me.' Here it is explained that the figure represents Love (*Caritas*) and this is confirmed later in Bk 1, vis. 2, ch. 46.

this is because in the strength of never failing divinity, Love is beautiful in election and marvellous in the gifts of the secrets of the most high Father and is in human form since when the Son of God assumed flesh he redeemed lost man through Love [*in caritatis officio*]. (*LDO*, Bk 1, vis. 1, ch. 3)

137

7 Caritas. A shining, four-winged figure is shown surmounted by a
venerable bearded head, holding the Lamb of God, and trampling beneath
its feet a monster and hideous serpent. Below, Hildegard records the vision
helped by Volmar and a nun. *Liber divinorum operum*, Lucca MS fo. lv.

8 The relation of man and universe, microcosm and macrocosm. Below,
Hildegard records the vision. *Liber divinorum operum*, Lucca MS fo. 9r.

The rest of the vision (which has seventeen chapters) describes the working of God, through Love, for the salvation of mankind, briefly encompassing the creation, Fall, and the obedience of the Virgin Mary to God, which counterbalances the disobedience of Eve and which was prefigured in the obedience of Abraham to God when he was told to sacrifice his son.[4]

The second vision introduces the theory of microcosm and macrocosm by means of a disk or wheel representing the universe located in the breast, or heart, of the image described in the first vision. In the centre of the universal wheel is a human figure, conveying the idea that mankind is the centre of creation with a pre-eminent relationship to other created things. It might be noted that the Lucca manuscript illustration, no doubt for reasons of symmetry and in order to fit everything in, represents the universal sphere as almost completely superimposed on the original figure of Love. In the illustration, the head of the figure appears at the top, the hem of its robe and bare feet at the bottom, and the hands and arms can be discerned embracing the upper circumference of the disk. The wings seem to have disappeared, although the Godhead is still present.

We cannot here discuss in any detail Hildegard's beliefs about the physical structure of the universe.[5] Suffice it to say that she has substantially modified her account since the *Scivias*. The independent movement of the planets is now explained by the expedient of introducing a supplementary wind. Indeed, the importance in the *Liber divinorum operum* of winds of all sorts – treated to some extent in *Causae et curae* – is striking. In the *Liber divinorum operum*, the universe is represented as disk-shaped, rather than ovoid as in the *Scivias*. A possible reason for the change in shape was a desire for symmetry, since exact measurement and symbolic equivalences play a much greater part in this account than in the earlier one; obviously, a sphere fits this schema more perfectly than an egg.

The second vision describes the six hollow spheres which surround the earth. It includes a great deal about the winds, represented as animal heads, together with the heavenly bodies and their inter-relations, usually described as rays joining one element in the scheme to another. These influences appear as a network of lines in the Lucca illustrations. An extract may make Hildegard's method clearer. Here is her description of the significance of the positioning of various planets and the interactions of the winds:

And as you see something like a ray ascending from the middle of the sign of the fifth planet, which is next under the sun, to the sign of the sun, so from the force of the spirit of understanding, which ought to be a near neighbour to the true operation of the spirit of fortitude, an exhalation goes out to fortitude, since knowledge is made strong by fortitude. . . . Another extends to the head of the crab and comes from the sign of the wolf's head since an exhalation . . . goes out to faith which arises from bodily tribulation . . . when man chastises his body and believes his sins are punished and purged. (*LDO*, Bk 1, vis. 2, ch. 36)

The next vision, after an introduction dealing in more detail with the winds and the planets, enlarges on their influence (especially that of the winds) on the health and well-being of man. Here the visionary mould into which Hildegard's thought is forced seems least appropriate, as the interaction of the humours is hard to represent pictorially. She implicitly acknowledges this herself by substituting a description of actual processes seen, for more abstract theorizing, as in the following passage:

Then I saw that by means of the different qualities of the winds and their concurrent airs, the humours which are in man are stirred up and changed, assuming their qualities. (*LDO*, Bk 1, vis. 3, ch. 1)

In this way the qualities of the various winds, represented in the vision by such animals as the lion, crab, wolf, and deer are transferred to the humours.

From time to time the humours in man rise up fiercely like a leopard but then they become softer and now like a crab going forward and then backwards, often show changes in themselves, and like the deer leaping and sparring, they often show their diversity. (ibid.)

There follows some more specific humoral description, including the incidence of specific diseases (epilepsy for one), before the voice from heaven is introduced to explain all.

What the voice first asserts is that the things God made to be of assistance to man are not just for his bodily health, but also for his spiritual needs, if only in an exemplary way. For instance, the combination of the east and south winds with their collateral winds (NE, SE, SW, etc.), which make the firmament revolve from east to west, stand for (*'designat'*) the breath of the fear of God, which, together with the breath of the judgement of God and other virtues, touching the interior spirit of man, make him persevere in his good intentions. This process is assimilated to the dawn which triumphs over the setting of the sun, a symbol of the flesh (*LDO*, Bk 1, vis. 3, ch. 2).

So, too, the arrangement of the organs in the body has a spiritual significance. The liver, Hildegard claims, is located in the right side of the body and is the chief source of its heat, which indicates 'that in the right side, that is in the prosperity of salvation of the good and righteous man, justice together with the Holy Spirit is at work' (*LDO*, Bk 1, vis. 3, ch. 10). Even physical illnesses have a spiritual counterpart, although it is not always clear whether a simple analogy is intended rather than a causal connection. Sometimes metaphor is the vehicle of expression, as in the following:

> For whoever does not afflict the flesh with fitting abstinence, but feeds it with vices and lusts, puts on the fat of sins and thus makes himself a filthy stench before God. (*LDO*, Bk 1, vis. 3, ch. 18)

The fourth vision, which concludes the first book, is an extended treatment of the influence of the heavenly bodies on the world of nature and man. Here, too, there is a moral dimension. Thus in chapter 59, Hildegard draws out the analogies between the waters of the earth (seas and rivers), the veins in the body, and human perseverance in virtuous actions:

> This air, with the watery air, moves the sea from which separate rivers flow, which water and bind together the earth as also the interconnected veins are manifestly strengthening the whole man with blood. And the soul which is airy and through which all the works of man are perfected, just as the fruits of the earth are by the air, proposes to man his works through the grace of the Holy Spirit, so that through thoughts, which flood like the sea, it discerns utility and uselessness.

The analogy now changes slightly:

> Thus when the mind of man, expanded by various virtues, is roused to praise God, he builds on rock with a stable foundation, which the wind, that is the various temptations of the Devil, cannot move, since just as the veins with the nerves of the body hold it together so it does not fall apart, thus the virtue of humility holds together and strengthens good works lest they be dissipated through pride.

So the fourth vision moves (with some digressions) in its description of the human constitution from head to foot (finally reached by ch. 94). In the course of this, Hildegard relates the seasons and months of the year to aspects of the body, the ages of man, and the seven gifts of the Holy Spirit. All is summed up in the climactic hundredth chapter, which reads in part:

For man is the work of God perfected, because God is known through him, and since God created all creatures for him, and allowed him in the embrace of true love to preach and praise him through the quality of his mind. But man needed a helper in his likeness. So God gave him a helper which was his mirror image, woman, in whom the whole human race lay hidden. It was to be brought forth in the power of God's strength, just as the first man was produced by him. And the man and the woman were thus complementary, so that one works through the other, because man is not called 'man' without woman, nor is woman without man, called 'woman'. For woman is the work of man, and man the form of woman's consolation. Neither can exist without the other. And man signifies the divinity of the Son of God; woman his humanity.

Next follows an anticipatory glimpse of the Last Judgement, where humankind will become the tenth order of heaven, to replace the fallen angels, before Hildegard's final words on the relationship of body and soul which conclude:

Therefore, as said above, such is the form of man, body and soul, the work of God brought forth together with all creation, as John, inspired with my spirit wrote, saying: In the beginning was the word. (*LDO*, Bk 1, vis. 4, ch. 104–5)

An explication of the Gospel of St John (John 1:1–14), follows. Hildegard's method is to proceed phrase by phrase and her explication is almost entirely confined to the literal level of the text, drawing on many of the correspondences and analogies described earlier in the work.

The fifth vision, which constitutes the entire second book of the *Liber divinorum operum*, is concerned principally with the structure and arrangement of the terrestrial sphere. Some details are obscure, even when the illustration in the Lucca manuscript is consulted. Here, it may be noted, the usual orientation with east at the top is abandoned in favour of one where south is uppermost and east on the left. The globe or disk Hildegard now sees is divided into five parts, roughly north, south, east, west, and a central section. The eastern section is bright, the west dark, and the northern and southern segments contain a mixture of torments and monstrous apparitions. The middle section includes hot, cold, and temperate zones. On the eastern side Hildegard sees a red and blue circle from which two sets of wings and a building project. In the northwest corner the mouth of hell seems about to devour the globe.

The explanation for this arrangement once more combines naturalistic and moralistic elements. The five different regions of the earth, for instance, with their varying climates, stand for the five senses. The senses in turn reflect the nature of the divisions. Thus for the east and west: 'the sense of smell, through the odour of virtues tends to the right; taste, through the savour of vices, to the left' (*LDO*, Bk 2, vis. 1, ch. 3). So also in the east we find the 'refreshment of blessed souls', the earthly paradise where the saved wait to enter heaven. Here too, Hildegard provides some sort of answer to the problem of where sinners, ultimately numbered among the saved, were to serve out their time of purgation. It represents a clarification of her thinking on the matter since the *Liber vitae meritorum*. Although she describes the places as located 'at the four corners of the earth', the chief sites of punishment seem to be in the north and south. They are obviously distinct from the hell of the damned which is here represented as a great mouth. That the places are actually on or near the surface of the earth, is suggested by her claim, in chapter 7, that God has fenced off these places of punishment with very high mountains so that their noxious vapours cannot spread to the habitable parts of the world.

Having set the scene, Hildegard returns to the theme of the history of salvation. This time it is described principally as a contest between God and the Devil, culminating in the latter's (provisional) routing by the Virgin Mary as described in Rev. 12:13 and explicated with many a backward look to the Old Testament. Thus:

When the time shining with the dawn came, that is of manifest justice, through my Son, the ancient serpent was astounded and greatly terrified, since through a woman, that is to say the Virgin, he was completely deceived. So in his fury he blazed up against her, as is written under my direction 'And the serpent cast out of his mouth water as a flood after the woman, that he might cause her to be carried away by the flood. And the earth helped the woman'. Which is to be understood thus: the ancient persecutor sent from his most wicked voraciousness [against] the righteousness of the woman who had produced the man, unbelief and lack of faith among the Jews and pagans, hoping by this that she, worn out by many persecutions, would subject herself to him, or be completely overwhelmed, like a ship in a shipwreck, so that her name should vanish from the face of the earth, like something thrown into a deep river. But the woman was helped by the earth since my Son assumed the garment of humanity from her, and bore in his body much opprobrium and suffering, to the serpent's confusion. (*LDO*, Bk 2, vis. 1, ch. 16)

The remaining chapters of this section of the work are devoted to a commentary on the first book of Genesis, where God's creation of the world in six days is described, before the seventh day of rest. This arrangement parallels that of the first section of the *Liber divinorum operum*, which is brought to a close by an exegesis of the opening chapter of the Gospel of St John. However, Hildegard's commentary on Genesis is much fuller, with each verse interpreted literally, allegorically (as referring to the progress of the faith and the growth of the church), and tropologically or morally, pertaining to the actions of the individual Christian. Her method can be illustrated by following her commentary on the words, 'And the earth was without form and void; and darkness was on the face of the deep.' On the literal level she writes:

The earth was formless, that is to say, lacking form, and invisible, having no light because it was not yet illuminated by the splendour of light, nor the brightness of the sun, moon or stars, and uncultivated because it had been tilled by no one, and void, that is without order because it was not yet full, as it did not yet have the greenness, promise or burgeoning of plants or trees. (*LDO*, Bk 2, vis. 1, ch. 17)

The same passage is explained allegorically as follows:

All the people, that is the Jews and Gentiles, who lived on the face of the deep, that is the earth . . . were blind and deaf to recognition of God, and empty of good works, since they did not live according to the teaching of the Son of the Highest, until he ascended to his Father. And thus on the earth, which is the face of the deep, was the darkness of unbelief, in which men lived, not recognizing God, as if they were blind. (*LDO*, Bk 2, vis. 1, ch. 20)

Finally Hildegard gives her tropological explanation:

> The person who can never be steadfast in his behaviour is quite formless and ever flooding like the sea ... surrounded by dark deeds which pertain to depraved actions ... and the body is like the face of the abyss, the soul like the abyss, because the body is visible and palpable like the face of the deep, the soul invisible and impalpable. (*LDO*, Bk 2, vis. 1, ch. 23)

The third section of the *Liber divinorum operum* consists of the remaining five visions and can be seen as the temporal fulfilment of the six days of creation and the seventh day of rest, in terms of world and salvation history. A secondary theme is the revelation of the mysteries of God and the nature of his church, first through his prophets and later the apostles and other teachers.

The sixth vision is static rather than dynamic and serves as an introduction for what is to follow. Here a shining white mountain, shaped like a volcano, represents the justice of God, while a well-defended city stands for the divine foreknowledge of the entire course of salvation. The figures of the dove and mirror are used to explain the revelation of God's secrets. Crowds of angels, some blazing, some shining, and others like stars, are in attendance.

The course of salvation begins to be traced out in the seventh vision, with references to knowledge of God's purposes before the Law, under the Law, and up to the Incarnation. Hildegard shows how the prophecies of the Incarnation were not recognized as such until they were fulfilled when God became man:

> And the incarnate Son of God completed in himself all the miracles of old which had gone before him. ... In his infancy when Herod, seeking to kill him, was misled by the wise men, he shows the fall of the old Serpent which tried to overthrow Heaven. In his childhood he represented the time which was between Adam and Noah, when unlike Adam, he possessed great knowledge. (*LDO*, Bk 3, vis. 2, ch. 14)

And so on for the rest of his life on earth. His youth is thus presaged by the time from Noah to Abraham, since the baptism of Christ in water replaces the circumcision enjoined on Abraham. His passion and death replicates the Babylonian captivity and his resurrection the return from it. His command for the disciples to preach and baptize and the bestowal of the Holy Spirit indicate the end of the old law of the flesh and the inauguration of the spiritual life. Hildegard concludes the section with another reference to prophecy, when she compares the words of the prophets of old to the noises made by an infant, not capable of being understood until the time is ripe and the baby has grown: 'and thus before the Incarnation of the Son of God, prophecy was unrecognized and not understood, in Christ however it was revealed, because he himself is the root and branch of all goodness.'

The eighth vision is very short and represents something of a departure from the otherwise linear progression of the third section of the *Liber divinorum operum*. Three female images, reminiscent of the virtues in the *Scivias*, are described, standing in or near a fountain. They are identified as Love, Humility and Peace, although Love appears here in a somewhat different manifestation from that of the opening vision of the *Liber divinorum operum*. This vision is, as it were, an aside, placed here to assure the reader that every action God performs, including the eventual destruction of the world, is perfected through love, humility and peace. Here too, Love confirms Hildegard's place in the line of prophets, wise men, and evangelists, a claim which Hildegard had so far only made by implication, as in the opening of the *Scivias*.[6]

My clarity overshadowed the prophets, who predicted what was to come through holy inspiration since in God all things which he wished to do were foreshadowed, before they came into being. But reason gives utterance and the sound is like thought and the word like a deed. And from this shadow the book *Scivias* came forth by means of a woman who was herself a shadow of health and strength, lacking such forces. (*LDO*, Bk 3, vis. 3, ch. 2)

The ninth vision is of a type familiar from both the *Scivias* and the *Liber vitae meritorum*:

And then near the north-eastern corner I saw a figure whose face and feet shone with such great brightness that it beat upon my eyes. She had on a garment as if made from white silk and over it a green coloured tunic which appeared decorated all over with pearls and she wore in her ears earrings, on her breast necklaces, on her arms, bracelets, all, it seemed, from purest gold and ornamented with precious stones. And I saw another figure standing erect as it were in the middle of the northern side, having a marvellous form, from the top of which, where the head should have been, shone such brilliance that it beat on my eyes. In the middle of its torso a head appeared, with white hair and beard, and its feet were like the feet of a lion. And it had six wings. (*LDO*, Bk. 3, vis. 4, ch. 1)

The images here stand for the wisdom of true blessedness and the Omnipotent God. The six wings, which are adorned with mirrors bearing inscriptions, stand for the six days of creation and also the six ages of the world, the time man has to turn to God. The heads and feet of the images are represented as too bright to see because mortals cannot comprehend the beginning or end of such august forms. The elaborate ornaments of Wisdom – necklaces, earrings, bracelets – are bestowed on her by the righteous actions of men:

> Man, fulfilling the commands of God's precepts, is the soft white garment of Wisdom and the green clothing through good intentions and the greenness of works adorned with many virtues, and [he is] the ornaments for her ears, when he turns from the hearing of malicious whispers, and her torque when he ignores illicit desires, and . . . her bracelets when he fights against sin. (*LDO*, Bk 3, vis. 4, ch. 2)

Once more the Incarnation plays a central role in the vision and history is divided into the periods which lead up to it, by reference to the mirrors on the wings of the figure of God. Incidents from the Old Testament, such as the precipitation of dew on the fleece of Gideon, which prefigured this central event in salvation history, are once more described, as is the possibility of seeing God while in the flesh. This last point is explained by means of analogies, without much reference to the vision, as follows:

> God too cannot be seen, but can be known through his creation, just as the body of man cannot be seen on account of his clothes. And just as the inner brightness of the sun cannot be seen, so God cannot be seen by mortal man, but he may be understood through faith as the external shape of the sun can be seen by the watching eye. (*LDO*, Bk 3, vis. 4, ch. 14)

After these several adumbrations of the theme, the tenth vision finally presents a picture of world history and an account of the end of time. Both time and eternity are envisaged as complementary and constituting a single whole, in the form of a wheel with a line projected across its centre. Love, now dressed in different symbolic garments, which are still related to the actions of mankind, presides over the wheel. Different colours on the wheel represent different stages of the history (and prehistory) of the church, starting with Adam and all tending towards the dawn of the Incarnation.

> And thus, having assumed flesh from the Virgin, he was born, and made clear all past and future through himself and turned all the accounts of the works of man to better ends, by destroying the futile and conserving the useful. . . . And in the Son of God justice and peace were united. (*LDO*, Bk 3, vis. 5, ch. 6)

From this, the process begun with the apostles and martyrs in working out God's purposes, is carried forth into the present, in the different orders and degrees of the church. There has, however, been a notable falling off in the faith, as well as a deterioration of the world at large. Hildegard here introduces once more her description of the present as a time of 'womanly weakness':

> And afterwards, through the teaching of the apostles and through the virtues of other saints, the times up to now were made pure and shining, but these times have declined from their strength, as if in womanly weakness. (*LDO*, Bk 3, vis. 5, ch. 7)

There follows a long digression praising the twelve apostles, who are described as representatives of different psychological types, and who are said to clothe and adorn Justice in a similar way to that in which mankind clothed Love. Here is Hildegard's description of Matthias, the twelfth apostle who was chosen to replace Judas:

> Matthias, being mild and humble, dovelike in behaviour, fleeing the inconstancy of men, their envy and hate, was a vessel of the Holy Spirit, who inhabits those who do not let their minds run freely and pry into everything. And he, in his humility, performed as if unaware many signs and wonders before the faithful and unbelievers and longed for martyrdom as for a feast. Whence he prepared a royal throne for Justice to sit rightly upon, with the heads of eagles and the feet of lions in four columns. (*LDO*, Bk 3, vis. 5, ch. 9)

The theme of Justice is extended by a dramatic monologue lamenting the activities of those who harm the church, some of whom are its very ministers. Here Hildegard no doubt had various contemporaries in mind.[7]

> Wherefore they soil my garment with the dirt of sins nor do they cleanse the dirt through penitence but pullulate like worms in the

149

filth of sins. For they are blind, deaf and dumb, not declaiming my office, or pronouncing my judgements, but they gulp down avarice and do not heal wounds because they themselves are full of wounds. And they are deaf to Scripture addressed to them and do not hear it, nor do they teach others. (*LDO*, Bk 3, vis. 5, ch. 11)

There follows a long description of the tribulations of the church as the end of the world draws near. Here reference is made to her previous description of the last days in the *Scivias*, where different historical periods were referred to under the guise of animals – a fiery dog, a reddish lion, a white horse, a black pig, and a grey wolf. It is noteworthy that these figures do not appear in the present vision, being merely used for purposes of explanation.

The fiery dog which was not burning in the book *Scivias* represents the days which are listless with injustice, while the others represent the stronger times which followed. (*LDO*, Bk 3, vis. 5, ch. 15)

As in the earlier work, it is difficult to decide what, if any, specific historical periods Hildegard intended by such figures. Her vagueness has allowed subsequent commentators to interpret her prophecies (mostly read in the form of Gebeno's *Pentachronon*) in varying, not to say contradictory ways, including anticipations of the Protestant Reformation and the suppression of the Jesuits.[8]

A disconcerting alternation of persecutions and regenerations of the faith follow fast upon each other. These lead up to the birth of Antichrist and his battle with Enoch and Elijah which heralds a final return to Christ before the Last Day.

And in those days an impure woman will conceive a wicked child ... he will be raised in diverse and hidden places, so he is not recognized by men, and he will be furnished with all the arts of the Devil and hidden until he reaches maturity, nor will he reveal the perversity which is in him.

While much of the intended chronology is uncertain, Hildegard clearly believes that the time of Antichrist has not yet come.[9] It also appears from chapter 23 that the time of the wolf extends until just before the Last Judgement. It is perhaps odd that Hildegard does not round out the whole production with an account of the Last Judgement and the bliss of the saved, together with the corresponding lamentations of the damned, but possibly she thought that she had sufficiently covered the theme in her earlier works.

I fear that in the space of this chapter and the earlier ones on the *Scivias* and *Liber vitae meritorum* I have not been able to do much more than hint at the richness of Hildegard's three great visionary works. What I hope to have shown, however, is something of their differences and interrelations as well as the kinds of material to be found in each. Systematic studies of Hildegard's thought, such as Newman's *Sister of Wisdom*, which locates aspects of Hildegard's theology within the sapiential tradition, are now beginning to appear, together with investigations of the theological foundations of her ethical views and her problematic relationship to the learned traditions of the various subjects towards which she turned her attention. The process will no doubt be encouraged by the recent completion of critical editions of the major theological works. Meanwhile, it is important to remember that wherever Hildegard originally derived her ideas, in viewing them in the refracting mirror of her visions, and incorporating them into her holistic picture of the world, she made them truly her own.

8

ADMONITION AND ADVICE

It is also clear that she replied judiciously to many letters sent her
from various provinces. (*Vita*, Bk 2)

I

This chapter is concerned with what might be called Hildegard's
pastoral activities. The fact that Hildegard toured as a preacher,
wrote letters of direction to correspondents (both lay and religious) of
all degrees, and acted as a consultant exorcist, at a time when women
were not expected to assume such a public role in church affairs,
clearly requires some explanation. The answer is to be found in the
recognition of Hildegard as a prophet. All these activities were in
some sense grounded in or justified by the prophetic role, which had
also enabled her to write the theological treatises discussed earlier.

However, it was not as an authority in her own right that
Hildegard's opinion and direction was sought, but rather as the agent
through which the will of God, or in some cases God's secrets, were
to be known. Much of the evidence for this side of Hildegard's life
is to be found in her correspondence. Although about 300 letters
purportedly written by Hildegard survive in one form or another,
together with a smaller number of letters addressed to her, the correspondence in some ways promises more than it delivers. This is partly
because, like most medieval letters, they were intended for public
consumption, rather than as intimate expressions of emotion or
thought – a factor heightened in Hildegard's case by her virtual
eschewal of her own voice in preference to that of God – and partly
because of the circumstances of their transmission.

The largest surviving body of her correspondence, in a manuscript
known as the Riesenkodex, now at Wiesbaden, consists of a series of
paired letters in which a letter supposedly written to Hildegard is

followed by her reply. While some of Hildegard's letters also appear in manuscripts other than the Riesenkodex, very few of the letters addressed to her are found in any other source, which, of course, is not to say that the others must therefore be rejected. The compiler of the Riesenkodex has also taken some liberties with Hildegard's letters, sometimes making two letters into one, or altering the name of the addressee.[1] This means that we cannot take the correspondence in the Riesenkodex at face value to represent Hildegard's particular responses to specific epistolary requests. On the other hand, even if the pairings are suspect, we can at least examine the sorts of request which Hildegard received, the kinds of question she was expected to answer, and often the basis for the confidence her correspondents placed in her. By the same token, her own letters, even if not always written in response to a specific request, do enable us to deduce something of the range and manner of Hildegard's pastoral activity, as well as the geographical and social spread of her spiritual clientele. As we might expect, the earliest correspondence dates from the time of her recognition at the Synod of Trier in 1147–8 and is maintained with increasing volume and diversity until her death in 1179.

II

There are letters to Hildegard from the pope and emperor at the top of the ecclesiastical and secular pecking orders, through titled nobility and princes of the church, down to humbler members of the laity and religious orders, covering an area from Prague in the east to Beauvais in the west. In the Riesenkodex the letters are arranged according to status, with those of the laity – king, emperor, and count – coming after the bishops and before the abbots.

The requests fall into two or three main groups, apparently with little differentiation according to the status of the questioner. There are general requests for Hildegard's prayers, or for letters of admonition or consolation, and more specific petitions for answers to questions of general or particular import to the questioner. Those concerned with exorcism will be treated separately below, as will the surviving papal letters and some from the archbishops of Mainz which arose in the context of particular disputes or problems.

Many of the letters ask Hildegard in fairly nonspecific terms to send the writer a message of encouragement, admonition, or consolation. The talismanic value of a letter from such an acknowledged source of spiritual strength should not be underestimated;[2] such a

153

connection provided virtue by association. Requests like this came from people who were known to Hildegard, including her relatives, as well as from strangers. Sometimes such a letter includes an additional request for Hildegard's prayers, while sometimes only her prayers are sought.

Thus Bishop Herman of Constance wrote to solicit Hildegard's prayers, remarking that 'earthly cares have almost entirely taken me away from the service of God'.[3] The idea of drawing upon someone else's holiness to counteract one's own shortcomings was well entrenched in the Middle Ages, being one of the principal rationales for lay support of monasteries.

A fellow bishop, this time from Liège, wrote to Hildegard 'in great turmoil of mind and body', conscious of having offended and irritated God in countless ways.[4] Nevertheless, he trusts that she will convey to him 'whatever is shown to you from the unfailing and living light to rouse me from my slumbers'. Less specifically, Archbishop Philip of Cologne, a frequent visitor to Rupertsberg, asks Hildegard for words of advice ('*commonitoria verba*') and remarks that it is common knowledge that 'you are infused with the divine gift of charisma, on account of which the band of the faithful of the Church rejoices'.[5]

There are many similar examples indicating that Hildegard's gifts were recognized and her prayers and advice sought by members of the upper clergy in her immediate area and beyond. Moreover, such recognition is spread over many years.[6] Hildegard's powers were acknowledged to come from a divine source and to embrace both theological and secular knowledge, as in a letter from Eberhard of Bamberg, who asks a specific question about the procession of the Holy Spirit, and seeks also more general wisdom.[7] For this reason Hildegard was often sought out by letter as counsellor and comforter.

The same sorts of request come from members of the monastic orders who contribute about a hundred letters to the collection and thus provide a valuable insight into the way in which Hildegard was viewed by her brothers and sisters in religion. While there are rather too many letters from heads of houses to represent grassroots opinion, it is perhaps here that we come closest to the popular monastic assessment of her.

As in the case of the letters from bishops, Hildegard's role in the minds of her monastic correspondents is revealed as much by what they ask her as by the formal opening address and words of praise their letters contain. Some, however, do make explicit mention of

Hildegard's prophetic gifts. Thus Adam of Ebrach, in a letter (Van Acker, 85) expressing his concern about how to care for his monks, refers in closing to 'the gift of the Holy Spirit, which works many marvels in you by the spirit of prophecy'. And Ludwig of St Eucharius (admittedly an old friend) writes: 'you surpass in keenness of mind not only philosophers and dialecticians, but even the prophets of old' (Van Acker, 215).

That this prophetic gift could be used to foresee the future is suggested by a letter (Van Acker, 149) from Abbot Werner of Kirchheim, who notes that her reputation depends not only on the performance of good works but also on her knowledge of the future. His specific request is for a copy of a sermon Hildegard preached 'to us and many more in Kirchheim about the failings of priests'. In a letter (Van Acker, 48) asking Hildegard for her prayers and letters of correction, a Benedictine monk and priest, Godfrey of Alpirsbach, expresses his belief that the secrets of his heart will be revealed to Hildegard by the spirit which enables her to see all things, past, present, and to come. He adds that he would be exceedingly pleased to receive any letters concerning her visions.

We find such lines of thought converging in a letter (Van Acker, 191) whose author identifies himself as 'a poor prelate' (possibly the Abbot of Rothenkirchen). The writer begins his letter by suggesting that Hildegard's special relationship with God is the result of her genuine faith and the consecration to him of her virginity since childhood. He who makes known his hidden secrets through Hildegard has also judged her worthy to give ear to those who question her in God's name. That such a gift has been bestowed on a woman does not perturb the writer, since God can, when he wishes, reveal his secrets through holy women just as through male prophets. He cites Joel 2:28 and adds that Deborah, Olda, Anna the mother of Samuel, Elisabeth the mother of John the Baptist, and other women possessed the spirit of prophecy, despite being married. Hildegard, he maintains, comes to prophecy from a position of spiritual superiority, as a virgin devoid of every carnal weakness.

It turns out that this correspondent was not a stranger to Hildegard, since his request was for written words of consolation conveyed in writing of the kind, which, he reveals, she had often given him face to face. He hopes that he will be able to refresh his memory by reading them. Likewise the Abbess of Bamberg, whom Hildegard had possibly met on one of her preaching tours, hoped to be strengthened by a letter from her and also expressed a wish that their two convents might be joined in a union of prayer (Van Acker, 61).

Many of the letters which come from the heads of houses reflect a renewed contemporary questioning of the form of life most appropriate for achieving the spiritual goals once thought to be almost exclusively obtainable in Benedictine communities. It was recognized, particularly by those in authority, that the burdens of office in such a community (or even the lifestyle itself, according to the more rigorous) might interfere with a truly spiritual existence. Such concerns contributed to the spectacular growth of orders such as the Cistercians who sought a stricter observance of the Benedictine Rule.

At the same time as the Cistercians were fleeing the world by withdrawing to uninhabited and waste places, other groups, including some orders of canons, were becoming more closely involved in teaching and ministering to the spiritual needs of the urban laity. While it was generally agreed that a person could move from a less strict to a more stringent order (especially by the Cistercians who tended to be the chief beneficiaries of such transfers), other possibilities were also canvassed, for example living as contemplatives within the ambit of an established Benedictine monastery, as at Cluny. It is against such a background that the uncertainty over the true apostolic lifestyle, found in many letters to Hildegard, should be viewed.

Although the question of whether to resign office voiced by many heads of monastic houses among Hildegard's correspondents could be considered from various perspectives, what most concerned them was the effect the decision might have on their ultimate salvation. The question uppermost in their minds is whether their proposed course of action accords with the will of God. Thus Abbot Eberhard of St Anastasius in Rome enquires

> whether the Spirit who reveals His arcane and hidden wisdom, will indicate to you what would serve me better in shouldering the burden of obedience to Christ, that is, whether to persevere, or to leave off so I could have time for contemplation. (Van Acker, 190)

Similarly, Abbot Conrad of Kaisheim (Van Acker, 144) begs Hildegard to ask the Spouse who reposes in the chamber of her heart, whether he should lay down the burden of pastoral care of his monks or rather continue to shoulder it. In much the same vein the Abbot of St Maria in Pfalzal (Van Acker, 182) asks Hildegard to find out whether it would be better for his future salvation to persevere in or relinquish that office which he finds at the same time both 'honourable and onerous, dignified and dangerous'.

Letters from women in like situations show similar concerns. Hildegard's advice is sought because she has the means of ascertaining God's will. As one abbess put it:

> heavenly wisdom has prepared her seat in you. Wherefore . . . I implore you to be so kind as to ask God whether it is His will that I support or relinquish this burden. (Van Acker, 237)

So too, Sophie of Kitzingen (Van Acker, 150) concludes a rather fulsome letter with the brief request: 'Let your voice sound in my ears and inform me, seeking word from above, whether it is safer to put aside the burden I carry or bear it longer?'

A comparable situation is outlined in the letter of a priest who appears to have charge of a hospice in the town of Lutter. Finding his work too demanding, he would like to seek the comparative peace of a monastery (presumably not as its abbot). He sums up his dilemma in the following way (Van Acker, 164): 'For we are bidden to serve the poor, yet cannot do so without our souls becoming seriously troubled', and asks Hildegard what course he should follow. His final words express the underlying wish of all such petitioners: 'May God show you what would be more pleasing to Him in this case.' Hildegard almost invariably advised such enquirers that they should persevere in the office to which God had called them. Her own preference was obviously for a mixed life, where the gifts of contemplation were to be used for the good of others. Having herself experienced the solitary life, Hildegard was also in a good position to counsel others about its difficulties.

In a large group of letters from clergy, monks, and nuns, Hildegard's prophetic powers are still more clearly implied. Thus almost one quarter of the letters ask either about the present state of the writer's soul (often in conjunction with the state of his or her monastery) or its ultimate fate. Sometimes this is expressed in quite general terms, as by the Abbot of Kempten (Van Acker, 148), who asks Hildegard for anything which has been divinely revealed about himself or the state of his monastery, or the Prior of Zwiefalten (Van Acker, 241) wishing to repair the failure of discipline in his monastery, who asks Hildegard what has been revealed to her on this subject.

A more personal enquiry, doubtless influenced by his state of health at the time, is to be found in a letter from the ailing Abbot of Haina (Van Acker, 112), who asks about his future prospects. Such knowledge, he asserts, is made possible through him who dwells within her. A member of the cathedral clergy of Mainz is likewise concerned with his personal standing in the eyes of God (Van Acker, 168). He asks Hildegard to write him a letter detailing his faults, as shown to her by God, and how best to amend them. The Abbot of Selbod (Van Acker, 204) is determined to leave nothing to chance when he asks Hildegard to send him a letter describing his spiritual state and everything that has happened, or will happen to him. Once more, the expectation is that all will be revealed to Hildegard through the Holy Spirit.

III

Clearly, then, Hildegard was consulted by members of the monastic orders and secular clergy on a wide range of subjects: from theological questions and matters of personal salvation, to problems of monastic discipline and church organization. Direct evidence, however, on the attitude of the laity is harder to come by. The Riesenkodex preserves only three letters (*PL*, CXCVII, 185–7) to Hildegard from laymen – King Conrad (1138–52), Frederick Barbarossa (1152–90), and Count Philip of Flanders. On the other hand, there is plenty of indirect evidence in the form of Hildegard's answers to people in secular life, from which the nature of their requests can be inferred.

Conrad simply sought Hildegard's prayers for himself and his son, Frederick, the heir apparent since the death of his elder brother, Henry, in 1150. Frederick Barbarossa's letter refers to a meeting he has had with Hildegard at the royal palace of Ingelheim and states that the things she predicted there have already come to pass. Of a more obvious personal nature is the letter of Philip of Flanders, which he wrote to Hildegard when considering a journey to the Holy Land. He asks Hildegard whether he ought to remain there or return home. In words reminiscent of the clerical and monastic correspondents, he asks her to tell him what she has heard, or may subsequently hear, about him. Hildegard's reply seems rather veiled, although she appears to favour the general idea of fighting the enemies of God.

To find other examples of lay attitudes to Hildegard, we have to rely on her answers. Often the nature of the request which produced the letter is easy enough to infer. In many cases, Hildegard's letter seems a direct response (much more direct, for some reason, than her replies to many letters from religious) to a particular personal enquiry, often about a member of the correspondent's immediate family. For example, we may take her letter to Luitgard of Karleburg:

O Luitgard, God's creature, arrange your affairs according to your needs, because I do not see your husband's illness lifting before his end. Therefore, beg, correct and warn him for the safety of his soul, because I see much darkness in him. May God look upon you, that you may live in eternity. (*Sanctae Hildegardis Opera*, ed. J.B. Pitra (Pi.) 560)

Another such letter is found in the same collection, addressed to Martin and Isabella of Lausanne. Here in a few lines she admonishes Martin to make good his intentions of drawing nearer to God, and praises Isabella for her spiritual progress while assuring them that Beatrice, perhaps their daughter, will be liberated from all her difficulties. Such letters suggest that in the minds of the laity Hildegard was credited with a straightforward clairvoyant capacity, a belief in which, at times, she seems to have acquiesced. Such a position could be justified by appeal to her moral intentions, since by such means she was getting people to lead better lives. The suspicion remains, however, that Hildegard was more circumspect in her answers to members of the clergy and the religious orders.

The recipients of these letters, who evidently knew some Latin, were presumably not much below Hildegard herself on the social scale. There are also examples of letters from Hildegard to members of the titled nobility, such as Gertrude of Stahleck, the former Countess Palatine (Pi. 552), who had entered a convent and sought words of encouragement. In a letter to Gerhard, Count of Wertheim (Pi. 550), Hildegard promises to pray for his mother and father in their troubles, and for his brother who is in prison, while the Count himself is to have thirty masses said for another brother now deceased. To Irmintrude, Countess of Widen (Pi. 546), she urges good works and almsgiving and undertakes to pray for the birth of a son to her. Nor should we omit her letters to the King and Queen of England, presumably Henry II and Eleanor of Aquitaine. If these last two letters were solicited, they must have been very general requests for words of encouragement and admonition, or at least this is what Hildegard provides.

The letters described above give some indication of the way in which Hildegard was consulted as a kind of spiritual counselling service, because she was thought to have knowledge of God's purposes and designs beyond that of ordinary people, whether lay or religious. Sometimes the requests are closely connected to her visionary work and sometimes (especially, it seems, in the minds of the laity) the original connection with her visionary writings appears to have degenerated into a kind of soothsaying. Of course, the human need for such guidance was not confined to the Middle Ages (when the world in its day-to-day aspect was a much more unpredictable and menacing place), as the advice columns of modern magazines, newspapers, and their equivalents on the electronic media clearly indicate.

IV

Other letters reveal more specialized concerns. One group opens a window on a fascinating case, described at some length in the third book of the *Vita*, in which Hildegard acted as consultant in the exorcism of a woman possessed (or rather obsessed) by a devil. Her name was Sigewize, a young woman of noble family from Cologne, as we learn from some oblique references to the case in correspondence between Hildegard, her nephew Arnold of Trier, and a deacon from Cologne. The most important exchange of letters, between Hildegard and the monks of Brauweiler, is incorporated into the text of the *Vita*.

The story as told in the third book of the *Vita* is woven from several different sources: Hildegard's own words in the autobiographical fragments, the authorial comment of Theodoric (who adds some colourful details, possibly to be taken with a grain of salt), and the letters between Hildegard and the monks which are presumably genuine. Hildegard's account begins by placing the incident in the context of her literary activity and her general health; it occurred after she had started the *Liber divinorum operum* and when she had been lying ill for a year, which suggests that the incident took place in 1169. She tells of hearing of the sad affliction of the woman from the lower Rhine, whose friends had conducted her around the shrines of the saints for many years in search of a cure, but without success. She also pondered upon the nature of such afflictions, concluding that they arise when the Devil clouds the intellect and moral senses rather than actually entering the body, as in a case of genuine possession.

There is some suggestion that the woman was suffering from a form of religious mania, since she is described as preaching and thereby inciting many to depravity and sin. Hildegard then adds that the woman had claimed that she would only be helped by 'a certain old woman further up the Rhine', an obvious reference to herself. So it was that Sigewize was brought to Rupertsberg in the eighth year of her illness. Theodoric adds in his commentary that the wicked spirit, speaking through the woman, referred to Hildegard mockingly as 'Scrumpilgard', which could be translated 'Crumplegard', presumably an allusion to her wrinkled face. What Hildegard does not mention in this account is her first, failed, attempt to exorcize the woman at the request of the monks at Brauweiler; that incident is described in letters inserted at this point by Theodoric.

After an extended and highly complimentary introduction, in which Abbot Gedolphus explains that although they have never met, Hildegard's reputation has ensured his love and admiration for her, he comes to the point of his letter:

> Therefore, O pious mistress, let not the sweetness of your sanctity repulse our boldness when we presume in the simplicity of our hearts, compelled by great need, to open to you the reason for our importunity. We do not doubt that we will receive good counsel from you. A certain noble woman, obsessed by an evil spirit these many years, was brought to us by her friends, to gain the help of the blessed Nicholas our patron, to free her of the devil which beset her. The cunning and wickedness of this most sly and wanton enemy led almost a thousand people into error and doubt, which we fear was greatly detrimental to the Holy Church. Now we all laboured for three months, together with a multitude of people for the liberation of this woman in all sorts of ways. But – we cannot say it without grief – since our sins weighed upon us we achieved nothing. Thus all our hope is in you, after God. Now one day when the devil was conjured, at last it revealed to us that this obsessed woman should be liberated by the virtue of your contemplation and the mightiness of your divine revelation. . . . We humbly and earnestly pray, therefore, that whatever God inspired you with in this matter, or revealed to you in a vision, your holiness may take care to set down in writing.

Hildegard, having digested the letter and asked her nuns to 'dwell humbly in their public and private prayers on the problem' and having herself 'lifted the eyes of her mind to the Lord' sent back her reply. In it she identifies the demon as an extremely recalcitrant type because it cannot be routed by 'the Lord's cross, the relics of the saints and other things that pertain to God's service'. Rather it must be dealt with by 'fasting, scourging, prayers, alms and the command of God himself'. She goes on to outline a ritual beating of the woman, combining actual and symbolic intervention, as follows:

Hear therefore the reply not of man, but of Him who lives: Choose seven priests of good repute, who are commended by the merit of their lives, the first in the name and order of Abel, the second in the name of Noah, the third in the name of Abraham, the fourth in the name of Melchisidek, the fifth in the name of Jacob and the sixth in the name of Aaron, who all offered sacrifice to the living God and the seventh in the name of Christ who offered Himself to God the Father on the cross. After fasts, scourgings, prayers, almsgiving, and the celebration of masses let them approach the patient with humble intention and in . . . priestly vestments and wearing their stoles. And let each one of them standing around her hold a rod in his hand as a symbol of the rod with which Moses, at God's command struck Egypt, the Red Sea, and the rock . . . the seven priests will also represent the seven gifts of the Holy Spirit. . . . And the first, in the name of Abel, holding his rod in his hand will say 'Hear, O wicked and foolish spirit, wheresoever you dwell in this person, hear these words not devised by man, but made manifest by Him who Is . . . and flee at his command.'

The order of the rest of the ceremony, squeezed into the margins of the Berlin manuscript of the *Vita*, is not altogether clear, but it involved the priests striking the woman 'lightly with their rods, on the head and back and breast and stomach and loins and knees and feet' and conjuring the spirit in the name of the personages they represent.[8]

It seems that Volmar himself was sent to oversee the ceremony, which apparently took place in the presence of a great many onlookers in the monastery church, the seven priests no doubt having been chosen from among the monks. The picture sketched by Theodoric, of the terror the spirit caused in the bystanders by its loud raving when the exorcism was performed, the weakness of the woman when the spirit left her and her feeble prostration before the altar of St Nicholas, the jubilation of the people who rang the bells and the monks who sang the *Te Deum* is most skilfully drawn, even if from his own imagination.[9] He concludes:

But alas, how wretched it is to relate, by a hidden judgement of God, the same old enemy returned and sought once more the vessel it had left. Then the woman shook all over, and rising, hooting and shrieking, became more insane than before.

It was only after the exorcism was tried again that the spirit revealed that Hildegard had to be there in person and so the monks sent Sigewize off with a letter of recommendation describing what had happened, admittedly in rather less colourful terms than Theodoric's. In it, they express the wish that greater spiritual benefits will result from Hildegard's closer physical proximity and that God might complete through her the cure they were denied because of the weight of their sins.

Theodoric then lets Hildegard resume the story. She describes the apprehension with which she and the nuns prepared to receive Sigewize into their midst. Once the patient had been installed in the sisters' quarters, Hildegard writes:

We never slackened – not for terror, nor for the disorder with which the demon confused those who pressed upon it for its sins, nor for the mocking and filthy words with which it sought to overcome us, nor for its terrible breath. (*Vita*, Bk 3)

Not only Hildegard and the nuns, but the whole community of the region seems to have been involved over a period of many weeks. 'So from the Purification of St Mary (February 2) until the Saturday before Easter the men and women of our region laboured for her, with fasting, prayer, almsgiving, and mortification of the flesh.' The woman seems to have been given leave to continue the activities which first led her into trouble. From Hildegard's description it sounds as if Sigewize continued to preach, but this time Hildegard kept a watchful eye on her doctrinal purity, as she says, 'Yet I did not prevent it [the devil] from addressing the people when it was speaking the truth.'

The climax came almost, it seems, by chance, when the woman was present on Maundy Thursday while the font was being consecrated by the breath of the priest, itself a form of exorcism. Here is how Hildegard describes what happened:

The woman was present and, seized with great fear, beat the ground with her feet and often emitted a blast from the terrible spirit that oppressed her. Then in true vision, I saw and heard that the might of the Most High, who always and ever brooded over

163

holy baptism, said to the devilish accumulation by which the woman was worn out: 'Come Satan from the temple of this woman's body and make room in it for the Holy Spirit.' Then the wicked spirit emerged, together with a terrible voiding from the woman's private parts. Thus she was freed and remained sound in mind and body for the rest of her life.

In fact, it would seem from a later letter that she joined Hildegard's community.

This detailed account of the case of Sigewize raises the question of the other cures Hildegard is said to have performed and their relationship to medical practice at the convent, especially in the light of Hildegard's writings on the medicinal uses of plants and animals. It is, however, the miraculous virtue of bread left over from Hildegard's meals, the girdle made from her hair (used by women in childbed), of water from her table, or, at a pinch, water taken from the Rhine, which interests her biographer.

This is not to say that Hildegard scorned such means. We are told, for example, in the same section of the *Vita*, about a certain Sybil from the city of Lausanne whom Hildegard cured of an issue of blood. The cure was performed by placing on her breast and waist a written text commanding the issue to cease, in the name of Christ – a rather simpler process than that employed with Sigewize. Moreover, we find among the letters of the Vienna manuscript (Pi. 521) what appears to be the very letter sent to explain what Sybil should do to effect the cure. Such cures, then, cannot be dismissed as merely the products of Theodoric's hagiographical imagination.

He does, however, remark in the second book of the *Vita* that many of the people who flocked to Rupertsberg 'consulted her about bodily afflictions from which they suffered and some were relieved of their illnesses by her blessings'. This, of course, does not mean that some were not cured by more natural means. The line between nature and supernature was not a clear one since, as we saw in the *Physica* and *Causae et curae*, God's will was thought to be an important element even in herbal and other remedies. Whatever her methods, there is plenty of evidence to show that Hildegard had a wide reputation as a healer. Indeed, she seems to have specialized in certain sorts of illness, being consulted by women in particular, and those suffering from what we might now call psychological ailments.[10]

The role of healer was traditional for women, and even in the case of exorcism, an act which had long been a prerogative of the male hierarchy of the church, Hildegard was careful to present herself as orchestrator rather than performer of the rite. The involvement of no less than seven priests would have sufficiently answered any claim that she harboured antisacerdotal attitudes. One area of her activity was, however, highly unconventional for a woman. I refer to her preaching, especially the occasions when she appeared publicly 'before the clergy and people'.

V

Although it is hard to reconstruct the chronology and itinerary of Hildegard's preaching tours, it is clear that they were only undertaken once her reputation had been well established by the *Scivias* and her charismatic personality widely recognized. We do not know whether she was asked directly to intervene in monastic disputes, or having been asked in a letter for advice, felt the reply would best be delivered in person. Her account of her first preaching exercise (c. 1159) in the *Vita* merely states: 'I took the opportunity to make a trip to other monasteries and expounded there the words God commanded.' She is a little more explicit about the fourth tour (c. 1170), where she writes:

> During this time [her forty-day illness] I was directed in true vision, to visit certain religious communities of men and women to reveal openly to them the words that God had shown me . . . and following God's instruction, I settled their internal quarrels.

Theodoric gives a list of twenty-one places Hildegard visited, 'not moved, but compelled by the Holy Spirit', making special mention of Cologne, Trier, Metz, Würzburg, and Bamberg as places where she preached 'to the clergy and people'. This list cannot be exhaustive, however, since no mention is made of Kirchheim, although other evidence shows she was here, presumably on her last trip, when she visited Swabia. The cases where Hildegard appeared 'before the clergy and people' suggest that she sometimes preached in the cathedral, while the other occasions would have been internal addresses, delivered most probably in the chapter house of the monastery, or possibly in the monastic church.

Some of these conjectures are strengthened by hints from the correspondence. For example, the numerous letters written by Hildegard to the Abbot of Hirsau about his administrative problems suggest a close interest in and knowledge of this particular monastery.

Another letter, mentioned above, from Werner, Abbot of Kirchheim (or perhaps strictly the head of a community of priests there), asks Hildegard to send a copy of the sermon she preached 'to us and many more in Kirchheim'. The survival of letters from members of the cathedral clergy of Trier, Cologne, and Mainz about her preaching also suggests that she spoke there under cathedral, rather than monastic, auspices.

While permission to preach within a monastic environment was largely up to the abbot (the fact that Hildegard allowed Sigewize to address 'the people' at Rupertsberg is significant), public preaching was controlled by licence from the bishop and was usually confined to priests. Thus Hildegard would have been twice disqualified: first by her non-priestly status, and second under the wholesale prohibition on women teaching or preaching, laid down by St Paul, and incorporated into canon law.

The obvious danger from unlicensed preachers was that they might mislead the people by presenting doctrines subversive of the established church. However, by the time Hildegard came to preach she was in her sixties, her bona fides had been well established, and her access to the Holy Spirit given papal endorsement. Thus her orthodoxy was hardly in doubt. Indeed, she had written a sermon against the Cathars, subsequently sent to the cathedral clergy of Mainz at their request. Her sermons criticizing priests might have been considered potentially more dangerous, except that she was there concerned to denounce the negligent minority who brought the whole body of the clergy into disrepute.

This sermon, or a version of it, has come down to us in the form of the reply sent to Werner of Kirchheim. The text (Van Acker, 149) shows strong affinities with Hildegard's other theological writings, and might indeed almost be extracted from one of her longer works, such as the *Liber divinorum operum*. Hildegard even introduces the sermon in the same way as her more extended visionary works:

> While lying for a long time on my bed of illness, in the eleven hundred and seventieth year of the Incarnation of Our Lord, I saw while alert in mind and body, a most beautiful image, having the form of a woman who was most choice in sweetness and most dear in the delights of all beauty, so that the human mind could not at all comprehend it and whose form reached from earth to sky.

The woman, representing the Church, is, however, begrimed with dirt and her beautiful clothes are torn. She begins a lament about her condition, caused by the negligence or downright criminality of priests:

> For they besmirch my face thereby, because they give and receive the body and blood of my spouse with the great filthiness of their lascivious lives, and the great foulness of fornication and adultery, and the dreadful rapaciousness of avarice, in buying and selling.

Her threat that such behaviour will lead to the downfall of priests by an uprising of the people and their leaders has been taken by some (especially nineteenth-century editors) to presage the Protestant Reformation of the sixteenth century. However, it should rather be seen as a return to the programme of reform of the clergy advocated earlier in the twelfth century by such writers as Rupert of Deutz.[11] The fact that Hildegard's strictures seem more radical here than in the *Scivias* may once more reflect her increasing age or the prolongation of the schism. However, she is far from completely rejecting the priesthood; her very criticisms underline the particularly high place she accords to it. Finally, she does see 'many Godfearing, pure and simple priests' surviving any such purges.

Another sermon she delivered in public at Trier, at Whitsuntide in 1160, is contained in a letter (Van Acker, 223r) she sent at the request of the provost of St Peter's on behalf of all the clergy of the city. Once more this sermon is similar in tone to the *Liber divinorum operum*, an apocalyptic warning to the spiritual leaders of the Church to reform themselves.

Likewise the sermon preached at Cologne, a written version of which was requested by Philip (Van Acker, 15 and 15r), later archbishop of that see, expresses many of the themes, such as that of the microcosm/macrocosm, found in Hildegard's last work. Philip describes himself in his letter as 'deacon' which dates the request to some time before 1165, when he was made provost. Once more the work seems directed principally at the clergy, whom Hildegard addresses as God's mouthpiece:

> O my dear sons, who feed my flocks. . . . I have placed you like the sun and other luminaries that you may give light to men through the fire of teaching, shining in good report and offering burning hearts. . . . Through teaching of the Scriptures which were composed in the fire of the Holy Spirit you should be the strong corners of the Church, holding it up, like the corners which hold up the ends of the earth; but you are prostrate and do not sustain

the Church. You flee to the cavern of your delight and because of the tedium of riches and the avarice of other vanities you do not fill those under you, nor allow them to seek teaching from you.

A disturbing consequence of this state of affairs is the progress made in the city by the Cathar sect who 'walk about in black robes, properly tonsured, and display themselves among men as serene and peaceful in all their ways. Moreover, they do not love avarice, and they do not have money, and, in their private lives, hold abstinence so highly that they can scarcely be reproached'. In short, they present a stark contrast to the legitimate clergy. Appearances, however, are deceptive since the Cathars are actually part of the Devil's forces in the great fight against the City of God. The sermon ends with a description of the Last Days, a topic Hildegard treats in her larger works, and a further call to those 'masters, teachers and other prudent men who hold the higher positions in the Church' for moral and institutional reform.

Some doubt arises in all these cases about the form which her preaching took. Was it in the vernacular? If not, the laity could hardly have gained much benefit from it. On the other hand, the sermons seem directed more at the clergy than the people themselves, and so it might have been felt desirable that the people should not be able to understand them. It may seem strange that the clergy, castigated by her sermons, should ask for further punishment in written form. Yet this is precisely what they seem to have done. Perhaps it was because Hildegard did not single out individuals, but rather criticized whole groups, and even then allowed that some might be blameless. Thus the hearers could applaud her fulminations, without feeling personally threatened.

If this was Hildegard in her public persona, reprimanding the church at large, how does she appear when giving direction at a more personal level, as she is known to have done in the case of the disputes which occurred in the monasteries she visited? Does she, for example, show an informed understanding of human psychology and moti-vation? An example of the sort of advice Hildegard gave can be seen in the exchange of letters between her and the Abbess Hazzecha of Krauftal. Hildegard had included this Benedictine nunnery in her second round of visits, in 1160, and had apparently made a great impact on the impressionable abbess. Hazzecha writes:

After your long desired presence and affability, by God's help, I was happily relieved and had some rest from wavering spirits and the previous tempests; and because I doubt not that your words come forth not from human intelligence but from the living light which has illuminated you more than other people, I have postponed doing what I purposed to do till now. (Van Acker, 159)

She then asks that Hildegard convey to her whatever words of correction the Holy Spirit might reveal.

What the abbess says she has postponed or put off – that she has renounced the idea completely is doubted by Hildegard – was her intention of becoming a solitary. Hildegard makes a reference to this in her reply:

> Take care that you bear your burden carefully and gather the good work in the wallet of your heart, lest you fail, for in the solitary life which you seem to be considering you will have no peace because of the instability of your ways, and then your end will be much worse than your beginning. (Van Acker, 159r)

Another letter in the Riesenkodex from A, Abbess of Krauftal (Van Acker, 160), may also be from Hazzecha. Here there seems to be no mention of leading a solitary life, although the terms of praise used for Hildegard are sufficiently extravagant to suggest they might be from Hazzecha. Hildegard's reply is fairly acerbic in tone and does suggest, under the symbolism of a tower fortifying a city, that charity is to be defended by obedience, faith, and hope (Van Acker, 160r). There might also be some allusion to her duty to remain with and sustain her community. A further letter (Van Acker, 162) to the community as a whole, suggests that matters stand in need of correction, but nothing very concrete is said, and nothing at all about the head of the house.

Much more specific, however, is a letter in the Berlin manuscript which Peter Dronke suggested very plausibly is also directed to Hazzecha of Krauftal.[12] Here Hildegard seems partly to abandon her prophetic tone so that the message comes across without fear of being misunderstood. This letter is remarkable for its direct approach to the problem. It seems that her correspondent had once more raised her proposal to become an anchoress or, alternatively, to make a pilgrimage to Rome. She may also have been indulging in extravagant penances. In this case Hildegard possibly felt that she was partly to blame for these excesses, since her earlier letters had been harsh in tone. In response, Hildegard's counsel is one of moderation, of knowing how far to go and when to stop. The advice is given without mediation of symbolism or allegory, except in a vestigial manner, represented by the personification of the virtue of moderation as the (female) figure Discretion.

Thus Hildegard begins:

> In true vision I saw and heard these words. O daughter of God, you who call this poor little woman Mother in God's love, learn to have Discretion, which in all heaven and earth is the mother of everything, since through her the soul is ruled and the body is nourished in proper austerity. The person who, amid sighs of repentance remembers her sins, which were committed at the suggestion of the Devil in thought, word and deed, shall embrace her mother Discretion and be supported by her, and amend her sins in true humility and obedience to the counsel of her directors.

She follows this advice with a warning that the Devil often sabotages one's best efforts at repentance by suggesting excessive mortification of the flesh, which leads to bodily illness. The task of repentance is thus left unfinished and so one is worse off than when one started. Hildegard had already used this line of argument, with its reference to Matt. 12:45, in her earlier letter to Hazzecha.

The practice of self-inflicted, excessive austerities was not unusual at the time; for example, Book 3 of the *Vita* mentions a similar case of a nun from Schaffenheim. What is interesting, however, is that Hildegard saw such behaviour as misguided, indeed diabolical, and sought to curb it. In Hazzecha's case it was by argument and explanation, and although the case of the nun of Schaffenheim is numbered among Hildegard's miracles, the means used to guide her do not seem to have been much more miraculous. The nun, we are told, having been sent to Hildegard, 'was comforted and freed from her diabolical error'.

Hildegard next turns to the problem of choice and, by locating the activity of the will firmly in the realm of the body, argues that whatever a person wishes to do herself – presumably when it is in conflict with the counsel of her spiritual advisers – should be treated as suspect. She then turns directly, as we must suppose, to addressing the proposals for another way of life put to her by the abbess.

> Dearest daughter, I cannot see how it will profit you and your two companions to seek out a wood, or cell or Rome itself [*limina sanctorum*] when you are signed with the sign of Christ which leads to the heavenly Jerusalem. For if you begin a greater labour than

you can sustain, through the Devil's deception, you will fall, as I said before.

The concluding part of the letter apparently deals with further questions of Hazzecha's. Hildegard asserts that it is not her practice to speak about what will befall people or about their achievements – a resolve which in fact she did not always stick to, as we have seen. She does, however, promise to pray for 'the men she had commended' to her, and especially for Hazzecha herself, that she may 'bring to fruit the labour of holy works with holy discretion'.

So far we have been dealing with matters where Hildegard's intervention, advice, or co-operation were actively sought. All such cases involved, either explicitly or implicitly, a recognition of her prophetic powers. More importantly, in responding to such requests, Hildegard always made the source of her knowledge and power apparent. She is not only performing God's will, but speaking his very words.

9

WORLDLY DISCORDS

A prophet is not without honour, save in his own country and in his own house. (Matt. 13:57)

I

But there were other, less gratifying occasions when Hildegard, rather than being in the position of giving advice or telling others what to do, found herself in conflict with her ecclesiastical superiors. In these circumstances Hildegard also had recourse to her prophetic persona.

Hildegard's first recorded difference of opinion with those in authority over her occurred when she expressed a desire to remove her convent from Disibodenberg to Rupertsberg in 1148. This plan, coming as it did after the papal recognition of her work at the Synod of Trier but before the completion of the *Scivias*, belongs to the earliest phase of her career when her prophetic persona had not been fully established. It is hardly surprising, then, that the abbot and monks of Disibodenberg were not immediately persuaded by her claim to have been divinely commanded to move, even going so far as to suggest that she 'was deceived by some foolishness'.

Faced with this failure to recognize the ultimate authority for the action she had planned, Hildegard took to her bed. She had a little earlier been similarly prostrated after failing to make known to the monks God's command to move. All work on the *Scivias* also came to a standstill and this circumstance, together, no doubt, with the more remarkable aspects of her illness forced the monks to reconsider.[1]

It should also be noted that Hildegard had enlisted impressive lay and ecclesiastical supporters in the Marchioness of Stade and Archbishop Henry of Mainz. But if, at the time, the way in which she obtained permission to move to Rupertsberg did not represent a clear-cut victory for Hildegard as prophetess, in retrospect it could be, and indeed was, considered to have helped establish her prophetic claims. In Hildegard's next battle, over the nun Richardis of Stade, we find Richardis's mother, the marchioness, and Henry of Mainz unexpectedly ranged on the opposing side, together with Archbishop Hartwig of Bremen and, ultimately, the pope. The facts of the matter seem fairly uncomplicated; the emotions engendered by them less so.

Richardis, it will be remembered, was the nun who stood by Hildegard during both the writing of the *Scivias* and the difficulties experienced in the early stages of the new foundation at Rupertsberg. The nature of the assistance Richardis gave in the writing of the *Scivias* is not described by Hildegard, although it seems likely that as well as moral support, Richardis may have acted as amanuensis when Hildegard was too ill to write herself.

Whatever the nature of her assistance, Hildegard resented its untimely removal when in 1151 Richardis was elected abbess of the Saxon foundation of Bassum in the diocese of Bremen, then held by her brother Hartwig. Hildegard's first letter in the exchange is to Richardis's mother. It is chiefly remarkable for the fact that it is written in her own persona and not as the word of God. The difference between this and the majority of Hildegard's letters is obvious from the opening words:

> I beg and warn you not to disturb my soul and draw bitter tears from my eyes and fill my heart with harsh wounds, on account of my dearest daughters Richardis and Adelheid.[2]

She has no hesitation, on the other hand, in declaring that the decision to make the girls abbesses 'clearly, clearly, clearly is not from God, nor pertains to their souls' health'. The marchioness is warned that she may bring ruin on the girls and sorrow to herself if she persists in this course.

Was there some impropriety in the elections, as Hildegard also seems to suggest? Although Adelheid (actually the marchioness's granddaughter) was extremely young – possibly not even professed at the time – Richardis herself must have been at least 28 years old, and on Hildegard's own admission, an exemplary nun. Of course, the proximity of Bassum to Bremen, where Hartwig was in bitter contention with Henry the Lion, may have suggested to Hildegard, among others, that considerations of *realpolitik* had entered into the election. Yet when Hildegard, in writing to Henry of Mainz, alludes to simoniacs, I do not think she is suggesting that Richardis was elected with bought votes, but rather that any ecclesiastical election against the manifest will of God renders its participants suspect of trafficking in the offices of the church.

This letter is a reply to the archbishop who had taken the precaution of writing to Hildegard to announce that messengers with his backing had come from Saxony to escort Richardis to her new post. Having apparently formed the impression that Hildegard might not relinquish her companion without a struggle, he added the warning:

> If you do this you will feel our pleasure, even more than hitherto. If not, however, we will demand it again more strongly and will not cease until you accord with our wishes in this matter.[3]

Hildegard's reply adopts from the outset a most uncompromising tone.[4] She begins her letter with the words: 'The pellucid fountain, which is not false, but just, says . . . ', thus indicating that it is God's word she is about to deliver and not her own. The message she has to convey is that Richardis's election has no standing in the eyes of God since it is the work of 'the conniving audacity of ignorant minds'. There follows a warning to bishops (*O pastores*) from the 'Spirit of God in his zeal' about the perversion of ecclesiastical offices. A change from the plural form of address to the singular signals the fact that the last part of the letter is addressed by 'Him who Is', specifically to Henry of Mainz. It contains a strongly worded, if rather cryptic rebuke:

> But arise since your time is short and remember how Nebuchadnezzar fell and how his crown perished. And many others have fallen who raised themselves boldly against Heaven.[5]

In this letter, unlike the one to Richardis's mother, Hildegard makes no personal appeals. In adopting the prophetic persona she insists on her divine source three times in the space of a brief letter, mingling judgements about the specific case with warnings which allude to a wider context.

Yet this tactic was apparently unsuccessful, since the next letter in the correspondence is from Hildegard to Hartwig of Bremen asking him to arrange for Richardis's return.[6] Here she puts the chief blame on 'a certain horrible person', apparently Abbot Kuno of Disibodenberg, together with Richardis's mother and the Count-palatine, Herman of Stahleck, rather than on Archbishop Hartwig, recognizing, perhaps, that he was also subject to family pressures. This letter, which lacks any formal prophetic indicators, begins

'O praiseworthy man' and continues in a tone of (qualified) intimacy, as she writes: 'My dear, your soul is greatly pleasing to me on account of your family'. Yet Hildegard's conviction that she knows God's will in the matter and that everyone else is going against it, remains unshaken.

Indeed, Hildegard maintains that God's plan for Richardis was a perpetuation of the status quo; that her destiny was to remain as her own collaborator and supporter. At the same time, she does seem willing to countenance some other position for Richardis at a future date, if she is willing to forego the present one and return to Rupertsberg forthwith. The closing words of the letter suggest that Hildegard's goodwill towards Hartwig is only provisional, when she writes:

> May God give you blessing from the dew of Heaven and all the choirs of angels bless you if you hear me, the handmaid of God, and if you carry out the will of God in this matter.

Having evidently failed to get her own way either by personal appeals or declarations of God's will, Hildegard wrote to the pope. Unfortunately this letter does not survive, so we do not know what approach she adopted. Clearly, however, Pope Eugenius wished to distance himself as far as possible from the dispute. His proviso about whether Richardis could adequately observe the Benedictine Rule at Bassum is a mere face-saving device, effectively putting the ball back into the archbishop of Mainz's court.[7]

The next letter, written by Hildegard to the nun Richardis, is a fascinating reflection of Hildegard's struggle to salvage something from her apparent defeat. In language which is, for Hildegard, intensely personal, meditative introspection alternates with lamentation. In the face of sustained lay and ecclesiastical opposition and the *fait accompli* of Richardis's removal, Hildegard seems, at least momentarily, to have doubted her apprehension of the will of God. And since this was the well-spring of Hildegard's way of dealing with the world, such a loss was even more threatening than that of Richardis. So we find in this letter Hildegard replacing her former certainty that the election was contrary to God's will, with a new one that in fact the election was contrived by God with the deeper purpose of displaying to Hildegard the vanity of earthly attachments. The logic of this situation demands that Hildegard reject such transitory affections, placing her gaze 'on God as the eagle on the sun' rather than on human nobility 'which fails just as the flower falls'.[8]

Yet this bleak analysis of the situation was clearly at odds with her experience and her feeling that there was something redeeming about her love for Richardis. Thus she writes: 'I loved the nobility of your behaviour, the wisdom and purity of your soul and your entire being.' Here Hildegard was obviously experiencing some of the paradoxes of human and divine love which received their definitive resolution in the contemporaneous *De spirituali amicitia* (*On Spiritual Friendship*) written by the English Cistercian, Aelred of Rievaulx.[9]

Indeed the reasons she gives for her attachment to Richardis were just those which were thought by Aelred to form the proper basis for spiritual friendship. It was, perhaps, fortunate for Hildegard that she evidently knew nothing of such a theology of friendship. If she had, it would have been harder to explain her failure to prevail. As it was, by localizing the fault within herself, and limiting it to a particular aspect of her behaviour, she was able to salvage her general position – that of God's confidante.

It was not long after this new equilibrium had been achieved, towards the end of 1152, that Hildegard received another letter from Hartwig, announcing the sudden death of his sister.[10] In it he assures Hildegard that Richardis had made a good end, and died

> having made a holy and pious confession . . . anointed with holy oil after the confession. . . . Committing herself to the Lord through his Mother and St John, thrice signed with the sign of the cross, believing in the unity and the Trinity in perfect faith, hope and charity.

He adds, moreover, that Richardis had shed many tears for her former cloister, having been about to make a visit to Hildegard when she was prevented by death.

Hildegard's reply to this letter has been much praised by scholars.[11] Yet, at the risk of sounding churlish, it must be pointed out that her generosity only became apparent when Richardis's death effectively put her out of reach of all contending parties and justified Hildegard's original stand. Gone is all thought of Hildegard's having been wrong in her attachment to Richardis, rather 'my heart was full of love for her since the living light taught me to love her in a most powerful vision'. That vision had showed Richardis among the virgin throng in heaven. So Hildegard had been justifiably worried lest Richardis were seduced from such high destiny by the worldly honours which her family connections had thrust upon her.

Now Hildegard can see Richardis's death as proof of God's special favour: 'But God loved her more. Therefore he did not wish to give his beloved to a rival lover, that is, the world.' Because of what happened, Hildegard was able to dispense with the idea that her separation from Richardis was intended by God as a rebuke. Now it seemed patently due to the malice of the 'old serpent', who wanted to deprive Richardis of the blessed place prepared for her.

In other words, as Hildegard had maintained throughout, with the exception of her moment of doubt in the letter to Richardis, the appointment had been a perversion of God's will, and she alone had recognized this. That her belief was vindicated in the end may go some way towards explaining why she was able to be magnanimous to Hartwig: 'Therefore I cast out the sorrow from my heart which you brought upon me, in the matter of my daughter.' Once again she was able to draw her prophetic mantle about her.

II

The last confrontation Hildegard had with her ecclesiastical superiors in 1178–9 was also the most serious. Since no mention is made of this incident in the *Vita*, the sequence of events has to be reconstructed from her letters and the *Acta*. The trouble arose over the burial at Rupertsberg of a man who had at one time been excommunicated. A few days after the burial, the clergy of Mainz, claiming that the sentence of excommunication had never been lifted, ordered the body to be disinterred and cast out of the cemetery, on pain of interdict. Hildegard believed that the man had been reconciled to the church before he died and cites the manner of his death and burial as 'confessed, anointed and having taken communion, and buried without anyone objecting'.

Faced with their decree, however, Hildegard consulted 'the living light' and was confirmed in her fear that to do as her superiors commanded would be highly dangerous. Rather than comply she concealed the grave. Then, although still believing that she held the moral initiative, she complied with the terms of the interdict. This meant that the nuns had to refrain from singing the divine office and were denied communion, a heavy deprivation.

After suffering this regime for some time, Hildegard felt compelled to take further action by appealing to her superiors in Mainz to restore the sacraments to her convent. The substance of her plea is contained in the letter headed 'To the Prelates of Mainz' in the Riesenkodex.[12] Failing in this effort to sway them, Hildegard returned home 'full of tears'. At this point Hildegard's friends intervened. Philip, Archbishop of Cologne, went to Mainz, bringing with him a certain knight who claimed to have been absolved at the same time as the man buried at Rupertsberg, together with the priest who had performed the deed.

Philip also seems to have taken it upon himself to lift the interdict, pending the return of Archbishop Christian of Mainz from Rome. However, soon after this a letter came from the archbishop himself, confirming the interdict and Hildegard felt bound to comply once more. This was the occasion of her second letter to Christian.

It was this appeal that finally obtained results. In a very diplomatic and conciliatory letter, Christian heaped praises on Hildegard and asked for the intervention of her prayers before answering her petition.[13] Here he attempts to rehabilitate his colleagues at Mainz in her eyes by pointing out that they were merely acting in her best interests 'so long as there was any uncertainty in their minds about his absolution'. Then in a manoeuvre much like that of Pope Eugenius in the Richardis dispute (but this time with a happier result), he says he has written to the clergy of Mainz, ordering them to allow the divine offices to be resumed if they are satisfied by witnesses about the status of the deceased. He closes his letter by requesting her forgiveness and expressing his hopes for a safe return to Mainz.[14]

Before examining the way in which Hildegard handled this dispute, we should ask whether the issues at stake were properly represented by the parties concerned. If we dismiss the possibility that Hildegard refused to exhume the body simply because to do so might have had adverse financial or social repercussions for her convent, how do we explain the position of the clergy of Mainz? It is true that since the intrusion of Christian of Buch into the see in 1165 and Hildegard's recognition of Pope Alexander, Rupertsberg and the Cathedral of Mainz had (until the schism was resolved in 1177) represented opposing loyalties. On the other hand, Hildegard numbered many prelates who supported the emperor among her friends and had accepted (indeed sought) a charter from Barbarossa at a time when he was already excommunicated. Moreover, Philip of Heinsberg, whose witnesses saved the day, was imperial chancellor and a frequent ambassador for the emperor.

Perhaps no animus was felt towards Hildegard, and the chief object of the clergy's displeasure was the deceased man himself. It is also possible that the prelates of Mainz were themselves acting in good faith and seeking to protect Hildegard from the dangers of having a suspected excommunicant buried within the monastery, as Christian suggested in his letter.

Yet Hildegard had good *a priori* reasons for believing that the man was no longer excommunicate when he died. She enumerates these in her letter to the prelates, her first salvo in the battle.[15] Thus her reaction – she describes herself as 'seized with great terror' – to their order to dig up the corpse is also understandable. Predictably, in the circumstances, Hildegard resorted to divine counsel to see whether the body should be exhumed. Her description of what happened is as follows:

> I looked, as is my wont, to the true light and saw in my soul with open eyes that if, according to their instruction, the body of this dead man be cast out, that act would threaten great danger to our place, like a great darkness, and the blackness of a cloud which presages storm and thunder would overcloud us.

Accordingly, Hildegard refrained from disturbing the body while avoiding direct confrontation with her superiors by accepting the interdict 'lest we be found entirely disobedient'. The grave consequences of this course of action should not be underestimated. Apart from the public shame involved, the interdict struck at the very foundations of monastic life, as Hildegard soon realized. Her feelings of 'great bitterness' and 'enormous sadness' which seemed like a heavy weight pressing on her, were followed by a vision.

Taken as a whole, the vision does not seem much concerned with the rights and wrongs of the particular case. In essence it is an explanation and defence of the high claims she makes for music and especially song, as an element in divine worship. She hopes, by the sheer force of her arguments for the primacy of divine praise, and the authority they derive 'from the living light', to put to shame those who would seek to curtail it in any way.

The first part of the vision deals with the nature and purpose of the mass. In it Hildegard hears the voice of God telling her not to neglect 'the sacrament of the Incarnation of the Word of God' for a mere human prohibition. Yet the voice does not recommend outright defiance, telling Hildegard rather to seek to have the interdict lifted. There follows an abbreviated version of the doctrine of redemption discussed at much greater length in *Scivias*. Because of the taint of original sin, only someone who partook of human nature but did not suffer this defilement could be man's defence against sin. Such a defence is to be periodically renewed by the sacrament of

179

communion. Those who are disobedient to God, like Adam, should be denied the sacrament, until, having performed a suitable penance, they are allowed by their pastors and masters (*magistri*) to partake once more.

Having dealt with the question of communion, Hildegard turns to that of the performance of the *Opus Dei*, the curtailment of which she apparently felt to be an even greater hardship. Although the nuns were permitted to repeat it in whispers, behind closed doors, she argues that this is, as well as a deprivation for her whole community, more importantly a slight to God. The argument, as told to her by the voice 'proceeding from the living light' once again hinges on the Fall of man. At the Fall man lost 'the voice like an angel's voice which he had in paradise' and the ability to hymn his Creator, which angels possess because of their 'spiritual natures'. The quality of Adam's voice before the Fall (and presumably Eve's, though she is not specifically mentioned), was such that 'mortal man in his infirmity could not possibly in any way bear its power and sonorousness'. Yet in order that God might not be completely deprived of the praise due to him from his creatures, he inspired prophets and other learned and holy men to compose psalms and hymns as well as to invent instruments to accompany such singing.

Not surprisingly, the nature of the instruments and the manner of singing held symbolic meanings for Hildegard. Even musical notation, represented by the Guidonian hand, reminds man that Adam was formed by the finger of God.[16] So too, the lyre mentioned in Psalms 32 and 91 with its lower note refers to the discipline of the body, while the higher ten-stringed psaltery reflects the aspirations of the soul.

In this way Hildegard shows that music and song have a high place in the divine plan, since they are 'rooted by the Holy Spirit in the Church'. Yet the argument does not rest here. As we saw in the dispute over Richardis of Stade, Hildegard was liable to attribute the (temporary) thwarting of God's plan to the machinations of the Devil. In that case, his attentions were directed at the individual. Here the claim is rather more general:

> When, however, the Devil, man's deceiver, heard that he had begun to sing by the inspiration of God and through this would be drawn to remember again the sweetness of the songs of the heavenly homeland, seeing the machinations of his guile coming to nothing, he was made frantic.

Thus Satan strove to pervert and prevent such divine praise by putting in the hearts of men 'evil suggestions and wicked thoughts or diverse attacks'. More to the point, he pursued the same end 'through dissension and scandals and unjust repression', perpetrated through 'the mouth of the Church'. So that no mistake can be made about the implications of this statement, Hildegard appends the following warning:

> Wherefore, you must strive with greatest vigilance, you and all prelates; before you close by your sentence the mouth of any church singing praise to God or you suspend it from offering or receiving the sacraments, you should carefully canvass the reasons why this is to be done.

Hildegard goes on to enumerate some of the unworthy motives which might move prelates to act in this way – 'indignation or an unjust movement of the mind or a desire for revenge' – thereby indicating her doubts about the purity of the motives of those who opposed her. After this pointed warning, a few more general considerations in favour of her argument are adduced, before she returns to her prophetic and minatory style. Here she declares that whoever silences the Church in its praise of God, without good reason, will themselves suffer the fitting punishment of being in turn deprived of the company of angels praising God in heaven. This can only be avoided if, in a striking reversal of roles, they perform 'true penance and humble satisfaction'.

Hildegard proceeds to warn particularly those who have the power to bind and loose, lest they 'open what should be closed and close what should be opened'. The concluding sentences of the letter maintain and extend the high prophetic tone. Once more she hears the voice speaking, though this time it produces only a menacing catechism designed to inculcate a proper fear of the Lord: 'Who created Heaven? God. Who opens Heaven to his faithful? God. Who is like him? No one.' In conclusion Hildegard alludes to a theme which she has treated at greater length elsewhere: 'This time is a womanish time because the righteousness of God is weak.' There is no reason to think that she intends to exclude the prelates of Mainz from implication in this state of affairs, or herself from the closing sentence where she writes: 'But the strength of the justice of God prevails with difficulty and there emerges a virago [*bellatrix*] against unrighteousness in its overthrow and destruction.'[17]

So the arguments by which Hildegard hoped to convince the

clergy of Mainz to restore the divine office to Rupertsberg consisted of a mixture of philosophical speculations on the nature and place of sacred music in the divine economy, leading to the conclusion that its performance should only be prohibited on impeccable grounds, together with the suggestion that in the case of the Rupertsberg interdict such grounds were lacking. The whole of the foregoing argument was presented to Hildegard by means of her vision. Moreover, the strictures about unjust judgements and the awesome responsibilities of those who have the power to bind and loose, combined with the heightened ending of the piece, clearly suggest that Hildegard was trying, by the means she knew best, to intimidate her superiors into changing their decision. Yet the attempt failed.

Then Hildegard, proving her adaptability once more, tried another tack. If the clergy were blind to her arguments and preferred to conduct the case on legalistic lines, she could match them at this. Thus the witnesses found by Philip of Cologne were brought in and were apparently accepted by all parties. The ban was then lifted and there the matter would have rested, save for the vexing arrival of Christian's letter, which forced Hildegard to write to him again. The letter she wrote on this occasion, although describing what happened and the part played in the process by the living light, does not reproduce the arguments which failed to convince the prelates of Mainz.[18]

In this confrontation, as in the earlier ones, Hildegard's strategy was to attempt to convert others to her point of view by claiming knowledge of the divine will, as against their ignorance or possible malevolence. One difference between the earlier and the later cases is the more explicit demonstration of her prophetic powers in the latter instance. Whereas in her letters to Henry of Mainz and the von Stade connection she was content to assert her privileged status, in her letter to the prelates of Mainz she expounded her vision in a form which would also have reminded them of her other prophetic works. Here she not only claims the powers of a prophet, but demonstrates them. Yet when she failed to get her way by such means she was quite prepared to countenance other methods.

This last dispute indicates both the advantages and disadvantages of the prophetic role in an adversarial situation. Even if her antagonists were prepared to admit her claims in a general way, or with regard to her major writings, it was also possible for them to hold that she was mistaken in the particular case at issue. Perhaps even the lack of observable phenomena accompanying her visions made her claims for their divine origin easier to ignore when greater issues were at stake. Moreover, the sanctions that Hildegard could apply to those who proved resistant to her point of view were limited.

It is hard to assess the subjective effect of the warnings and threats with which she peppers her letters. Did her allusion to the fall of Nebuchadnezzar produce a *frisson* in Henry of Mainz? Did her warnings about the fate of those who resist the will of God give the clergy of Mainz cause to think again? Whatever their immediate shock value, their long-term coercive effects were not great. It seems, in fact, that Hildegard's use of the prophetic persona in adversarial situations was never in itself sufficient to prevail over the opposition. In the confrontations that she won, there was usually some other factor involved which tended to strengthen her claims. Often it was the manifestation of some illness, as in the case of the financial settlement at Disibodenberg or the proposed move to Rupertsberg.

Why, then, did Hildegard continue to use her prophetic persona even when it offered no guarantee of success? It is here that the peculiar strength of the position she adopted becomes apparent. Hildegard persisted because no rebuff by mortal man could undermine her faith in herself. To those who proved obdurate she had a ready answer: they were spiritually blind, to take the charitable view, of worse, led astray by the Devil.

Where such rationalizations could not be employed Hildegard was able to entertain the idea that some fault in herself was interfering with the way things ought to be. Thus at one stage in the Richardis affair Hildegard, while still maintaining that the move to Bassum was against God's will in an absolute sense, saw its accomplishment as a particular rebuke to herself and so continued to recognize it as God's plan. When Richardis died, Hildegard was able to make a triumphant reassertion of her knowledge of the divine will and her championing of it throughout the case.

Thus, while the belief in her prophetic powers could not be undermined by mere human opposition and indeed appeared to be confirmed in many cases by events, it served another purpose. The shifts to which Hildegard was prepared to resort to maintain her own belief in her prophetic persona suggest that it served a psychological rather than a polemical purpose.

The way Hildegard used her prophetic role in her life paralleled her use of it in her writings. Her conviction that she was privy to God's will gave her the courage to assert herself where she might otherwise have hesitated, and to stand up to her superiors when she thought they were in the wrong. In cases where there was a clear legal remedy she was prepared to appeal to it, but not without also insisting on her superior knowledge of God's intentions.

But her faith in her infallible spiritual rectitude was even more essential in situations which did not hinge on legalistic determinations, as in the case of her move to Rupertsberg, her financial arrangements with Disibodenberg, and the Richardis affair. Even in the matter of the excommunicant, where the alternatives presented to Hildegard seemed clear, her decision to reject them both and hold out for a third way could not have been reached without an inner struggle.

In many cases such conflict was accompanied by some form of physical illness, which was felt by Hildegard to be God's way of ensuring that she should perform what had been commanded. The close connection in Hildegard's mind between the vision which showed her the course to follow, and the illness which compelled her to pursue it, is indicated by such statements as 'in a true vision of my soul from the highest Judge, whose precepts I have not dared to resist, compelled by the weight of a very grave illness, I came to our prelates of Mainz' (Van Acker, 24) with which she tended to explain her actions. In the next chapter I shall examine further the interaction between Hildegard's physical states of health and her visions.

10

POTENT INFIRMITIES

And she suffered this kind of illness . . . whenever she delayed or doubted to perform the business of the heavenly will through womanly fear. (*Vita*, Bk 1)

We have already seen that many of Hildegard's contemporaries thought of her as a prophet, empowered to know and make known the '*secreta Dei*', whether past, present, or future. Hildegard, too, assiduously promoted herself in this role, both in her writings and in her daily dealings with others. That her prophetic role was no mere literary device is most clearly evident in the personal and institutional confrontations described in chapter 9. Her maintenance of this stand in the face of its obvious lack of success as a bargaining position, together with the positive shifts to which she resorted in order to safeguard her prophetic integrity (such as her changes of position in the Richardis case) suggest a very strongly-held belief – one might almost say, an article of faith. Like other articles of faith, it provided psychological benefits for Hildegard, giving her the courage and authority to act in ways which would otherwise have been difficult, perhaps impossible, for reasons of status, education, and gender.

In all her public pronouncements Hildegard claimed to be acting as God's mouthpiece rather than expressing her own thoughts and opinions. The benefits of such a course of action might seem obvious, as also the temptation to identify one's own will with the will of God. In this case, Hildegard's appeal to her privileged source of authority could be seen as cynically manipulative in her personal dealings and intellectually dishonest in her writings. That such doubts about her integrity have not been more generally expressed is probably because her eventual enrolment among the saints has, to some extent, insulated her from vulgar historical scrutiny.

185

Still, the issue cannot be dismissed out of hand. Since the basis of Hildegard's conception of herself as a prophet was her 'vision', we must start with a closer examination of this phenomenon. The first thing to note here is that her use of the word '*visio*' is as ambiguous and hard to grasp as are some of the visions themselves. It seems, for instance, that Hildegard sometimes employs the word to refer to the experience of the vision (the act of seeing), and sometimes to denote what is seen by this means. It is often hard to decide between the two senses and quite possibly Hildegard herself did not intend to make a clear distinction. Thus her most commonly used phrase '*in vera visione . . . vidi*' could be read as either 'by means of true visionary experience . . . I saw', or 'in a true vision [object-specific] . . . I saw'. The same goes for Hildegard's use of such formulae as '*in vero lumine*', and '*in vera luce*', which she uses in contexts which seem interchangeable with those of the 'vision' formulae. Here we might ask whether Hildegard implies that the light is what she saw, or rather the means by which she apprehended the vision. Once again, the experience of seeing the light is hard to separate from the light itself.

In terms of what was seen, the visions fall into several distinct types. The simplest seems to have been an experience of a great light or brightness, often accompanied by a speaking voice. Hildegard recalls her first visionary experience in the following way: 'In the third year of my life I saw such a great light that my soul quaked, but because I was an infant I could reveal nothing of it.' So too, the vision that led to the writing of the *Scivias* was apprehended, at least in the first instance, as 'a great splendour, in which there was a voice from Heaven speaking to me'. Many of her letters appear to refer to the same sort of experience or same type of vision – a heavenly voice emanating from, or accompanied by, an intense experience of light. Indeed, although the word '*vidi*' ('I saw') is often used, the voice seems in many cases to be the main element. The connection between seeing and hearing in Hildegard's visions may well have been one of 'synaesthesia', where there is a transference between the senses – colour, for example, being experienced as sound.

But the visions which Hildegard describes in her extended written works are not of this simple kind, although simple visions may form the initial stage of a more complex vision. The visions described in Hildegard's theological works are filled with complex, highly-coloured images of mountains, buildings, composite animals, people, denizens of heaven, and representations of the cosmos and the Deity. Sometimes the visions appear as static tableaux and sometimes as dynamic processes, complete with speech and movement. What relationship, if any, existed between the two kinds of vision?

In the 1170s similar questions exercised the monk Guibert of Gembloux, who wrote to Hildegard seeking definitive answers.[1] Her reply seems to confirm some of the conclusions reached by a study of her usage of the terms in other letters and writings. For instance, she seems to identify the visionary experience (*visio*) with the light present in, or to, her soul.

Hildegard's account of the location of this light is ambivalent. At times it appears to be external, presumably from heaven, like the voice, or at least somewhere outside Hildegard. At other times it seems to be located inside her, particularly 'in her soul'. Hildegard refused to be pinned down on this question, declaring that the light had no location and no measurable extent. Yet it seems probable that this light is to be identified with the vision which Hildegard claims to have seen from her infancy 'in my soul up to the present time'. The light, however, presented itself to her in two forms. The first, of which she was always conscious (in the sense of being able to address it at will) she calls the '*umbra viventis luminis*', 'the shadow of the living light'. This, she says, 'my soul does not lack at any time'.

The relationship between this light and her more elaborate visions is that their various elements appear reflected in it, just as the heavenly bodies are reflected in the water. Indeed, Hildegard sometimes speaks as if the light is a kind of reflecting pool or even a mirror, and often refers to the source of her knowledge by water imagery. The words that she hears are not audible in the usual sense, but are presented to her understanding 'like flashing flames and clouds moving in the pure air'. Furthermore, the apprehension by which she understands what she sees and hears, is both immediate – 'I see and hear and understand at one and the same time' – and more or less permanent. Thus she is able to record and elaborate her works over many years.

She also claims to produce answers for her correspondents from this light. But if this is only the 'shadow of the living light', why do so many of her letters refer to the '*lux vivens*', the living light itself, or some equivalent, as the source of the answer, rather than its shadow or reflection? It seems that Hildegard used this phrase as a kind of personal shorthand, only spelling out the relationship between the two in her letter to Guibert. Here she writes that the 'living light' is immanent in that light which she calls the shadow of the living light.

The light itself she is only able to glimpse occasionally, but when she does, the experience fills her with joy. She writes:

And in that light occasionally and infrequently I see another light, which I have been told is the living light, and I am unable to say when and how I see it, and while I apprehend it, all sadness and all pain is lifted from me, so that then I feel like a simple girl and not an old woman.[2]

Since this light is the ultimate source of her knowledge, she can describe herself as giving answers 'from the blaze of the living light'. It is for this reason that she describes herself as directing her gaze to the living light. Even if she cannot be sure of seeing it every time, she knows that the things she does apprehend will appear in its shadow.

In the same letter to Guibert, Hildegard also makes a definitive statement about the circumstances in which she sees her visions. She sees them fully awake and conscious, but not by means of her bodily senses:

I hear these things not with the bodily ears, nor the thoughts of my mind, nor perceive them through any combination of the five senses, but entirely within my soul, with my external eyes open, so that I never suffer a lapse into ecstasy, but I see them fully conscious by day or night.

Hildegard was particularly anxious to deny that her visions were obtained from dreams. This is not surprising, considering the theory of dreams she propounds in *Causae et curae*. Here she describes the thoughts and emotions felt during the day as working like yeast in the sleeping mind and giving rise to further thoughts. Sometimes God can indicate true things by this means, but often the Devil takes a hand, introducing falsity and temptations into the mix.[3] She also makes a point of denying that her visions come through dreams in the prefaces of the *Scivias* and the *Liber divinorum operum*. She was equally adamant that she remained fully conscious throughout her visions with no diminution of her normal faculties.[4] Guibert of Gembloux, by asking Hildegard whether she experiences her visions in dreams or by means of trances, seems to envisage only these two possibilities.

In order to see what Hildegard was distinguishing herself from, we might look more closely at the experiences of Elisabeth of Schönau (b. 1129), her younger contemporary and (to some extent) protégée.

This is how Elisabeth described the typical onset of one of her visions:

Then when the Mass of Our Lady the Blessed Virgin was begun, it being Sunday, I fell into an ecstasy, and my heart was opened, and I saw above the air . . .

Her brother, Eckbert, who recorded the accounts of her visions, describes her as showing no signs of life – apparently not even breathing – when in such a trance.[5]

Another point of difference between Hildegard's descriptions of her visions and those of Elisabeth of Schönau is the comparative degree of reality which the objects of the vision had for each woman. Although neither writer discusses this particular aspect of her experience, significant differences in the way they experienced their visions are evident from their writings. The difference, in its most pronounced form, is that between vision and hallucination. Hildegard is generally somewhat distanced from the objects of her vision, which are almost like images projected on a screen before her. The images are not localized by reference to Hildegard herself. They do not occupy the same physical space as the visionary. Her references to directions – north, south, east, and west – are only relative to the visionary scene itself. She often employs the words 'like' or 'just as' in connection with what she sees. Hildegard is an observer who has little interaction with the figures which people her visions. Since she retained her ordinary bodily sensations, there was no danger of mistaking the nature of her experience.

With Elisabeth the case was quite different. Since her normal senses were overwhelmed by her vision, she sometimes shows herself uncertain about how to classify what she sees. On one occasion, for instance, she sees a rainbow, 'solely with the intuition of the mind' but asks to be able to view it 'even with the eyes of the body' so that the spiritual nature of the experience might be reinforced for her (*Visionen*, 10). Sometimes, indeed, she is doubtful about the source of the vision, as in the case of a dove which she fears might be a diabolical manifestation. She is reassured when it perches on a crucifix, since she knows that a devil would flee its presence (*Visionen*, 8). (Her demonology was less sophisticated than Hildegard's, who recognized the insufficiency of such a sign with certain kinds of devil, for instance the one who afflicted Sigewize.) This account also shows how in Elisabeth's case the apparitions occupy the same physical space as the seer and indeed interact with real objects.

Elisabeth describes an even clearer case of hallucination which she experienced when in the grip of a severe fever. She wished for extreme unction, but had to await her abbot's return from a visit to a neighbouring place. At about dusk

> when my mistress was sitting with me, a venerable man came in and stood where I could see him and thinking it was my abbot, I was glad. (*Visionen*, 31)

Elisabeth then chides him for being late, asks him to recite the Lord's Prayer and creed over her and anoint her. When the rite has been performed he gives his blessing and departs. When her mistress, who has heard her speaking, asks what is going on, Elisabeth records that she replied:

> Was not my Lord Abbot here and did he not anoint me? But she swore she saw no one there. Then I understood for the first time that I had seen a spiritual vision.

Even in the later books of her visions, where Hildegard's own influence becomes more apparent, Elisabeth seems to participate much more in her visions than does Hildegard. So we read:

> the angel of the Lord took me to another place of most cheerful pleasantness, and set me under a tree, which was covered with most beautiful flowers. Soon I sat on the grass and picked a handful of flowers, which were lying all around me. (*Visionen*, 46)

If Hildegard's visions were not of this overtly hallucinatory kind, we must next ask to what altered state of consciousness they belong. In some ways the visions claimed by Elisabeth of Schönau are more readily explained, since the neurophysiological causes of hallucinatory states, whether induced by ascetic practices, disease, or drugs, are relatively well known. However, since Charles Singer first made the suggestion (see his *Studies in the History and Method of Science*, Oxford, 1951), it has become something of a medical, although not a hagiographical, orthodoxy to claim Hildegard among other distinguished sufferers from migraine. Indeed, illustrations from the Eibingen manuscript of the *Scivias* form the cover of a recent popular work on the subject. Two questions now arise. The first is whether Hildegard's descriptions of her visions accord with accounts of migrainous phenomena. If they do, the second question is whether the visions are then reducible to this physiological cause.

The conclusions reached on these questions must obviously have a significant bearing on our interpretation of Hildegard.

Singer's original identification of what he took to be 'scintillating scotomata' in the manuscript illustrations to the *Scivias* led him to suggest that Hildegard's visions contained elements derived from migrainous experiences.[6] (While it is unlikely that Hildegard was her own illustrator, the possibility of such features being introduced at this stage from the illuminator's experience is not great, since it is generally agreed that the pictures bear a very close relationship to the text.) Yet Singer's approach was not wholly reductive in the sense that he thought Hildegard's visions were nothing more than a record of her medical condition. On the contrary, he went to the opposite extreme in claiming that Hildegard used the visionary form as a literary device, albeit one suggested by her experience of migraine. It is thus somewhat ironic that his account is often criticized for concentrating on the 'pathological basis of the visions' rather than their intellectual content, especially when he was one of the earliest commentators to recognize the *Pastor Hermas* (*The Shepherd of Hermas*) as a source for parts of the *Scivias*. But to see the visionary form as no more than a literary device does greatly strain Hildegard's credibility, and leads to the conclusion that the circumstantial details with which she bolsters her visionary and prophetic claims are merely factitious.

I believe that Singer's suggestions about the place of migraine in Hildegard's work, far from being too reductive, do not go far enough or in the right direction in linking other aspects of Hildegard's life and work with this underlying explanatory factor. In order to redress the balance some discussion of the nature of migraine will be necessary. For our purposes an understanding of the biochemical nature of the mechanisms at work in a migraine attack is not essential. Indeed, the current state of medical opinion on the matter is not unanimous. My approach will be phenomenological, concentrating on the ways in which the condition affects its sufferers. To this end I have drawn largely on the material provided by Oliver Sacks in his analysis of the case histories of migraine sufferers.[7]

At this point the reader may feel that the migraine theory is inherently unlikely, since no mention has been made, in connection with Hildegard's illnesses, of headaches. However, the identification of migraine with headache is apparently a common mistake, and not only of laymen. In his *Migraine: Understanding a Common Disorder*, Sacks wrote:

I thought of migraine as a peculiar type of headache, no more and no less. As I saw more patients, it became apparent to me that headache was never the sole feature of a migraine, and, later still, that it was not even a necessary feature of all migraine. (xvii)

In discussions of migraine two basic types are generally distinguished: the common and the classical migraine. It is possible for the same person to experience both types, either at different stages of his or her life or concurrently. From the descriptions of her illnesses it seems that Hildegard was such a person.

Sacks describes the migraine as a sequence consisting of 'prodromal stages, "attack proper", resolution, and rebound'. Symptoms characterizing the prodromal stage may be physical (thirst, water retention, constipation) and/or emotional (hyperactivity, insomnia, emotional arousal, irritability). These merge imperceptibly into the attack proper which is marked by vascular headache, nausea, weakness, drowsiness, and depression. The resolution of the attack may come in sleep or by 'lysis', a gradual lessening of the symptoms. Alternatively, the attack may pass through a 'crisis', typified by a sudden burst of physical or mental activity which brings it to an end. Some migraines are followed by a rebound phase which leaves the patient feeling even better than before the attack.

The classical migraine can be distinguished from the common form by the nature of the prodromal phase or 'migraine aura'. Sacks lists the following symptoms, which may be present at different times during the phase or occur together:

(i) specific visual, tactile and other sensory hallucinations;
(ii) general alterations of threshold and excitability;
(iii) alterations in levels of consciousness and muscular tone;
(iv) alterations of mood and affect;
(v) disorders of higher integrative functions: perception, ideation, memory and speech (ibid., 59).

It should be noted here that Sacks uses 'hallucinations' in a more attenuated sense than usual, which does not weaken the distinction drawn between Hildegard's visions and those of Elisabeth of Schönau. Writing of the 'pseudo-objectivity' of migraine hallucinations, he comments 'there exists even in the most sophisticated patients a *tendency* to objectivise the sensations of the aura' (ibid., 76).

Although any number of visual hallucinations may occur in the course of a migraine aura, some visual effects seem to be specific to it and are not encountered, for example, in an epileptic aura. These are the so-called 'scotomata' which often follow the perception of phosphenes in the visual field. They are sometimes called 'migraine spectra' because of their shape and colour, or 'scintillating scotomata' because of their characteristic flickering (estimated to be at a rate of something like 10 per second). They have also been called 'fortification spectra', because of the castellated structure of their margins, which are said to be 'reminiscent of the ramparts of a walled city'.[8] Scintillating scotomata are also associated (either before or after their passage) with areas of total blindness in the visual field. Such phenomena were detected by Singer in 'the extinguished stars vision' in the third book of the *Scivias*.

But even such an apparently clear-cut example contains elements which are not explicable in terms of a simple procession of phosphenes. The first problem concerns the extent and nature of the visions themselves and the relationship between the illustrations and the written accounts of what Hildegard saw (or says she saw). Although it was the illustrations of the Wiesbaden codex that alerted Singer to the migrainous origins of the visions, they should not be viewed in isolation from the text.

Let us take an example. The first vision of the third book of the *Scivias* is illustrated by two miniatures, the second of which is the 'extinguished stars' vision. The first illustration depicts a bearded male figure, dressed in a blue gown, green mantle, and red and gold cope, sitting on a golden throne with his feet on a red and gold cloud above a set of concentric circles of varying shades of blue. It is only by a willing suspension of disbelief that the figure on the throne can be assimilated to a play of scotomata. Yet when we turn to the written description of the vision we find:

> and there I saw . . . a round kingly throne on which sat a certain living light of wondrous glory, of such brilliance that I could in no way apprehend him clearly . . . and from that light seated on the throne there extended a great circle of colour like the dawn. (*Scivias*, 3, 1)

So here the illustration contains elements of interpretation and iconography which appear to be much more concrete than they were in Hildegard's description.[9] What was to her a brilliant but undefined light has become a traditional representation of God sitting like a king on his throne. Where we could easily allow that Hildegard

The manuscript text to the right of the illustration is in medieval Latin script that is largely illegible.

prima uisio tertie partis:

EGO
homo
sumpta
ab alus
homm
uisque
ñ sudig
na nomi

nari homo ppr̄ tñsgreshionē legis
di̅ cū deberem ē uisia & sum inuisia.
ñ q̄d di creatura sum ipsi grā. que
me eria saluabit uidi adorientem.
& ecce illic conspexi uelut lapidem
unū torū integrū unse latitudi
nis atq̄ altitudinis. habentē ferreū
colorē. & sup ipsum candidā nube.
ac sup ea posirū regalem tronum ro
tundū inquo sedebat quidā uiuen
lucidus mirabilis glē tanteq̄ clarita
tis ut nullatenī eū pspicue possem
inueri. habens q̄si in pectore suo li
mū nigrū & luculentū tanteq̄ lati
tudinis ut alicui magni hominis
pectus ē. circūdatū lapidib̄ pciofis
atq̄ margaritis. Et de ipso lucido
sedente in trono prendebat magnus
circulus aurei coloris ut aurora. cui
amplitudinē nullom cōphendere
potui. quani ab oriente ad septentio
nē & ad occidentē atq̄ ad meridiem.

9 Extinguished stars. An instance of scintillating scotomata? *Scivias*, 3, 1,
Eibingen MS.

194

i. Quod corda fideliu timore & uene xvi. Qd gia splendoris illi que diabo
tari debet magnitudine. latitu lus p supbia pdidit: seruata e ille
dine. atcitudine timoris dni. creto patris alii facti luce.

ii. Quod omis fidelis anima sapienti xvii. Qd diabolus accidit absq, herede.
tinens dnm p fide sedes dci e. homo aut accidit habens herede.

iii. Quod pfunditas misteriorum dei xviii. Exemplu de goliath & de dauid
hominib; incopjhensibilis e n qm ad candem rem.
tu ipso donante fide concipit.

iiii. Qd in sapientia di patris p amo
re filii siu pfecto oinium elec
torū coputata e.

v. Qd exemplu metiglio de eade re.

vi. Qd significet luceus unis specto
re. & cur homo ab anglo risper.

vii. Verba ysaie ad eande re. § nat.

viii. Verba dauid.

viiii. Qd ds pat in filio sio ab autora
ungine incarnato. opat ordi
nat. ac pficit omia opa sia.

x. Vo e circulo gtiante.

xi. Qd potestas di altior e qm homi
nu eiendu sit. & cur angli lau
dent dm.

xii. Quod ds e pspicua iusticia. uer
& iustus absq, comutatione.

xiii. Qd uirtus iusticia. & iudicii diuid
tum fine habet qui cophendi pos
sit humano sensu.

xiiii. Vo e casu pmi angli & sibi consentien
tib. & qre. & quom. & q acciderunt.

xv. Verba ezechielis de eadem re.

10 The living light enthroned. *Scivias*, 3, 1, Eibingen MS.

experienced the first as part of a migraine aura, the second might give us pause.

Migraine sufferers, however, do sometimes interpret the phenomena of the aura as formed images. Selby, in commenting on this tendency, notes:

> the fact that Hildegard was a mystic and a highly imaginative writer may help to explain why the majority of our patients do not describe similar experiences.[10]

But this is perhaps putting the cart before the horse.

Are we then, with Singer, to recognize the migrainous origin of the visions but to conclude that they bear little relationship to their source, thus relegating much of Hildegard's evidence about her writings to the realm of pious fraud? I believe the relationship between her experience and her writings is both more and less direct and one which indeed owes much of its characteristic ambiguity to the nature of the migraine experience. Although Sacks's book is useful for its illustrations of particular clinical aspects of migraine, his insight into the overall understanding of the condition is even more fruitful for a study of Hildegard.

Sacks outlined his approach to the topic in the preface to the book, describing it as 'simultaneously envisaging migraine as a *structure* whose forms were implicit in the repertoire of the nervous system, and as a *strategy* which might be employed to any emotional, or indeed biological, end' (*Migraine*, xviii). I have earlier suggested that various episodes of illness in Hildegard's life seem to have been used in this strategic way. The task now is to see whether they fit the overall migraine picture. Therefore we must examine further the relationship between Hildegard's visions and her reported illnesses.

Hildegard's description of her health as a child exhibits several features typical of migraine sufferers. They include the early onset of the condition and the picture of her generally 'delicate' constitution. We might surmise that in childhood Hildegard suffered from isolated migraine auras (that is, manifestations not followed by an attack proper) and common migraines or possibly migraine equivalents which she did not connect specifically with her visions. As she reached middle age, however, there was some change in the pattern of her illness, or in her perception of it, which she describes in several different contexts. The simplest possibility is that the earlier mixture of isolated migraine auras and common migraines coalesced to give Hildegard her first experience of a classical migraine. Such shifts in the overall pattern of the disease throughout a sufferer's life are well attested.

The autobiographical portion of the *Vita* suggests a close connection between the vision of 1141 and the illness which forced Hildegard to reveal it, when she writes: 'In that same vision I was forced by a great pressure of pains to manifest plainly what I had seen and heard.' Her account in the *Scivias* introduction suggests a more extended sequence. Here she says, 'But I . . . not out of stubbornness, but in humility, refused to undertake the writing, until I fell into a sickness, cast down by the scourge of God.' A classical migraine attack lasting up to thirty-six hours is not unknown, and might well be apprehended as 'the scourge of God'. That the attack was terminated when Hildegard decided to take positive action suggests the 'crisis' resolution described above. Finally, Hildegard seems to refer to the 'rebound' reaction when she writes about 'arising from my illness with my strength restored'.

Besides a change in the pattern of her illness, the vision of 1141 marked a change in the way Hildegard perceived her visions. The change in perception may have been implicit in the experience itself or, if it was her first experience of a classical migraine, brought about by the physical sequel to the vision. In the preface to the *Scivias*, Hildegard describes a sudden access of understanding. What she understands has a strongly theological colouring, which is not surprising given her position and the surroundings in which she had lived since childhood. This characteristic also has a place in the migraine theory. Thus Sacks:

> Among the strangest and most intense symptoms of migraine aura, and the most difficult of description or analysis, are the occurrence of feelings of sudden familiarity and certitude . . . or its opposite. . . . Such states are experienced, momentarily and occasionally, by everyone; their occurrence in migraine auras [as in epileptic auras, psychoses, etc.] is marked by their overwhelming intensity and relatively long duration. (*Migraine*, 89)

It was, I believe, such a combination of factors that finally allowed Hildegard to capitalize on her accumulated visionary experience by recording it in written form. Significantly, the early parts of the *Scivias* contain visions which can be closely linked with migraine aura effects, are relatively discontinuous, and are interpreted by Hildegard in terms of fairly basic Christian teachings. It seems likely that in her first theological work Hildegard was drawing on a series of different aura experiences which led up to the major integrative episode described in the *Scivias* introduction. This is also suggested by her words in the *Vita*, Book 2: 'then in that vision I was compelled . . . to show forth what I saw and heard; but I was greatly afraid and embarrassed to offer what I had kept silent for so long'.

The employment of material accumulated over the years may also explain the lack of structure of the *Scivias* compared with Hildegard's later works. It seems also to reflect a less mediated or less refined interpretation of actual visual experiences. How close does this come to saying that, henceforth, everything Hildegard thought was interpreted by her as coming from God? Was it, as Newman writes, simply that

> when she took stylus and wax tablets in hand, she did not under-stand herself to be thinking, imagining, inventing or composing at all. Unversed in the subtleties of modern psychology or hermeneutics, she was simply 'writing the words and visions that [were] revealed to her'. (*Sister of Wisdom*, p. 248)

Hildegard could certainly distinguish between human invention (*adinventio mentis*) and divine inspiration and was careful to make all her public writings and pronouncements dependent on the latter. This was not, however, because she lacked modern psychological under-standing or was ignorant of medieval epistemology, but because of her particular neurophysiological makeup. She was careful never to take stylus and wax tablets in hand until she had a vision to reveal.

Supposing that Hildegard was preoccupied with a particular problem, such as the role of the priesthood, it seems likely that she would tend to interpret any particular migraine experience she had at the time as related to this problem. Moreover, once she was convinced of the divine source, and symbolic and allegorical nature of her visionary experiences, the harder it would be to separate the raw data of the experience from her subsequent, but sometimes more or less immediate, interpretation.

This tendency to interpret such an experience, or even to precipitate an attack, in connection with a current preoccupation is indicated by other events in Hildegard's life. An example is her decision to move to Rupertsberg. The references in the *Vita* to the physical strains caused by overcrowding of the nuns' quarters at Disibodenberg suggest that it was no sudden whim. We can only guess at the psychological strains occasioned by Hildegard's increasing fame.

The illness which followed the revelation of God's plan for the move seems to have been of some duration and to have been marked by different stages. The immediate effect of the vision was apparently partial blindness, accompanied by paralysis and pain – effects which can also be attributed to the aftermath of a severe migraine. In Hildegard's account her sight returned when she told what she had seen, although the paralysis persisted for some time.

The task of identifying each illness described by Hildegard as a manifestation of migraine is greatly helped by its protean forms. Thus the thirty-day illness where Hildegard's death was thought to be imminent can be accommodated to the pattern of the disease, as can the symptom she describes in the words 'my innards burned with the heat of the airy fire'. Once again, the vision she experienced at this stage had much to do with her current concerns, including the problem of the disaffected nuns.

A further insight into Hildegard's visionary methodology may be gained from her description of the events which preceded the writing of the *Liber divinorum operum*. There seems little doubt that when she writes of the event: 'I saw a marvellous and mystic vision such that my inmost core was convulsed and I lost all bodily sensation' (*Vita*, Bk 2), she is describing an example of migraine syncope or loss of consciousness. The vision that accompanied this was interpreted by Hildegard as a partial glimpse and anticipation of a work she would be called upon to write in the future. No doubt this knowledge served to prepare her mind for the next visitation. About this time news of the demoniac Sigewize reached Rupertsberg; Hildegard turned her attention to the problem of the ways of demons and was favoured with a vision on the subject which allowed her to direct the exorcism.

In the last decade of Hildegard's life, the migraines could be seen as clustering together, as they had earlier in the lengthy illness of 1158–61. Thus the illness which she describes as lasting for six months was probably not continuous, since she was able to recognize within it several different visions and, more importantly, was able to make visits to other religious establishments in order to deliver her messages.

In this way the genesis of Hildegard's major visionary works, as well as the feeling of being coerced to make them public, can be attributed to her own particular neuro-physiological profile. Their random occurrence, leading to the false start on the *Liber divinorum operum* and minor works interrupting the writing of major ones, also supports a migraine theory. But what of the cases where she claims to have looked to the living light in order to secure an answer for a particular questioner? A possible explanation is that Hildegard saved up such questions till she found herself experiencing a migraine attack or isolated migraine aura. Given the apparent frequency of these occurrences this seems a reasonable assumption. It might also explain why some correspondents complained of delay or even a complete lack of response to their questions. Thus the monks of the Cistercian monastery of Villers, near Gembloux, sent a series of thirty-eight questions to Hildegard through their friend Guibert of Gembloux. Subsequent letters show their increasing impatience as the answers were not forthcoming. Eventually Hildegard provided answers to some of the questions but not the full set.

On the other hand, Hildegard claimed that the living light was always with her. Possibly we could interpret this as meaning that by the time she made this assertion, Hildegard had discovered a technique for tapping the source of her knowledge at will. Whether this means she could produce an aura of the elementary 'photism' kind, or simply that she was so convinced of the reality of her source of knowledge that a conscientious meditation on the question produced the subjective effect of a migraine, is impossible to say. It does mean, however, that Hildegard's claims to be able to provide answers from the living light to particular problems need not be dismissed as charlatanism, however well-intentioned.

So far, the analysis of Hildegard's visions and illnesses in terms of the migraine theory has given coherence and credibility to what might otherwise be though of as a random collection of rather unlikely episodes. But while such experiences might make someone a visionary (though on the whole, according to medical case histories, they do not), the step from visionary to prophet is not automatic.

As the description of Hildegard's writings has shown, her interests were intellectual rather than mystical. She sought to understand the world in all its aspects, natural, human, and divine – or, to put it another way, she sought to understand the divine in its human and natural aspects. Understanding and explanation were her aims, rather than union with or assimilation to the Godhead. But as well as understanding, Hildegard wanted to change the world: in a general sense, by making public her knowledge and understanding of God's ways for man's salvation in her writings, and more particularly, by recommending certain attitudes and positions. To these ends the migraine experience was a wonderfully adaptable instrument, as was Hildegard herself. Let us look more closely at how the two interacted.

Hildegard's account in the *Vita* of her migraine experiences as a child suggests that they were not understood or used by her in any positive way. Rather, they were a cause of embarrassment and inconvenience. It was only during her adolescence that she began to understand their privileged nature. The positive attitude towards her experiences was no doubt aided by Jutta's and Volmar's acceptance, although as yet Hildegard was not confident enough to declare them to a wider public. We may surmise that Hildegard, by now satisfied that her visions were indeed from a divine source, began to make more structured interpretations of them, literally, to see more in them. At the same time, Hildegard's exposure to monastic thought and culture was expanded, whether orally, in conversation with Volmar, or by reading, or both, is not clear. So things went on for two decades. Then, suddenly, as described in the *Scivias*, Hildegard experienced a migraine which she recognized as having peculiar subjective significance. In it she found a way of combining such experiences with her own thoughts and meditations. What were in fact two 'inner experiences' – the migraine vision and her own mental processes – coalesced to form the vision and its interpretation, perceived by her as coming from a divine source.

But why had Hildegard waited so long before declaring herself? This can only be explained in terms of the internalization of the prevailing attitudes towards women in general and the male monopoly of the written word. The wording of Hildegard's description of her years of silence in the *Scivias* preface is here most suggestive where she writes 'I repressed [the visions] in quiet obscurity.' So too is her attribution to men of vindictive and derogatory attitudes towards her work.[11]

While the actual timing of the decisive event may best be explained in terms of a developmental psychology such as Erik Erikson's, since there was no obvious external or environmental stimulus, Hildegard's reaction to what happened is very significant. Even when she was convinced that her visions were intelligible, formed communications from God which she had been commanded to promulgate in writing, she hesitated to obey. Whether the intense suffering connected with the vision was an integral part of the migraine, or whether it was caused in some less obvious way by Hildegard's response to the conflict occasioned by the message she received, is not clear. Hildegard, however, believed it was a sign of God's displeasure at her failure to carry out his command. The fact that she recovered as soon as she made up her mind to perform the task put upon her, while attributable to the normal course of a migraine attack, would also have acted as a strong reinforcement both of Hildegard's understanding of the situation and of the behavioural patterns involved.

Since the factors controlling the occurrence of different forms of migraine in the same person are unknown, and since migraine auras, classical, and common migraines all seem to have been experienced by Hildegard at different stages of her life, it may be hazarded that she experienced classical migraines when the contents or interpretation of the vision placed her in a state of profound conflict. The paradoxical effect of this was that she then became able to perform the threatening action because the illness was interpreted by her, and perhaps more importantly by others, as a sanction. The pattern can be traced from the first explicit description of her vision of 1141, through the proposal to move to Rupertsberg and the settlement of financial affairs with the parent house to her final confrontation with the prelates of Mainz in the last year of her life.

The complex interaction of such physical and psychological factors finally enabled Hildegard to assume a role which, we may conclude, she had long desired, consciously or more probably unconsciously. There was, after all, good reason for disquiet about the state of the Church and its relationship with the secular powers, as well as about institutional and intellectual trends within it. The prophetic role was not only self-reinforcing but also endorsed by her ecclesiastical superiors, as she wrote:

> When these matters were brought to the hearing of the Church of Mainz and discussed, everyone said that they were from God and of the nature of prophecy which the prophets had prophesied in former times. (*Vita*, Bk 2)

Soon, indeed, this view received the ultimate authority of the pope at the Council of Trier. Before long the attitude had filtered down to the clergy and members of the laity who wrote to Hildegard for advice. The correspondence proved another opportunity for mutual reinforcement of the role.

By the time Hildegard came to start her second major theological work, the *Liber vitae meritorum*, she could only have abandoned the visionary form at considerable risk to her credibility. Besides, there is no reason to doubt that her visionary experiences were continuing and that her interpretation of them as direct communications from God had become second nature, even if these later reports may seem somewhat more mediated than those of the *Scivias*. Hildegard suggests how this might be rationalized when she explains that she saw, heard, and understood in an instant, thus allowing for further extrapolation over the years.

The initial visionary impulse for the *Liber divinorum operum* is described in the *Vita*. This makes it clear that Hildegard had been thinking over the problem (of the Incarnation and its relationship to the creation story in Genesis) for some time before she felt able to give written expression to her ideas. The fact that the *Liber divinorum operum* presents a revised version of the cosmology first outlined in the *Scivias* suggests that Hildegard had been pondering such questions in the intervening years.

The increasing sophistication of Hildegard's cosmological and theological explanations is paralleled by her growing facility in expressing herself in Latin, although it seems that she never gained a full mastery of the syntax. It is difficult to believe that someone as perceptive as Hildegard would have been unaware of her own intellectual development.[12] That such progress did not allow Hildegard to gain confidence in her own capacities indicates that she was, to some extent, a victim of her own mythology. The combination of inner and outer circumstances that led Hildegard to believe that the products of her own intelligence were the *secreta Dei* (secrets of God) allowed her to overcome what would otherwise have been a crippling diffidence, but once that was achieved she became locked into a pattern, not only of behaviour, but of belief.

Hildegard was aided and abetted in this by those of her contemporaries who saw her as an exponent of traditional monastic wisdom, bestowed by the Holy Spirit, as opposed to what they thought of as the laboriously acquired pseudo-learning of the schools. Thus Guibert of Gembloux describes to Hildegard some of the comments of the admiring circle to whom he read one of her letters. He puts these words in the mouth of the learned Dom Rupert, ex-abbot of Vallis Regia:

> I do not think . . . that the greatest masters of the age in France, powerful and keen of intellect as they are, could equal the force and profundity of some of the words written in this letter.

Guibert himself was not uneducated, having received a solid monastic grounding at Gembloux. His writings show more than a nodding acquaintance with such classical authors as Ovid and Horace. He was suspicious, however, of what he saw as the overuse of dialectic and speculative theology in the schools. He describes those who frequented them as 'resounding with dry hearts and rattling cheeks'. The intellectual aspirations of the monks of Villers are sufficiently indicated by the questions they were at such pains to have Hildegard answer. They included queries about the nature of Pentecostal fire and that of the burning bush which appeared to Moses on Mt Sinai and the bodies of the angels encountered by Abraham. Hildegard returned answers to only fourteen of them before she died, and for want of a better alternative, Guibert finally told the monks to direct their questions to one of the 'masters of France'.[13]

Volmar expresses the same intellectually conservative views when writing to Hildegard during one of her absences from Rupertsberg, presumably towards the end of her life. He also paints an unflattering picture of the lengths to which men will go in pursuit of learning. No room for doubt is left about his opinion of such people and the fact that their search for knowledge is not disinterested. Their aim, he suggests, is to acquire the kind of learning that will gain them positions in the Church, a course of action which is tantamount to simony.

> O vanity of vanities! Why do many following difficult paths to far-flung corners of the world vainly examine the teachings of various masters? Why, afflicted with thirst, hunger and cold, through litigious declamations of disputes, through burning the midnight oil, do they sweat over the profundity or rather conundrums of opinions? Surely, surely we know that they do all this not with the simple eye of intention but for private advancement. (Van Acker, 195)

But why should Hildegard need to be told this? Were not Volmar and Guibert preaching to the converted? Perhaps such outbursts served more as a compensation for what they felt was their own increasing intellectual marginalization. Hildegard, having 'chosen the better part' as a matter of necessity, since the option of the schools was hardly open to her, may not have felt so threatened. It was, however, a happy choice for us. Although Hildegard's learning and approach may have represented something of a backwater in her own day, the wave of scholasticism has long since peaked. Yet aspects of Hildegard's thought have contributed to a broader and more enduring stream of speculation about the interrelations of divinity, humanity, and the natural world.

NOTES

1 LIFE AND DEATH

1   *Vita domnae Juttae inclusae*, ed. Franz Staab, in Stefan Weinfurter (ed.), *Reformidee und Reformpolitik im spätsalisch-frühstaufischen Reich*, Mainz, 1992, 172–87. Although this work, apparently written by a monk of Disibodenberg around the middle of the twelfth century, is useful for the light it throws on Jutta's spirituality (or at least her spirituality as perceived and promoted by the monks of Disibodenberg) I believe that the wholesale adoption of its chronology and the resulting revision of that of Hildegard's early life has been premature. According to the new account, Hildegard must have been committed first to the care of the widow Uda of Göllheim, together with Jutta, for some years at Disibodenberg before being formally enclosed there in 1112. (Not that Jutta's *Vita* actually states that such was the case; this is a conclusion drawn by commentators who try to accommodate the traditional account given by Hildegard herself and her biographers with the evidence from the new *Vita*. See for example Barbara Newman's Introduction to *Voice of the Living Light: Hildegard of Bingen and Her World*, Berkeley, 1998.) However, until more persuasive evidence, whether external (to corroborate or disprove some of the many dates given in the text) or intertextual (to settle the relationship between the *Vita* and other sources, particularly the *Annales Sancti Disibodi*), is discovered, I prefer to follow what might be thought of as the traditional account, given by Hildegard and her more or less contemporary biographers.

2   It is possible that the *lingua ignota* was meant to approximate the language of the virgin throng in heaven, knowledge of which Hildegard obtained from her visions. Hildegard was accustomed to apply certain aspects of what she learnt in them to her daily life. The clothes that her nuns wore on feast days (see p. 213, n. 15) is another example of this.

3   According to the *Acta*, Rupertsberg had about fifty nuns, while Eibingen had places for thirty more. If we add to this a number of servants and pensioners, not to mention priests, the total under Hildegard's care might be well over a hundred.

4   Such arrangements typify the interdependence of the medieval monastery and lay society. The layperson received spiritual benefits by

association with the continual prayers and intercessions of the religious community. They, on the other hand, received material benefits from the person to be buried there, or later, from his family. The process operated at several levels of society, from royal foundations such as Quedlinberg, where a king might be buried, to comital establishments like Maria Laach, to the more modest example of Rupertsberg, where the deceased was merely 'a certain noble man'.

5   See, for example, the death of St Aelred in F. M. Powicke, *The Life of Ailred of Rievaulx by Walter Daniel*, London, 1950, and that of St Hugh of Lincoln in D. Douie and H. Farmer, *The Life of St Hugh of Lincoln*, 2nd edn, London, 1985.

6   Indeed, Barbara Newman argues that such ends had shaped Hildegard and her supporters' output during her lifetime. See 'Three-part Invention: The Making of the *Vita S. Hildegardis*', in Burnett and Dronke (eds), *Hildegard of Bingen: The Context of her Thought and Art*, London, 1998.

7   For a description of this document and its illuminated initial, see H. Hinkel, 'St Hildegards Verehrung im Bistum Mainz' in A. Brück (ed.), *Hildegard von Bingen 1179–1979. Festschrift zum 800. Todestag der Heiligen*, Mainz, 1979, 385–411.

8   J.-P. Migne's *Patrologia Latina*, 221 vols, Paris, 1841–64 a monument to nineteenth-century publishing zeal, claims to contain all such writings. The works of twelfth-century authors fill over forty of its substantial volumes. Migne's work is now being replaced by the editions of the *Corpus Christianorum* published by Brepols, Belgium. Volumes covering the eighth to twelfth centuries, including editions of Hildegard's work, will appear in the Corpus Christianorum Continuatio Mediaevalis (CCCM).

2   WORLD AND CLOISTER

1   Many books and articles have been written on this subject since C. H. Haskins first published his *Renaissance of the Twelfth Century* in 1927. For a representative selection of more recent scholarship with useful bibliographies see R. Benson and G. Constable (eds), *Renaissance and Renewal in the Twelfth Century*, Oxford, 1982, and now, Giles Constable, *The Reformation of the Twelfth Century*, Cambridge, Cambridge University Press, 1996.

2   Lay investiture refers to the practice of a king or noble investing a bishop (or sometimes an abbot) with ring and staff in return for homage, before consecration. Other planks of the policy included measures against simony, the buying or selling of spiritual offices, and the enforcement of clerical celibacy, especially for priests.

3   Quoted by G. Constable in 'Renewal and reform in religious life' in Benson and Constable, *Renaissance and Renewal*, 41.

4   *Annales Sancti Disibodi*, Monumenta Germaniae Historica (MGH) SS. XVII 4ff.

5   Another instance where the foundation date of a monastery does not coincide with the first occupation of the site by the monks is to be found in

the Chronicle of Melrose (Scotland), where Premonstratensian canons are first described as arriving at Dryburgh in 1150, but electing an abbot and establishing the monastery two years later.

6   R. W. Southern, *Saint Anselm and his Biographer*, Cambridge, 1963, 9.

7   M. Schrader, *Die Herkunft der heiligen Hildegard*, 2nd edn, Mainz, 1981.

8   Drutwin was the eldest brother. Two of her brothers also entered the church: Hugo was precentor of Mainz Cathedral and Roricus was a canon of Tholey in the Saar. Of the four sisters known by name, Irmengard, Odilia, Jutta, and Clementia, the last mentioned was a nun in Hildegard's convent.

9   Bruno Scott James, *The Letters of St Bernard of Clairvaux*, London, 1953, esp. Letter 1.

10   This passage appears in the *Acta* in a context which suggests that the story is taken from Godfrey and Theodoric's *Vita*. However, it is not found in any of the surviving manuscripts. Possibly the story comes from an earlier version of the *Vita*, which is known to have been abridged by Abbot Godfrey of Echternach.

11   The fact that she describes it as occurring when she was 5 years old in the *Scivias* preface may perhaps be explained if we posit a shift of two years in the chronology of the *Vita*, on the supposition that Hildegard was dating the event in this passage as if she had been born in 1100 rather than in 1098.

12   The placement of the cell is somewhat problematical. If it were actually attached to the church, the south side would seem the most likely place, since otherwise it would abut the monks' cloister on the north.

13   R. Foreville and G. Keir (eds), *The Book of St Gilbert*, Oxford Medieval Texts, 1987, 32. For the 'Institutiones' see W. Dugdale, *Monasticon Anglicanum* VI(2), London, 1846, i–lix.

14   See 'De Institutione Inclusarum' in A. Hoste and C. H. Talbot (eds), *Aelredi Rievallensis Opera Omnia*, CCCM 1, Turnhout, 1971, 637–82, esp. 640.

15   See C. H. Talbot, *The Life of Christina of Markyate*, London, 1959, 102, 104.

16   See 'Servicium recludendi' in H. A. Wilson, *The Pontifical of Magdalen College*, Henry Bradshaw Society, 39, 1910, 243–4.

17   The psaltery, a common instrument in Europe of the later Middle Ages, was thought to have been introduced from the East by Crusaders early in the twelfth century.

18   See G. Constable, *The Letters of Peter the Venerable*, 1, Harvard, 1967, 27–41.

19   Cited in Talbot, *Life of Christina of Markyate*, 9.

20   See H. Mayr-Harting, 'Functions of a Twelfth-Century Recluse', *History*, 60, 1975, 337–52.

21   'De consecratione virginis' in Wilson, *Pontifical of Magdalen College*, 84–7. See also *Pontificale Romano-Germanicum Saeculi Decimi*, (ed.) Cyrille Vogel, Studie Testi 226, 1963–72: 'Consecratio sacrae virginis quae in Epiphania vel in alvis paschalibus aut in apostolorum nataliis celebratur', 38–46.

22 *Annales Rodenses*, MGH, SS. XVI, 688–723.
23 For the works of Elisabeth of Schönau, see F. W. E. Roth, *Die Visionen und Briefe der heiligen Elisabeth*, Brünn, 1884.

3 OPPORTUNITIES AND CONSTRAINTS

1 P. Dronke, *Women Writers of the Middle Ages*, Cambridge, 1984, 147.
2 Jutta's recently discovered *Vita* may give some clues to possible reasons for this circumstance. In it Jutta is described as following a rigorously ascetic lifestyle, praying barefoot in winter, mortifying her flesh, refusing dietary indulgences even when sick, and wearing a penitential chain beneath her clothes. It is, perhaps, significant that on the question of personal austerities Hildegard always preaches moderation.
3 Hildegard's claim to divine understanding, although it may sound strange to modern ears, might well have been seen by her contemporaries as theologically unexceptionable and one which would tend to align her with admired contemporaries. There is a superficial resemblance between her account and claims made for St Bernard by William of St Thierry, his first biographer (see G. Webb and A. Walker (transl.), *St Bernard of Clairvaux*, London, 1960). It must be admitted, however, that Hildegard's are more extreme and far reaching. William writes, for instance, that St Bernard was favoured with a vision of Christ one Christmas and that this experience had given him a special understanding of and veneration for the mystery of the Incarnation. He also writes that St Bernard reached his profound understanding of the scriptures by praying and meditating outdoors, so that he would ' jokingly say to his friends that it was only the oaks and beeches who were his masters in the subject' (ibid., 42). However, William also describes St Bernard's education at the school of Châtillon-sur-Saône, to which he applied himself enthusiastically 'as a way of coming to know about God in the scriptures' and relates that he continued to read theological commentaries even when he felt that he could understand the Bible more easily than its explicators. Here he differed from Abelard, who boasted of being able to understand such secondary sources quite unaided. It seems almost as if what was, in William's biography, something of a topos or conventional description for a thoroughly holy person, Hildegard acted out literally. Bernard, for example, never claims to be delivering God's words. He speaks in his own person, passing on to his audience his own understanding and insights. The fact that he issued retractions of some of his works shows how far he is from Hildegard, who could never be mistaken in what she wrote since it was all received directly from God.
4 On the question of whether monks or canons had the right to preach, a contentious issue in the twelfth century, see C. W. Bynum, 'The spirituality of regular canons in the twelfth century' in *Jesus as Mother*, Berkeley, 1982, 22–58.
5 On education and learning see G. M. Paré, A. Brunet and P. Tremblay, *La Renaissance du XIIe siècle: Les Ecoles et l'enseignement*, Paris and Ottawa, 1933.

6   See M. M. McLaughlin, 'Peter Abelard and the dignity of women: twelfth-century "feminism" in theory and practice' in *Pierre Abelard, Pierre le Vénérable: Les courants* . . . , Paris, 1975, 287–333. The story of the brilliant Abelard's seduction of his young pupil, Heloise, and their subsequent ill-fated love affair which ended with Abelard's castration and their entry into separate monasteries can be followed in B. Radice, *The Letters of Abelard and Heloise* (Penguin Classics), 1974, whose numbering of the letters I follow here. For the Latin texts of the *Historia calamitatum* and other letters see J. T. Muckle and T. P. McLaughlin (eds), *Mediaeval Studies*, vols 12, 15, 17, 18, Pontifical Institute of Mediaeval Studies, Toronto, 1950, 1953, 1955, 1956.

7   Latin text in *Mediaeval Studies*, vol. 18, 1956, 241–92.

8   Dronke, *Women Writers*, 132.

9   Indeed, there is a possible example in the *Acta*, where a certain young woman called Gerdrudis is said to have 'transformed herself into a scholar'. Hildegard miraculously saw through the disguise, called her by her real name, and predicted her death. At this Gerdrudis confessed she was a woman and resumed 'the better part'. At one time I was tempted to see Hildegard's confrontation with this girl, who had appropriated for herself male educational prerogatives, as indicating her own usually repressed wish to have done likewise. However, I am now inclined to think that Hildegard did see her own as 'the better part', especially in the light of what we know of monastic opinions of the schools. For another, later, example see M. Shank, 'A female university student in late medieval Krakow', *Signs*, 12, 1987, 373–80.

10   See James, *Letters of St Bernard*, Letter 177 . For a translation of the *Speculum charitatis* see G. Webb and A. Walker, *The Mirror of Charity*, London, 1962.

11   E.-R. Labarde (ed.), *Guibert de Nogent – Autobiographie*, Paris, 1981, 134 ff.

12   *Ortleibi Zwifaltensis Chronicon*, MGH, SS. X, 70 ff.

13   J.-P. Migne, *Patrologia Latina (PL)*, 221 vols, Paris, 1841–64, CLXIX, 1215.

14   See *Vita S. Malachiae, PL*, CLXXXII, 1073–1118.

15   *PL*, CLXXXVIII, 1142.

16   See *PL*, CII, 1147.

17   *PL*, CLXXVI, 741.

18   J. H. Van Engen, *Rupert of Deutz*, Los Angeles, 1983, 48.

19   M. Reeves, *The Influence of Prophecy in the Later Middle Ages*, Oxford, 1969, 16.

20   Possibly the fact that Jutta never commanded Hildegard to write her visions down was another cause for her apparent coolness towards her mistress.

4   THE WAYS OF GOD

1   Now that critical editions of Hildegard's three principal works have been published, in-depth studies of her theological ideas are beginning to appear. For an overview see the essay by Constant Mews in Barbara

Newman (ed.), *Voice of the Living Light: Hildegard of Bingen and Her World*, Berkeley, 1998.

2 The opening words of the *Scivias* preface: 'And behold in the forty-third year of my life . . . I saw a great brightness' may be compared to the prophetic diction of the Old Testament prophets. See Führkötter and Carlevaris, *Hildegardis Scivias*, xviii for further examples. See also Kathryn Kerby-Fulton, *Reformist Apocalypticism and Piers Plowman*, Cambridge, 1990.

3 St Jerome, Letter 22 (to Eustochium).

4 It seems unlikely that she would have gone as far as the Cistercians who refused to admit novices below the age of 15. The only evidence we have for Hildegard's practice is a description in the *Acta* of a witness as 'Beatrix of Cologne, oblated at the age of twelve' at Rupertsberg. Of course, this does not rule out the possibility that Hildegard accepted younger oblates.

5 B. Newman, *Sister of Wisdom*, Berkeley, 1987.

6 They are as follows: celestial love, discipline, humility, mercy, victory, patience, lamentation; abstinence, generosity, piety, truth, peace, blessedness, discretion, salvation of souls; wisdom, justice, fortitude; constancy, heavenly longing, compunction of heart, rejection of the world, and concord. The discrepancy between the number of virtues in the *Scivias* and the vices in the *Liber vitae meritorum* arises because some, like anger, are subdivided and treated separately.

7 See L. Sherley-Price, *Bede: A History of the English Church and People* (Penguin Classics), 1955, 284 ff.

8 It is interesting to compare this more developed theology of purgatory with the vision of Jutta's passage to Heaven attributed to Hildegard (as her closest disciple) in Jutta's *Vita*. The motif of a vision to reassure those who have been left behind about the ultimate destination of the deceased's soul is common in monastic literature of the time. The intervention of named saints (such as St John and St James, in this case) as facilitators is also commonplace and is much used in the work of Elisabeth of Schönau. This vision is markedly different in tone and approach from the visions recorded by Hildegard herself.

5 THE SUBTLETIES OF NATURE

1 A further collection of material, usually referred to as the 'Berlin fragment', similar in style and content to parts of the *Causae et curae*, appears in Berlin Cod. lat. 674. See H. Schipperges, 'Ein unveröffentliches Hildegard-Fragment', *Sudhoffs Archiv*, 40, 1956, 41–77.

2 C. Singer, 'The scientific views and visions of St Hildegard (1098–1180)' in C. Singer, *Studies in the History and Method of Science*, First Series, Oxford, 1951, 1–59.

3 Although P. Kaiser's edition of *Causae et curae*, Leipzig, 1903, is divided into five books, the only authority for this in the manuscript is the placement of large illuminated letters at the beginnings of the different sections. In fact, a sixth letter (H in '*homines*') similar to the others, but

slightly smaller in size, marks the beginning of the '*lunaria*' section (Kaiser, *Causae et Curae*, 235). This section, sometimes referred to as Book 6 of the *Causae et curae*, is the one most frequently rejected as an interpolation or addition. On this now see the article by Florence Glaze in Barbara Newman (ed.), *Voice of the Living Light: Hildegard of Bingen and Her World*, Berkeley, 1998.

4   It should be noted, however, that Hildegard appears to refer to her medico-scientific works as a 'vision' in the preface to the *Liber vitae meritorum*, while Theodoric in the *Vita*, Book 2 seems to include them among the works written by Hildegard 'in a spirit of prophecy'.

5   Two very important sources of medieval scientific lore were Pliny's *Historia naturalis* (*Natural History*) and the works of Isidore of Seville (†636), especially his *Etymologiae* (*Etymologies*). Some elements of Greek medical (Hippocratic) thought had been transmitted through the writings of Galen (in translations of Constantine of Africa) to become part of the accepted medical background. When Hildegard wrote, the major translations of Aristotle's works on natural history and translations of Arabic medical writings were only just appearing. A flourishing school of medicine existed in Salerno in southern Italy, the teachings of which circulated in more or less popular forms. Whether Hildegard had any acquaintance with such specialized works on women as Soranus' *Gynaecology* is doubtful. These sources were supplemented by the fantastic lore of the bestiaries, and the more empirical traditions of Greek herbalists such as Dioscorides. However, Glaze identifies Constantine of Africa's *Pantegni* as a source for Hildegard's treatment of such topics as hernia.

6   On Hildegard's classification of plants and animals see the article by Kenneth Kitchell and Irven Resnick in Maud McInerney (ed.), *Hildegard of Bingen: A Book of Essays*, New York, 1998.

7   For the development and transmission of the theory see R. Klibansky, E. Panofsky, and F. Saxl, *Saturn and Melancholy*, London, 1964.

8   If such an exception could be made for the duck, it might be wondered why the same could not be said for fish which eat unclean food. Once more it seems likely that Hildegard was rationalizing medieval practice.

9   These are sometimes given as fixed weights (the '*nummus*' or pennyweight which was twice as much as the '*obolus*'), not simply proportions of one ingredient to another.

10   The difference here appears to lie in the greater extent to which the well water, being confined in one place, is 'tempered' by the air.

11   See further, Sabina Flanagan, 'Hildegard and the Humors: Medieval Theories of Illness and Personality', in Andrew Weiner and Leonard Kaplan (eds), *Madness, Melancholy and the Limits of Self*, Madison, WI, 1996.

12   Hildegard once defended her practice of permitting only the daughters of the nobility to enter her convent by asking rhetorically whether a farmer would put his oxen, asses, sheep, and goats in the same stable. Her description of what would ensue if people were treated in the same way, with the higher rank besetting the lower and the lower mounting above the higher, is strongly reminiscent of her description of conflict among the

humours. See her letter to Tengswich (Tengswindis) of Andernach, Van Acker, 52r. See also Sabina Flanagan, 'Hildegard of Bingen's Social Ideas', forthcoming, *Journal of Religious History*, 1998.

13 See Kaiser, *Causae et Curae*, 76. Hildegard could have found the idea that woman contributed seed to conception in Isidore, but she emphasizes that the woman's contribution of seed is much weaker, smaller in quantity, and less frequent than that of the man.

14 In fact, in Book 2, ch. 257, Hildegard compares tears produced by immoderate laughter to the production of semen from the blood.

15 B. Lawn, *The Prose Salernitan Questions*, London, 1979, 4.

16 Dronke, *Women Writers*, Cambridge, 1984, 175–6.

6 CELESTIAL HARMONIES

1 For discussion of dating and composition see P. Dronke, *Poetic Individuality in the Middle Ages*, Oxford, 1970, ch. 5; and 'Problemata Hildegardiana', *Mittellateinisches Jahrbuch* 16, 1981, 97–113. See also Barbara Newman's Introduction in *Symphonia: A Critical Edition*, Ithaca, 1988.

2 In the edition of Pudentiana Barth, M. Immaculata Ritscher and Joseph Schmidt-Görg, *Hildegard von Bingen: Lieder*, Salzburg, 1969, which includes a transcription of the music in plainchant notation, three pieces, 40, 41, and 71 are not otherwise classified.

3 See J. Leclercq, *The Love of Learning and the Desire for God*, trans. C. Misrahi, 2nd edn, London, 1978, 292.

4 See W. von den Steinen, *Notker der Dichter und seine geistige Welt*, Berne, 1948.

5 My understanding of the subject is based largely on W. Apel, *Gregorian Chant*, Bloomington, 1958.

6 See, for example, Part 2 by Greta Mary Hair of '*O Ecclesia*: the text and music of Hildegard of Bingen's sequence for St Ursula', *Tjurunga*, 30, 1986, 3–62. (Part 1: 'The text', is by Janet Martin.) Now see also Marianne Richert Pfau, 'Music and Text in Hildegard's Antiphons' in Barbara Newman (ed.), *Symphonia* and the essays by Margot Fassler in Barbara Newman (ed.), *Voice of the Living Light*, and Kathryn Bumpass in Maud McInerney (ed.), *Hildegard of Bingen: A Book of Essays*.

7 The fact that there are no antiphons for St Eucharius or St Maximin suggests that Hildegard did not always provide a complete set of liturgical pieces for all the offices of a saint's day.

8 I have tried to keep my translations close to the Latin of the originals, while conveying some sense of their poetry and Hildegard's verbal felicities. In the last line, for instance, alliteration has to do duty for her play on words '*suscitans et resuscitans*'.

9 See note 1, and also his analysis of the sequence for St Maximin in *The Medieval Lyric*, London, 1968. Several other poems, including the sequence for St Disibod, are treated in Dronke, *Poetic Individuality*, ch. 5.

10 I take stanza 7 to be a medical metaphor, looking forward to the imagery of stanza 10, rather than a musical one, as suggested by Dronke.

11 '. . . et cum sequentiam instinctu sancti Spiritus, quae sic incipit: O virga ac diadema, per claustram ambulando decantabat'.

12 Sleeve notes, *A Feather on the Breath of God: Sequences and hymns by Abbess Hildegard of Bingen*. Hyperion A66039 (recorded, 1981) and note 1.

13 See notes 1 and 6 above; Newman, *Sister of Wisdom*, 225–8.

14 See Dronke, *Poetic Individuality*, which includes a critical edition of the play. B. Hozeski, '"Ordo Virtutum": Hildegard of Bingen's liturgical morality play', *Annuale Mediaevale*, 13, 1972, 45–69.

15 Tengswich (Van Acker, 52) asks if it is true that Hildegard's nuns wear rings and elaborately wrought diadems bearing symbolic images on feast days. The descriptions of these accessories recall strongly the allegorical trappings of some figures in the *Scivias*. It is possible that the rumour, which, incidentally, Hildegard does not deny but justifies by argument, arose from a garbled account of a performance of the *Ordo virtutum*.

7 MAN AND THE COSMOS

1 See A. Derolez, 'The genesis of Hildegard of Bingen's "Liber Divinorum Operum". The codicological evidence', *Litterae Textuales. Essays presented to G. I. Lieftinck*, 2, 1972, 23–33.

2 This work can also be seen as Hildegard's most perfect formal and structurally articulated one. The structural features all serve to emphasize the divine source of her writing, as they did in the *Scivias* and *Liber vitae meritorum*. While the prophetic markers are very much in evidence, there is little or no direct apologetic writing. Hildegard does not portray herself in this work as doubting her capacities, at least not her intellectual ones.

3 See Charles Singer, 'The scientific views and visions of Saint Hildegard (1098–1180)' in his *Studies in the History and Method of Science*, 1–59.

4 Barbara Newman, in *Sister of Wisdom*, 69–71, sees this representation of Love or *Caritas* as a female aspect of the divine and uses feminine pronouns in her description. However, it is not clear to me that Hildegard herself intended the image to show specifically female traits. She refers to it as being in 'human form' ('*quasi hominis forma*'), rather than in 'female form' ('*forma mulieris*') as she had described the church in the *Scivias*. The image is said to be wearing a tunic, a garment which could be assumed by either sex. The illustrator of the Lucca manuscript maintains the ambiguity, although the short hair of the figure resembles the subsequent representations of men – the universal man superimposed on the globe, for instance, rather than the bejewelled female forms with long hair in the later visions.

5 See Singer, 'Scientific views and visions of Saint Hildegard' and H. Liebeschütz, *Das allegorische Weltbild der heiligen Hildegard von Bingen*, Leipzig, 1930.

6 For Hildegard's use of prophetic formulae see ch. 4, note 2 above.

7 Hildegard's castigation of the ministers of the church is more hardhitting in this later work than in the *Scivias*. Possibly this was due to the

prolongation of the schism, in its fifteenth year when Hildegard was completing the *Liber divinorum operum*.

8   Gebeno, Prior of the Cistercian monastery of Eberbach, made a collection of the eschatological portions of Hildegard's writings and issued them under the title *Pentachronon* (*The Five Ages*) in 1220. Many more manuscripts of this compilation survive than of Hildegard's own works. See J. B. Pitra, *Sanctae Hildegardis Opera*, Monte Cassino, 1882, 483–9.

9   Although the basic outlines of the Antichrist legend appear in Adso's *De ortu et tempore Antichristi*, written in the tenth century, there was some margin for speculation about the timing of the event. Bernard of Clairvaux, for instance, reports that Norbert of Xanten believed Antichrist would appear in his generation, but Bernard adds that he found Norbert's reasons for this belief less than convincing. See James, *Letters of St Bernard*, Letter 58.

8   ADMONITION AND ADVICE

1   For the identification of Hildegard's nephew Wezelin as the compiler and his method of approach see M. Schrader and A. Führkötter, *Die Echtheit des Schrifttums der heiligen Hildegard von Bingen*, Cologne and Graz, 1956, esp. 59–154. Lieven Van Acker has elucidated many of these problems in his (unfortunately uncompleted) edition of the correspondence and two earlier articles, 'Der Briefwechsel der heiligen Hildegard von Bingen: Vorbemerkungen zu einer kritischen Edition', *Revue Bénédictine* 98 (1988) 141–68 and 99 (1989) 118–54.

2   Guibert of Gembloux has a revealing description of how he received a letter from Hildegard. He first placed it unopened on the altar and prayed that he might be worthy to read and understand it. He then read it over silently two or three times, before allowing numerous others to read and even copy it.

3   Van Acker, 35. Herman of Arbon († 1165–6) was much concerned with the Emperor's affairs, annulling Frederick Barbarossa's marriage to Adelheid of Volsberg in 1153, and joining his Italian campaign in 1154.

4   Van Acker, 37. This may have been Rudolph of Zahringen († 1191), accused at various times of dereliction of duty, incompetence, and simony, or possibly Henry of Liège (1145–64).

5   Van Acker, 16. Philip of Heinsberg, provost of Liège, deacon (1156) and provost (1165) of Cologne Cathedral, chancellor of the kingdom (1166) and Archbishop of Cologne (1167). Died in 1191 near Naples while accompanying Henry VI to Italy.

6   Although there are many difficulties in dating individual letters, her correspondence covers the years from around the Council of Trier (1148) to the end of her life.

7   Eberhard II of Bamberg (1146–1170); Van Acker, 31.

8   See Klaes, *Vita Hildegardis*, Appendix I, pp. 11–12.

9   For a similar example of signalling a miracle by ringing bells and singing the *Te Deum* see Douie and Farmer (eds), *Life of St Hugh of Lincoln*, II, 230.

10 Although quantification of the types of cures effected by different saints is fraught with difficulty, some interesting trends emerge. Compared with the English and French examples in R. Finucane, *Miracles and Pilgrims*, London, 1977, Hildegard deals with a much greater proportion of mental afflictions than would be expected.

11 Hildegard may also have had in mind the actual example of the anticlerical, communal movement in Rome in the late 1140s, led by Arnold of Brescia (c. 1100–55), although she would hardly have condoned it. For the relation or such movements to ideas of canonical reform see L. K. Little, *Religious Poverty and the Profit Economy in Medieval Europe*, London, 1978, ch. 7.

12 Dronke, *Women Writers*, 186 ff. For the text of the letter from the Berlin manuscript see p. 257. According to Van Acker this is a composite letter, the first part of which was possibly written for Elisabeth, Abbess of St Thomas an der Kyll (Van Acker, 198).

9 WORLDLY DISCORDS

1 According to Godfrey in Book I of the *Vita*, the course of Hildegard's illness reflected the progress of her battle to gain permission to move: 'Sometimes rising suddenly from her bed she would walk through all the rooms and corridors of the convent, entirely unable to speak. Then, returning to bed, unable to walk, she would speak as before.'

2 This letter from the Stuttgart manuscript is edited by F. Haug, *Revue Bénédictine*, 43, 1931, 64. Adelheid († 1184) was actually the granddaughter of the marchioness (and the niece of the nun Richardis of Stade). She was the daughter of Luitgard of Stade and Count-palatine Friedrich of Sommerschenberg, entrusted to her grandmother's care when her parents divorced and her mother married King Eric of Denmark, c. 1144.

3 Van Acker, 18.

4 Van Acker, 18r, with Peter Dronke's emendation of '*conniventi*' for '*conviventi*'; see his *Women Writers*, 308.

5 Henry of Mainz was archbishop from 1142 to 1153, when he was deposed by the papal legates. Hildegard wrote on his behalf to the pope and the papal legates, but without success. See Pitra, *Sanctae Hildegardis Opera*, 520. Van Acker presents this as a separate letter, (Van Acker 19).

6 Van Acker, 12.

7 See Schrader and Führkötter, *Die Echtheit*, 117–18. Van Acker, 4.

8 Van Acker, 64.

9 See H. Talbot, *Christian Friendship by St Ailred of Rievaulx*, London, 1942.

10 Van Acker, 13.

11 Van Acker, 13r.

12 See Van Acker, 23. Another version is found as the last letter in manuscript B (54rb–56rb), parts of which are edited by Dronke, *Women Writers*, 314–15.

13 Van Acker, 24r.

14 The archbishop seems to have been denied this wish. Towards the end

of 1179 he was captured by the Marquis of Montferrat and imprisoned for over a year. He died in Italy in 1183.
15   See above, note 12.
16   Guido of Arezzo († c.1050) was credited with introducing this mnemonic device for singers whereby the tips and joints of the fingers all have notes allotted to them.
17   I take Hildegard to be alluding to herself as the 'virago' although it is possible that she meant this to be a description of 'fortitude'. In the *Scivias*, 3, 9 'fortitude' is represented as a fully-armed warrior, although there is nothing in the illustration or description to indicate the sex of the figure. The use of feminine pronouns is required because of the grammatical gender of the Latin word '*imago*' ('image').
18   Van Acker, 24.

10   POTENT INFIRMITIES

1   For Guibert's correspondence see Albert Derolez (ed.), *Guiberti Gemblacensis. Epistolae* 2 vols, in *Corpus Christianorum: continuatio mediaevalis*, vols 66, 66a, Turnhout, 1988–9. His letters to Hildegard are found in vol. 1, nos. 16–20. For Hildegard's replies see Van Acker 103r and 106r.
2   Van Acker, 103r.
3   *Causae et curae*, Bk 2, ch. 110.
4   Hildegard here discounts the one instance in which this seems to have happened: see p. 135.
5   See F. W. E. Roth, *Die Visionen und Briefe der heiligen Elisabeth*, Brünn, 1884, 2, and more generally, Anne Clark, *Elisabeth of Schönau: A Twelfth-Century Visionary*, Philadelphia, 1992. For useful background discussion of medieval visions and visionaries see Peter Dinzelbacher, *Vision und Visionsliteratur im Mittelalter*, Monographien zur Geschichte des Mittelalters, 23, Stuttgart, 1981.
6   For support of this view see the essay by Madeline Caviness in Barbara Newman (ed.), *Voice of the Living Light: Hildegard of Bingen and Her World*, Berkeley, 1998.
7   O. Sacks, *Migraine. Understanding a Common Disorder*, Berkeley, 1985.
8   Compare the illustrations of the walled city in *Scivias*, Bk 3; p. 122 above.
9   See further the essay by Caviness in Newman (ed), *Voice of the Living Light*, and references.
10   G. Selby, *Migraine and its Variants*, Sydney, 1983, 40.
11   These are expressed at various places in the *Scivias* e.g. preface, Bk 2, 1 and in the *Vita*, Bk 2.
12   Indeed, she does seem to recognize it, as far as the visions are concerned, in her preface to the *Liber vitae meritorum*.
13   Albert Derolez, (ed.), *Guiberti Gemblacensis: Epistolae*, vol. 2, letter 26.

SELECT BIBLIOGRAPHY AND DISCOGRAPHY

PRIMARY SOURCES

1 Works of Hildegard, editions

Scivias

Führkötter, Adelgundis, and Angela Carlevaris (eds) (1978), *Hildegardis Scivias*, in *Corpus Christianorum: continuatio mediaevalis*, vols 43 and 43a. Turnhout, Brepols.

Liber Vitae Meritorum

Carlevaris, Angela (ed.) (1995), *Hildegardis Liber vitae meritorum*, in *Corpus Christianorum: continuatio mediaevalis*, vol. 90, Turnhout, Brepols.

Liber Divinorum Operum

Derolez, Albert, and Peter Dronke (eds) (1996), *Hildegardis Liber divinorum operum*, in *Corpus Christianorum: continuatio mediaevalis*, vol. 92, Turnhout, Brepols.

Causae et Curae

Kaiser, Paul (ed.) (1903), *Hildegardis Causae et curae*, Leipzig, Trubner.

Correspondence

Van Acker, Lieven (ed.) (1991, 1993), *Hildegardis Bingensis Epistolarium*, Parts 1 (letters 1–90) and 2 (letters 91–250), in *Corpus Christianorum: continuatio mediaevalis*, vols 91 and 91a, Turnhout, Brepols (to be completed by Monika Klaes).

Symphonia

Newman, Barbara (ed.) (1988), *Symphonia: A Critical Edition of the Symphonia Armonie Celestium Revelationum*, Ithaca, Cornell University Press.

Music Editions
Barth, Pudentiana, Maria-Immaculata Ritscher, and Joseph Schmidt-Görg (eds) (1969), *Hildegard von Bingen: Lieder*, Salzburg, Otto Müller.
Page, Christopher (ed.) (1983), *Abbess Hildegard of Bingen: Sequences and Hymns*, Newton Abbot, Antico.

Ordo Virtutum
Dronke, Peter (ed.) (1970), in *Poetic Individuality in the Middle Ages*, Oxford, Clarendon Press.

Music Edition
Davidson, Audrey (ed.) (1985), *The 'Ordo virtutum' of Hildegard*, Kalamazoo, The Medieval Institute.

For the remaining works of Hildegard, *Physica, Explanatio Regulae S. Benedicti, Explanatio Symboli Sancti Athanasii, Expositiones in Evangelium, Vita sancti Ruperti, Vita sancti Disibodi, Solutiones XXXVIII Quaestionum, Lingua ignota, Litterae ignotae* and the balance of the letters, see:

Migne, J.-P. (ed.) (1976), *Sanctae Hildegardis Abbatissae Opera Omnia*, in *Patrologia Latina Cursus Completus*, vol. 197. Paris, 1855; Turnhout, Brepols.

Pitra, J.-B. (ed.) (1882), *Analecta S. Hildegardis*, in *Analecta Sacra*, vol. 8. Monte Cassino.

2 Works of Hildegard, translations

Correspondence
Baird, Joseph and Radd Ehrman (trans) (1995), *The Letters of Hildegard of Bingen*, vol. 1. New York, Oxford University Press. (A translation of the letters in Van Acker's volume 1; further volumes are planned.)

Scivias
Hart, Columba and Jane Bishop (trans) (1990), *Hildegard of Bingen: Scivias*, New York, Paulist Press.

Symphonia
Newman, Barbara (ed. and trans.) (1988), *Hildegard of Bingen: Symphonia*, Ithaca, Cornell University Press.

Ordo Virtutum
Dronke, Peter (ed. and trans.) (1994), in *Nine Medieval Latin Plays*, Cambridge, Cambridge University Press.

SELECT BIBLIOGRAPHY

Explanation of the Rule of St Benedict
Feiss, Hugh (trans.) (1990), *Explanation of the Rule of St. Benedict by Hildegard of Bingen*, Toronto, Peregrina.

Vita Hildegardis
Feiss, Hugh (trans.) (1996), *The Life of the Saintly Hildegard*, Toronto, Peregrina.

Silvas, Anna (trans.), (1985, 1986, 1987) 'Saint Hildegard of Bingen and the *Vita Sanctae Hildegardis*', *Tjurunga* 29 (1985) pp. 4–25; 30 (1986) pp. 63–73; 31 (1986) pp. 32–41; 32 (1987) pp. 46–59. Anna Silvas is preparing a new set of translations which will include, as well as Jutta's *Vita*, further biographical material on Hildegard.

3 Works of Hildegard, anthologies

Bowie, Fiona and Oliver Davies (eds) (1990), *Hildegard of Bingen: An Anthology*, London, SPCK.

Flanagan, Sabina (ed. and trans.) (1996), *Secrets of God: Writings of Hildegard of Bingen*, Boston, Shambhala.

Other translations of Hildegard's works are published by Bear and Co., Santa Fe and the Liturgical Press, Collegeville, MI. These should be used with caution since they are often translations from German translations of Hildegard's works rather than the original Latin. German translations of Hildegard's writings, sometimes abbreviated, are published by Otto Müller Verlag, Salzburg.

4 Related primary sources

Acht, Peter (ed.) (1968), *Mainzer Urkundenbuch*, II, part 1: 1137–1175, Darmstadt, Selbstverlag der Hessischen Historischen Kommission Darmstadt.

Beyer, Heinrich, Leopold Eltester and Adam Goerz (eds) (1974), *Urkundenbuch zur Geschichte der Mittelrheinischen Territorien*, 2 vols, Koblenz, Hölscher, 1860, Frankfurt, Olms.

Bruder, Petrus (ed.) (1883), *Acta inquisitionis* in *Analecta Bollandiana*, 2, pp. 118–29.

Derolez, Albert (ed.) (1988, 1989), *Guiberti Gemblacensis. Epistolae*, in *Corpus Christianorum: continuatio mediaevalis*, vols 66, 66a. Turnhout, Brepols.

Klaes, Monika (ed.) (1993), *Vita Hildegardis*, in *Corpus Christianorum: continuatio mediaevalis*, vol. 126, Turnhout, Brepols.

Roth, F. W. E. (ed.) (1884), *Die Visionen der hl. Elisabeth and die Schriften der Aebte Ekbert und Emecho von Schönau*, Brünn, Verlag der Studien aus dem Benedictiner-und Cistercienser-Orden.

Stimmung, Manfred (ed.) (1932), *Mainzer Urkundenbuch*, I. Darmstadt, Verlag des Historischen Vereins für Hessen.

Staab, Franz (ed.) (1992), *Vita domnae Juttae inclusae* in Stephan Weinfurter (ed.), *Reformidee und Reformpolitik im spätsalisch-früstaufischen Reich*, Mainz, Selbstverlag der Gesellschaft für Mittelrheinische Kirchengeschichte.

Vogel, Cyrille (ed.) (1963, 1973), *Pontificale Romano-Germanicum Saeculi Decimi*, Studi e Testi 226, 227.

Waitz, Georgius (ed.) (1861), *Annales Sancti Disibodi*, Monumenta Germaniae Historica SS. 17, Hannover.

Wilson, H. A. (ed.) (1910), *The Pontifical of Magdalen College*, Henry Bradshaw Society, 39.

SECONDARY WORKS

1 Books

Clark, Anne (1992), *Elisabeth of Schönau: A Twelfth-Century Visionary*, Philadelphia, University of Pennsylvania Press.

Dinzelbacher, Peter (1981), *Vision und Visionsliteratur im Mittelalter*, Monographien zur Geschichte des Mittelalters, 23, Stuttgart, Hiersemann.

Dronke, Peter (1984), *Women Writers of the Middle Ages: A Critical Study of Texts from Perpetua (†203) to Marguerite Porete (†1310)*, Cambridge, Cambridge University Press.

Kerby-Fulton, Kathryn (1990), *Reformist Apocalypticism and Piers Plowman*, Cambridge, Cambridge University Press.

Lautenschläger, Gabriele (1993), *Hildegard von Bingen: Die theologische Grundlegung ihrer Ethik und Spiritualität*, Stuttgart-Bad Cannstatt, Frommann-Holzboog.

Liebeschütz, Hans (1930), *Das allegorische Weltbild der hl. Hildegard von Bingen*, Leipzig, Studien der Bibliothek Warburg Bd 16.

Müller, Irmgard (1993), *Die pflanzlichen Heilmittel bei Hildegard von Bingen*, Freiburg, Herder.

Newman, Barbara (1987), *Sister of Wisdom: St Hildegard's Theology of the Feminine*, Berkeley, University of California Press.

Petroff, Elisabeth (1986), *Medieval Women's Visionary Literature*, Oxford, Oxford University Press.

Sacks, Oliver (1985), *Migraine: Understanding a Common Disorder*, Berkeley, University of California Press.

Schrader, Marianna, and Adelgundis Führkötter (1956), *Die Echtheit des Schrifttums der hl. Hildegard von Bingen*, Cologne, Böhlau-Verlag.

Schrader, Marianna (1981), *Die Herkunft der heiligen Hildegard*, 2nd edn., Mainz, Gesellschaft für Mittelrheinische Kirchengeschichte.

Singer, Charles (1951), 'The Scientific Views and Visions of Saint Hildegard', *Studies in the History and Method of Science*, vol. 1. Oxford, Oxford University Press, pp. 1–55.

2 Collected essays

Barton, Julie and Constant Mews (eds) (1995), *Hildegard of Bingen and Gendered Theology in Judaeo-Christian Tradition*, Clayton, Victoria, Monash University.

Brück, Anton (ed.) (1979), *Hildegard von Bingen, 1179–1979: Festschrift zum 800 Todestag der Heiligen*, Mainz, Gesellschaft für Mittelrheinische Kirchengeschichte.

Burnett, Charles and Peter Dronke (eds) (1998), *Hildegard of Bingen: The Context of Her Thought and Art*, London, Warburg Institute.

Davidson, Audrey, E. (ed.) (1992), *The Ordo Virtutum of Hildegard of Bingen: Critical Studies*, Kalamazoo, Medieval Institute.

——, (ed.) (1996), *Wisdom Which Encircles Circles: Papers on Hildegard of Bingen*, Kalamazoo, Medieval Institute.

McInerney, Maud (ed.) (1998), *Hildegard of Bingen: A Book of Essays*, New York, Garland.

Newman, Barbara (ed.) (1998), *Voice of the Living Light: Hildegard of Bingen and Her World*, Berkeley, University of California Press.

Rath, Philippa (ed.) (1997), *Hildegard von Bingen Prophetin durch die Zeiten*, Freiburg, Herder.

Schmidt, Margot (ed.) (1995), *Tiefe des Gotteswissens – Schönheit der Sprachgestalt bei Hildegard von Bingen*, Stuttgart-Bad Cannstatt, Frommann-Holzboog.

3 Articles

(see also collections listed above)

Bartlett, Anne (1992), 'Commentary, Polemic and Prophecy in Hildegard of Bingen's *Solutiones triginta octo quaestionum*', Viator 23, pp. 153–65.

Cadden, Joan (1984), 'It Takes All Kinds: Sexuality and Gender Differences in Hildegard of Bingen's "Book of Compound Medicine"', *Traditio* 40, pp. 149–74.

Dronke, Peter (1981), 'Problemata Hildegardiana' *Mittellateinisches Jahrbuch* 16, pp. 97–131.

Flanagan, Sabina (1996), 'Hildegard and the Humors: Medieval Theories of Illness and Personality', in Andrew Weiner and Leonard Kaplan (eds), *Madness, Melancholy, and the Limits of the Self*, Madison, WI, University of Wisconsin Law School.

Haverkamp, Alfred (1984), 'Tenxwind von Andernach und Hildegard von Bingen: Zwei "Weltanschauungen" in der Mitte des 12 Jahrhunderts', in Lutz Fenske, Werner Rösener and Thomas Zotz (eds) (1984), *Institutionen, Kultur und Gesellschaft im Mittelalter: Festschrift für Joseph Fleckenstein*, Sigmaringen, Thorbecke, pp. 515–48.

Hotchin, Julie (1996), 'Enclosure and Containment: Jutta and Hildegard at the Abbey of St Disibod', *Magistra* 2:2 , pp. 103–23.

Mews, Constant (1996), 'Seeing Is Believing: Hildegard of Bingen and the *Life of Jutta, Scivias* and the *Commentary on the Rule of Benedict*', *Tjurunga* 51, pp. 9–40.

Newman, Barbara (1989–90), 'Flaws in the Golden Bowl: Gender and Spiritual Formation in the Twelfth Century', *Traditio* 45, pp. 111–46.

Rissel, Hiltrud (1990), 'Hildegard von Bingen an Elisabeth von St Thomas an der Kyll. Die heilige Hildegard und die frühesten deutschen Zisterzienserinnen', *Cîteaux* 41, pp. 5–44.

Schnapp, Jeffrey (1991), 'Virgin Words: Hildegard of Bingen's *Lingua Ignota* and the Development of Imaginary Languages Ancient to Modern', *Exemplaria* 3, pp. 267–98.

Scholz, Bernhard (1980), 'Hildegard von Bingen on the Nature of Woman', *American Benedictine Review* 31, pp. 361–83.

Thompson, Augustine (1994), 'Hildegard of Bingen on Gender and Priesthood', *Church History* 63, pp. 349–64.

Wiethaus, Ulrike (1993), 'In Search of Medieval Women's Friendships: Hildegard of Bingen's Letters to Her Female Contemporaries', in Wiethaus, (ed.) (1993), *Maps of Flesh and Light: The Religious Experience of Medieval Women Mystics*, Syracuse NY, Syracuse University Press, pp. 93–111.

4 Bibliography

Lauter, Werner (1970, 1983), *Hildegard-Bibliographie I, II*, Alzey, Rheinhessische Druckwerkstätte. (A third volume is planned for 1998.)

SELECT DISCOGRAPHY

Sequentia, the Early Music ensemble, is in the process of recording the complete musical works of Hildegard in 8 CDs. So far available are:

1) *Hildegard von Bingen: Ordo virtutum* Sequentia. Deutsche Harmonia Mundi BMG 77051-2-RGD, 2 CDs (1982).

2) *Hildegard von Bingen: Symphoniae (Geistliche Gesänge)* Sequentia, Deutsche Harmonia Mundi EMI 49251 (1985).

3) *Hildegard von Bingen: Canticles of Ecstasy* Sequentia, Deutsche Harmonia Mundi, DES 77320 (1994).

4) *Hildegard von Bingen: Voice of the Blood* Sequentia, Deutsche Harmonia Mundi, DES 77346 (1995) (St Ursula and the 11,000 virgins).

5) *Hildegard von Bingen: O Jerusalem* Sequentia, Deutsche Harmonia Mundi, DES 77353 (1997).

Other recommended recordings

1) *11,000 Virgins: Chants for the Feast of St Ursula*, Anonymous 4, Harmonia Mundi 907200 (1997).

2) *A Feather on the Breath of God: Sequences and Hymns by Abbess Hildegard of Bingen*, Gothic Voices, Hyperion DCA 66039 (1981).

3) *Hildegard of Bingen: The Harmony of Heaven*, Ellen Oak, Bison Publications 1 (1996).

4) *Hildegard von Bingen: Symphoniae*, Schola der Benediktinerinnenabtei St. Hildegard, Rüdesheim-Eibingen, Bayer 100116 (1994) recorded 1979.

5) *Hildegard von Bingen und ihre Zeit*, Ensemble für frühe Musik Augsburg, Christophorus 74584 (1990).

6) *Jouissance: Hildegard and Abelard*, Viriditas, CD Spectrum Publications, Richmond, Vic., Australia 3121 (1994).

7) *The Lauds of St Ursula*, Early Music Institute, University of Indiana, Focus 911 (1991).

8) *Sinfonye: Symphony of the harmony of celestial revelations*, Stevie Wishart, Celestial Harmonies 13127 (1996).

New Age derivatives

1) *Diadema*, Vox, Real Music 8999 (1990).

2) *Illumination. Hildegard von Bingen: The Fire of the Spirit*, Richard Souther, Sony 62853 (1997).

3) *Vision: The Music of Hildegard von Bingen*, Richard Souther, EMI/Angel 55246 (1994).

223

INDEX